A Very Special Relationship

British Atomic Weapon Trials in Australia

Lorna Arnold

London
Her Majesty's Stationery Office

© Crown Copyright 1987
First published 1987

ISBN 0 11 772412 2   623. 45119

HMSO publications are available from:

HMSO Publications Centre
(Mail and telephone orders only)
PO Box 276, London, SW8 5DT
Telephone orders 01-622 3316
General enquiries 01-211 5656
(queuing system in operation for both numbers)

HMSO Bookshops
49 High Holborn, London, WC1V 6HB   01-211 5656 (Counter service only)
258 Broad Street, Birmingham, B1 2HE   021-643 3757
Southey House, 33 Wine Street, Bristol, BS1 2BQ   (0272) 24306/24307
9-21 Princess Street, Manchester, M60 8AS   061-834 7201
80 Chichester Street, Belfast, BT1 4JY   (0232) 238451
13a Castle Street, Edinburgh, EH2 3AR   031-225 6333

HMSO's Accredited Agents
(see Yellow Pages)

and through good booksellers

Contents

Note on Documentation

The author is grateful to the Controller of HM Stationery Office for permission to reproduce and quote Government documents. She also acknowledges her indebtedness to the authors and publishers of all those books that have been mentioned in this work.

In accordance with the usual practice of official histories, references to official papers have been omitted; references in the notes are, with one exception, confined to published material. A list of references will however be available later and will be accessible to scholars on request.

LA

Acknowledgements

Photographs 1–7 and 9–14, and Maps 2–5, are reproduced by kind permission of the Ministry of Defence (AWRE, Aldermaston).

Photograph 8 is reproduced by kind permission of the Ministry of Defence (Air Historical Branch).

Foreword

I have published three volumes of the history of the British atomic energy project: *Britain and Atomic Energy 1939–1945* (1964), *Britain and Atomic Energy 1945–1952* (1974), Vol. 1 *Policy Making* and Vol. 2 *Policy Execution*. Lorna Arnold was associated with me in the last two volumes and we have been working together on further volumes covering the 1950s; for them, Mrs Arnold had been doing research on British nuclear tests. However, in view of renewed public interest that led to the establishment of the Australian Royal Commission on the tests, I thought it desirable that Mrs Arnold's work should be expanded into a separate book. The Ministry of Defence have given her every possible help and very little indeed has been omitted on security grounds; she has been given free access to official documents but the selection and interpretation of the material for the book are entirely hers.

Margaret Gowing
Oxford

Abbreviations and Acronyms

Note Most of the organizations referred to are United Kingdom (UK) or Australian (A). The American and French entries are indicated by (US) or (F), respectively.

AAEC	Australian Atomic Energy Commission (A)
ACAE	Advisory Committee on Atomic Energy (UK)
AEA	Atomic Energy Authority (UK)
AE(M)	Ministerial Committee on Atomic Energy (UK)
AE(O)	Official Committee on Atomic Energy (UK)
AERE	Atomic Energy Research Establishment, Harwell (UK)
AHPR	Australian Health Physics Representative (A)
AIRAC	Australian Ionising Radiation Advisory Council (A)
ANU	Australian National University, Canberra (A)
ARC	Agricultural Research Council (UK)
ARDU	Australian Radiation Detection Unit (A)
AWRE	Atomic Weapons Research Establishment, Aldermaston (UK)
AWTC	Atomic Weapons Tests Committee (A)
AWTSC	Atomic Weapons Tests Safety Committee (A)
BEIR	Committee on Biological Effects of Ionising Radiation (US)
CAE	Controller, Atomic Energy, Ministry of Supply (UK)
CAW	Controller, Atomic Weapons, Ministry of Supply (UK)
CDEE	Chemical Defence Experimental Establishment (UK)
CEA	Commissariat à l'Energie Atomique (F)
CND	Campaign for Nuclear Disarmament (UK)

CPAE	Controller of Production (Atomic Energy), Ministry of Supply (UK)
CSAR	Chief Superintendent, Armament Research, Ministry of Supply (UK)
CSHER	Chief Superintendent, High Explosives Research, Ministry of Supply (UK)
CSIRO	Commonwealth Scientific and Industrial Research Organization (A)
CXRL	Commonwealth Xray and Radium Laboratory (A)
DAWRE	Director, Atomic Weapons Research Establishment (UK)
DAW(T)	Director, Atomic Weapons (Trials), Ministry of Supply (UK)
DGAW	Director General, Atomic Weapons, Ministry of Supply (later, Ministry of Aviation) (UK)
DRPC	Defence Research Policy Committee (UK)
G1, G2	The two shots fired in the *Mosaic* series 1956 (UK)
GZ	Ground Zero
HER	High Explosives Research—early code name for atomic weapon research (UK)
ICBM	Intercontinental ballistic missile
ICRP	International Commission on Radiological Protection
IF	Indoctrinee Force
IRBM	Intermediate Range Ballistic Missile
kt	Kiloton—equivalent to 1000 tons of TNT
LWRE	Long Range Weapons Research Establishment, Salisbury, South Australia (A)
MARSU	Maralinga Range Support Unit (A)
MBWP	Monte Bello Working Party (A)
MOS	Ministry of Supply (UK)
MPD (or mpd)	Maximum permissible dose. Similarly maximum permissible body burden (MPBB), concentration (MPC) or level (MPL)
mSv	Millisievert, a unit of radiation (see Appendix G)

MRC	Medical Research Council (UK)
Mt	Megaton—equivalent to 1 million tons of TNT
NRAC	National Radiation Advisory Council (A)
NRPB	National Radiological Protection Board (UK)
NTS	Nevada Test Site (US)
R, r, rad, rem, rep	Units of radiation dose (see Appendix G)
RAAF	Royal Australian Air Force (A)
RAE	Royal Aircraft Establishment (UK)
RAF	Royal Air Force (UK)
RAN	Royal Australian Navy (A)
RE	Royal Engineers (UK)
RN	Royal Navy (UK)
T1, T2	The two shots fired in the *Totem* series, 1953
UKAEA	United Kingdom Atomic Energy Authority (UK)
UKMOSS(A)	United Kingdom Ministry of Supply Staff in Australia (UK)
UNSCEAR	United Nations Scientific Committee on Effects of Atomic Radiation
USAEC	United States Atomic Energy Commission (US)
USAF	United States Air Force (US)
X200	Code name for Emu Field site

Introduction

America's, and the world's, first atomic weapon test was in July 1945. The first Russian test was in 1949. Britain came third in 1952; France followed in 1960 and China in 1964. The Partial Test Ban Treaty, which was signed in July 1963 and came into effect in October of that year, ended nuclear weapon testing in the atmosphere by the United States and the Soviet Union who by this time had carried out, in all, nearly 400 atmospheric detonations. Britain, after carrying out 21, had ceased atmospheric testing five years earlier, in 1958; subsequent British tests were conducted underground at the United States' site in Nevada.

This book is neither an apologia for nuclear weapons or weapon tests, nor an argument against them. Defence policy, nuclear strategy, weapons research and development, and the ethics of nuclear weaponry are not its business. It is concerned to show why Britain adopted certain postwar defence policies that entailed nuclear weapon tests; why more than half of them—and all the earlier ones—were in Australia; where and how they took place; how the two nations cooperated; and what was achieved, and at what cost. It looks at the radiation safety standards of the time and of the present day; it considers how the safety aspects of the trials appeared then and how they appear now.

The book covers only the five series of trials in Australia (and the experimental programmes, not involving nuclear explosions, that took place there). The *Grapple* tests—nine shots off Malden and Christmas Islands in the Pacific during 1957 and 1958—merit a separate study.

The British trials began in 1952 in the Monte Bello Islands, an uninhabited group off the northwest coast of Australia. Three shots were fired in these islands and nine on the Australian mainland during the five years from 1952 to 1957. This was a unique episode in the history of Britain and Australia, with lasting and extremely important results. No other nuclear power developed its nuclear weapons as Britain did by testing them with the cooperation, and in the sovereign territory, of another independent—but non-nuclear—nation. This was only possible because of the very special relationship between the United Kingdom and Australia. The relationship was intensified by the test programme itself, although tensions and misunderstandings inevitably occurred in what was a generally close, friendly and effective collaboration. By the 1960s, the relationship was, for many reasons, beginning to change and weaken.

What actually happened during the years of testing? There is no dearth of information; the problem is not to find material but to extract the essentials from a vast mass of papers and to present a balanced and comprehensible picture. The sources are contemporary official records, published material, and oral evidence from test veterans and others. The present account is based mainly on contemporary documents— files, committee papers and scientific reports—from United Kingdom archives, especially, but not only, at the Atomic Weapons Research Establishment (AWRE), Aldermaston. There are also voluminous official records, estimated at two and a half thousand files, in various places in Australia; some but by no means all are counterparts of documents in the United Kingdom. I have been able to use some information from Australian sources, though not to study the Australian records at first hand, or to look at the terrain.

My confidence in the contemporary records, particularly the scientific files and reports, is strengthened by their unselfconscious quality and candid objectivity. There was then no thirty-year rule—not even a fifty-year rule—and certainly no thought of a Freedom of Information Act; the Public Records Act, embodying a fifty-year rule, was passed in 1958 and the thirty-year rule dates only from 1964. So the writers were not looking over their shoulders and they had no notion that their notes, correspondence and reports—including Top Secret papers— would ever be open to the public, certainly not within a few years. Far from trying to cover up anything that went wrong, the scientists discussed it *ad nauseam*; they had every incentive to study each trial exhaustively, to learn as much as possible from it, to identify and understand errors and shortcomings, and to improve and refine their methods for future trials. This is clear from reading the stream of scientific reports and notes that appeared for months or years after each of the trials.

Some of this material will soon be available in the Public Record Office. In the meanwhile I am grateful to the Ministry of Defence—in particular to AWRE, Aldermaston, which comes under its jurisdiction—and also to the United Kingdom Atomic Energy Authority, for allowing me to use their archival material. I have also been able to look at relevant records at No 10 Downing Street and in the Cabinet Office. I thank all the archives and library staff who have given me unstinting help.

A few problems arise in writing about radiation, since the units of measurement and some of the terms used in the 1950s are now obsolete. In the text, I have where necessary used both old and new units, and explanatory notes are given in Appendix G.

Books and articles that have helped me, especially on the political and scientific background to the weapon trials, are listed in the Bibliography.

I was already working on this subject before the Royal Commission into British Nuclear Tests in Australia was set up. Much oral and written evidence, from over four hundred witnesses, was given to the Royal Commission both in Australia and in the United Kingdom. Its papers—which include proofs of evidence and statements, thousands of pages of transcripts of the hearings, the numerous Australian and British documents tendered to it, and the final submissions of all the Counsel involved—are a rich store of information. However the contemporary United Kingdom records have been my main source.

I have talked to a small number of people who were engaged in the tests, had some special knowledge of them, or were the authors of scientific reports. Otherwise I have not attempted to interview any of the thousands of test participants. It would have been too lengthy a task to identify from the records a sufficiently large and representative selection of people for my purpose, to interview them all, and to check the collected material thoroughly. Such checking of oral evidence is essential; experience of talking to people about events twenty or thirty years ago shows that some valuable information may be gained, but that errors abound, for even the best memories are fallible.

Friends and colleagues have greatly assisted me with information, comments, corrections; any errors that remain are my own. So are the opinions expressed. I am grateful to my colleagues and to my friend Dr John Symonds of Cronulla, NSW, whose work in Australia and England on the trials produced an admirable chronology and report.

My special gratitude is due to Lord Penney who has been most generous with his time, and to Professor Margaret Gowing, who gave me her uniquely well qualified advice and criticism, as well as much-needed encouragement.

Carol Dines deciphered my drafts with praiseworthy success and was tireless in typing them.

1 Atomic Policies and Policymakers

Origins

Why, and how, did Britain decide at the end of the Second World War to develop her own atomic weapons?[1]. The origins of the decision go back to 1939, the year that saw both the outbreak of the war and scientific discoveries that were to lead to the atomic bombs that ended it.

During 1939 it was found that when neutrons—uncharged particles from the nucleus of an atom—bombarded atoms of uranium not only were fission fragments and an immense amount of energy released, but also some spare neutrons that could then split other uranium atoms, so that a chain reaction was possible, releasing more and more energy. It was only two days before war broke out in September that the great Danish physicist Niels Bohr, with an American colleague, published the theory that gave understanding of uranium fission. That is, the basic scientific knowledge was openly available to the whole world.

Scientists in several countries had seen during 1939 that uranium fission might be a source of heat and power far beyond anything ever known. It also seemed that it might provide an unprecedentedly powerful explosive. If so, would German scientists be able to develop it for Hitler? Bohr's paper made this seem unlikely, as it showed that fission is much more likely to occur in one kind of uranium atom—the fissile isotope uranium-235—than in uranium-238 atoms. But natural uranium consists mainly of uranium-238 (99.3 per cent), with only 0.7 per cent uranium-235, and a chain reaction can be achieved in natural uranium only if the neutrons are slowed down (or moderated) to increase their chances of hitting the fissile uranium-235 atoms. Slow neutrons, however, cannot produce the tremendously fast reaction required for an atomic explosion. Scientists who realized that the fast neutron reaction was necessary for an atomic bomb thought it would be possible only by using pure uranium-235; they did not think a bomb feasible, therefore, since the task of separating uranium-235 from the slightly heavier but chemically identical uranium-238 would be impossible. So although physicists in Britain and America continued with uranium research—which might prove very important in the long run—they did not see it as contribution to winning the war. Britain had other more urgent wartime projects, such as radar research, and the United States did not enter the war until December 1941, when Japan attacked Pearl Harbour.

In the spring of 1940 there came a turning point. Two physicists in Birmingham, England—Rudolf Peierls, a refugee from Germany, and Otto Frisch, a refugee from Austria—wrote a memorandum that showed that a lump of uranium-235 of about 5 kg would give the prodigiously fast reaction needed for an atomic explosion equivalent to several thousand tons of dynamite. It then suggested an industrial method for separating uranium-235. It drew attention to the radiation hazards such a bomb would create. Finally it emphasized the strategic and moral implications.

As a result of the Frisch–Peierls memorandum, a scientific committee, code-named the Maud Committee[2], was set up. Soon after, as France fell, two French scientists, Halban and Kowarski, escaped to England. They came from a Paris team that had been the first to report early in 1939 the possibility of achieving a slow chain reaction in ordinary, natural uranium. Even though scientists believed by 1940 that this slow reaction would be useless for a bomb, it held out to them the hope of nuclear power. The two French physicists carried with them to England the total world stock of heavy water that they had brought from Norway; this was the best known and most efficient moderator for slowing down neutrons. The Frenchmen settled in Cambridge at the Cavendish Laboratory, and here two of their colleagues predicted that in the course of slow chain reactions in ordinary, unseparated uranium a new element almost completely unknown in nature would be formed, which would behave like uranium-235 and would be usable for bombs. This was the element later called plutonium.

The Maud Committee, fearful of possible German progress, worked with frantic haste. In the summer of 1941, it presented to the British government a brilliant and comprehensive report showing the possibility of an atomic bomb—certainly with uranium-235 and possibly with plutonium—and described the processes and plant required. It even estimated the cost. A copy of the report was taken to the still neutral United States where groups of scientists were, rather desultorily, studying bomb possibilities. It was only after they received the Maud Report that the Americans took the project seriously and, even before Pearl Harbour, launched what was to be the huge Manhattan Project.

The British Government, meanwhile, immediately set up an organization with the code-name 'Tube Alloys'. Clearly the project would mean an enormous industrial effort. Was it possible to build the plant in beleaguered Britain, which was under enemy air attack and short of manpower and materials? British scientists and politicians decided that the first pilot plants ought to be built in Britain, and later full scale plants in North America, preferably in Canada with United States help. But the project had such vast implications that there was a fear of transferring all the work from Britain to the United States, which was still neutral and might become isolationist after the war as after the 1914–18 war.

At the end of 1941, the British were ahead and the United States suggested a joint project. But the proposal was treated with cool condescension; the British wanted exchanges of information, no more. By the summer of 1942 the Americans had forged ahead very fast. The British, still struggling to build a few pilot units for a uranium separation plant, now wished to be partners in the American project, but they were too late and were not wanted; even the exchange of information ceased. The British were desperate: they realized that the atomic bomb would be the key to national power in the postwar world, and they also had great hopes of peaceful nuclear energy, but they could not make progress alone and were cut off from knowledge of the United States project.

After great efforts, Churchill eventually persuaded Roosevelt to sign the Quebec Agreement in August 1943[3]. It enabled the British to participate in the Manhattan Project, and also set up arrangements for joint exploitation and purchase of uranium supplies. There were two other important provisions: first, that neither side would use the bomb without the other's consent; and, secondly, that neither would communicate any atomic information to third parties except by mutual consent. After the Quebec Agreement, nearly all the British scientists working on uranium-235 or on fast neutrons for bombs joined the United States project; most went to Los Alamos, the atomic bomb laboratory in New Mexico. The British contribution to the Manhattan Project, though on a very small scale, was of high quality, and of key importance in some crucial areas of research, so that again it hastened the completion of the bombs.

Meanwhile the French and British scientists at Cambridge engaged in slow neutron work had been moved to Canada where a joint research establishment was set up, and after the Quebec Agreement the Americans underwrote the project, which was directed by the British scientist, John Cockcroft[4].

When the war ended, there was almost no doubt in the mind of British politicians and scientists that Britain must have her own nuclear programme. It was a flexible and open-ended programme, to carry out research 'covering all uses of atomic energy'[5] and to produce fissile material in sufficient quantity to enable Britain to develop a programme 'for the use of atomic energy as circumstances may require'. At first this did not mean atomic bombs, for there were hopes that international control of atomic energy might be established, but the Atomic Energy Commission of the new United Nations Organisation, set up in January 1946, failed and was wound up in May 1948[6]. However it was generally assumed that Britain would make atomic bombs, and the engineers given the task of constructing reactors to produce plutonium had been told that it was for bombs, to be made with utmost urgency in the vital interests of the nation.

A very secret decision to make atomic bombs was taken by Ministers in January 1947—it was not disclosed to Parliament[7] until May 1948—and from this time an independent nuclear deterrent became a cornerstone in British government policy. It was endorsed by both the major political parties (except for a twelve-month interval, 1960–61) and supported by the majority of the public; there was little criticism or questioning before 1954 and no substantial organized opposition until CND was founded at the beginning of 1958.

What were the reasons underlying the 1945 and 1947 decisions? There were strategic grounds; there were considerations of status; and there was Britain's relationship with the United States.

Strategic reasons

Strategic ideas about atomic weapons were very general at first. In 1945, shortly before the bombing of Japan, an advisory committee of British scientists (at least two of whom later strongly opposed the British weapons programme) concluded that the only answer to an atomic bomb was to be prepared to use it in retaliation—i.e., deterrence.

The 1947 decision was not made in response to an immediate military threat. It was based, rather, on an intuitive feeling that Britain must possess this climacteric weapon. It was seen as a manifestation of the scientific and technological strength on which Britain must depend. At the end of the war, it must be remembered, though there were American occupying forces in Germany and Austria, there was no formal United States commitment to defend Britain or Western Europe and no 'nuclear umbrella'. NATO was not set up until 1949.

Even in the closing stages of the war some people, notably Churchill, had become increasingly apprehensive about a postwar Soviet threat. But for a while after the end of the war no immediate danger to the peace of the world seemed very likely. However, by early 1948 the developing cold war made the military threat much closer and more menacing. A Communist regime was established in Czechoslovakia in February 1948; in June the Soviet blockade of Berlin began, and lasted nearly a year; the three year long Korean War broke out in June 1950. In September 1950 the Labour government undertook a general rearmament programme.

Status

The second reason for Britain's decision to possess nuclear weapons was her belief in her great power status. Her wartime achievement, without which Germany would probably have been victorious, and her crucial atomic role hid her changed status in the world. There were indeed two superpowers: the United States, with its atomic monopoly and economic might; and the Soviet Union which became the second nuclear power with its first atomic test in 1949—fully three years before Britain's. This was a shattering blow to Britain, who had expected to be second in the field. But although Britain was not a superpower, she was, amidst the devastation of other European countries, a great power only one step below the superpowers. If, in the new atomic age, she did not make atomic bombs she would (to quote Lord Cherwell, Churchill's friend and scientific adviser) 'rank with other European nations who have to make do with conventional weapons'. 'If we are unable to make the bomb ourselves', he wrote, 'and have to rely entirely on the United States for this vital weapon, we shall sink to the rank of a second-class nation, only permitted to supply auxiliary troops, like the native levies who were allowed small arms but not artillery'[8]. Atomic weapons seemed to guarantee continuing great power status for Britain. Hardly anyone except Sir Henry Tizard, then chief scientific adviser to the Ministry of Defence, questioned this view. In 1949 he wrote, 'we persist in regarding ourselves as a great power . . . we are *not* a great power and never will be again. We are a great nation but if we continue to behave like a great power we shall soon cease to be a great nation. Let us take warning from the fate of the great powers of the past and not burst ourselves with pride. (See Aesop's fable of the frog)'[9].

The Anglo-American relationship

The partnership embodied in the 1943 Quebec Agreement had been re-affirmed by Churchill and Roosevelt in another agreement signed in September 1944 at Hyde Park (Roosevelt's country home in New York State)[10]. It said *inter alia* that full Anglo-American collaboration in developing atomic energy for civil and military purposes would continue after the war 'unless and until terminated by joint agreement'. But after Roosevelt's death, the agreement turned out to be worthless, as no one in the United States Administration knew about it.

Yet another agreement, promising 'full and effective collaboration' in atomic energy, was made in November 1945 in Washington by Truman, Attlee and Mackenzie King, the Canadian Premier[11]. But in a few months these agreements were swept aside when in August 1946 the United States Congress passed the Atomic Energy Act, known as the McMahon Act, which prohibited the passing of classified atomic information to any foreign country, including Britain, and imposed the severest penalities, including the death penalty. At one blow it ended the Anglo-American cooperation of the Quebec, Hyde Park and Washington agreements of 1943, 1944 and 1945. Only one area of partnership remained: the arrangements set up by the Quebec Agreement, for joint procurement and allocation of uranium, the indispensable raw material of atomic energy.

The McMahon Act meant that Britain must develop her atomic project on her own, without American help. Despite forebodings in Whitehall, this was not a serious obstacle to the building of the original atomic plants and a simple Nagasaki-type bomb. The withdrawal of Anglo-American atomic collaboration however was of the utmost political and strategic concern to Britain, and of great technological importance for more advanced weapons.

While the British atomic energy project developed independently, successive British governments strove ceaselessly in the next twelve years to regain the Anglo-American atomic partnership. There were hopeful moves and disappointing failures. In 1948, a secret arrangement—the *modus vivendi*—was made that offered some scientific and technical collaboration[12]. But it amounted to very little and entailed the surrender of the clause in the Quebec Agreement which provided that neither country would use the atomic bomb without the consent of the other. (A right to consent before atomic bombs were used from United Kingdom bases was regained in 1951, but it did not apply to any use of bombs from overseas bases.)

There was, however, one concession to Britain's Commonwealth ties. The Quebec Agreement had forbidden the passing of any atomic information to third parties, but now the *modus vivendi* made provision for 'areas of cooperation between members of the British Commonwealth'. The nine areas specified included health and safety, detection of distant nuclear explosions, survey methods for uranium and treatment of uranium ores, and research reactors. It was this annex to the *modus vivendi* that from January 1948 governed the supply of information by Britain to Australia (see Appendix B).

The next initiative was at the end of 1949. So far Britain had simply wanted an independent deterrent and a full exchange of information with the Americans, but the vastly increased American technological lead (and the Soviet test detected in August 1949) made much closer collaboration desirable. Talks began in Washington in late 1949, but they broke down in January 1950 after the arrest for espionage of Klaus Fuchs, the German-born British-naturalized scientist at Harwell who had worked at Los Alamos during the war[13].

There was a further slight advance in cooperation in 1955 when an amendment to the McMahon Act permitted further limited exchanges of information. But the breakthrough did not come until 1958. Before then the Americans were not particularly impressed by what Britain had to offer as a partner. While Britain was beginning to acquire atomic bombs, the United States and the Soviet Union were already acquiring the infinitely more powerful thermonuclear bombs. Only a month after the first British atomic test in October 1952, the Americans exploded the world's first thermonuclear device, and the Russians tested a thermonuclear bomb nine months later. One United States Congressman, asked for his views on atomic cooperation with Britain, said 'We would be trading a horse for a rabbit'[14].

The Churchill government decided in June 1954 that Britain, too, must have thermonuclear weapons. A new programme of weapon development began that resulted, in the short space of three years, in a series of high yield weapon tests in the Pacific. By 1958, the success of the British independent nuclear weapons programme had been demonstrated in Australia and at Christmas and Malden Islands in the Pacific. Moreover in 1956 Britain had opened Calder Hall, the first land-based nuclear power plant on an industrial scale in the world. All this convinced the United States that Britain was a worthwhile partner with a valuable contribution to make to the partnership. After the necessary amendments to the McMahon Act, a bilateral agreement, this time in treaty form, on 'Co-operation on the Uses of Atomic Energy for Mutual Defence Purposes', was concluded in July 1958[15]. It included exchanges of technical information and weapon designs and an Agreement in 1959[16] extended the exchanges to fissile materials; later, nuclear weapon test facilities were shared—the first joint test was in Nevada in March 1962—and the United States agreed to supply missiles to Britain, who was to fabricate her own warheads. After twelve years of enforced independence, a new era of nuclear interdependence began. It had been one of the main objectives of successive British governments and its pursuit had overridden all other such relationships whether with European or Commonwealth countries.

Organizations and men

The Attlee organization

Who made these atomic decisions, who advised on them, and who were the men who carried them out?[17].

In the Attlee government the crucial decisions were taken, not by full Cabinet, but by a small and active Ministerial committee known as Gen 75—called by Attlee 'the Atom Bomb Committee'. Because of its exceptional secrecy, its decisions were not even reported to the Cabinet. A still smaller group of Ministers, Gen 163, took the January 1947 decision to make an atomic bomb. The Prime Minister, Lord President of the Council, and Foreign Secretary were in both these groups; the Chancellor of the Exchequer was on Gen 75 only, and the Minister of Defence and the Dominions Secretary were on Gen 163 only. In February 1947, a proper Ministerial committee—the AE(M) Committee— was set up to handle policy questions requiring the consideration of Ministers, under the chairmanship of the Prime Minister, but it met infrequently and Gen meetings, variously numbered, were still used to deal with the highest matters of policy.

The other Ministerial committee that discussed atomic energy was the Defence Committee, also under the Prime Minister's chairmanship, but it was not kept regularly informed on the atomic project and took no decisions on the programme until 1950, when it had to deal with important questions of priority between atomic and other weapons.

So atomic policy was made, under the especially close direction of the Prime Minister, by small ministerial groups with varying membership, but an almost constant inner core—the Prime Minister himself, Ernest Bevin, the Foreign Secretary, and the Minister of Supply, who was departmentally responsible but who had much less influence on policy than Bevin.

Ministers were at first advised on policy by an advisory committee of Service and official representatives (the ACAE) chaired, for the sake of continuity, by Sir John Anderson, an Independent MP who had been the Cabinet Minister in charge of atomic energy in the wartime coalition government and who now sat on the Front Bench of the Conservative Opposition. These strange arrangements never worked well, and the ACAE was disbanded in 1947. A new official committee, the AE(O), was set up in late 1946 and became very hardworking and effective after Roger Makins (now Lord Sherfield) took the chair early in 1947 on returning from the Embassy in Washington, where he had dealt with atomic energy matters from 1945 to 1952. He had unrivalled experience of Anglo-American relationships in atomic energy, and the connection was maintained when he became Ambassador in Washington (1952–56) and, later, chairman of the United Kingdom Atomic Energy Authority (1960–64).

On the Defence side, the Ministry of Defence was created in October 1946, and in January 1947 a scientific adviser was appointed (Sir Henry Tizard) and a Defence Research Policy Committee (DRPC) was set up. It was to advise the Minister of Defence and the Chiefs of Staff on defence science policy, but was forbidden to encroach on the territory of the Anderson Committee (the ACAE) and was starved of information until after the ACAE was wound up. Then the DRPC was allowed an atomic energy sub-committee.

The Minister departmentally responsible for atomic energy was the Minister of Supply, in whose vast department atomic energy was placed by the 1946 Atomic Energy Act. It provided a ready-made infrastructure for the new project, and there it remained until mid-1954 when, as we shall see, the United Kingdom Atomic Energy Authority was formed.

Britain was unusual in not creating at once a new single-purpose organization to accommodate this new project. The Americans had set up the United States Atomic Energy Commission (USAEC), the French had set up the Commissariat à l'Energie Atomique (CEA), and other nations followed suit. Britain alone poured new wine into old bottles. There were some advantages, but the results did not look logical or tidy.

Within the Ministry Lord Portal, the impressive ex-Chief of the Air Staff, was appointed to head the atomic energy project, aided by a small staff of civil servants, some with experience of Tube Alloys. He was responsible to the Prime Minister and tended to bypass his departmental Minister. His special strengths were the weight he carried with the Americans and his influence with the Chiefs of Staff and the Service departments. At first he was Controller of Production (Atomic Energy)—CPAE—but in 1950 became Controller, Atomic Energy—CAE—with his jurisdiction extended to include the research establishment at Harwell, under Cockcroft, and the weapons establishment under Penney, as well as the industrial organization under Hinton[18] which had the task of producing fissile material.

When Portal retired in 1951 he was succeeded by the much less weighty but amiable General Sir Frederick Morgan[19]. He remained in the CAE post until 1954, and after the Atomic Energy Authority was formed he continued in the Ministry of Supply as Controller of Atomic Weapons (CAW). When he retired in 1956 the post became DGAW—Director General of Atomic Weapons—and was occupied by officials who were birds of passage.

Of the three separate parts of the project—Cockcroft's research establishment at Harwell, Hinton's industrial complex based at Risley in Lancashire, and the weapons establishment under William Penney—only the third concerns us here. It was a small highly secret staff, drawn in 1947 from the Armaments Research Department of the Ministry of Supply, of which Penney had been appointed Chief Superintendent (CSAR), with responsibility for conventional weapons research of all kinds, at the beginning of 1946. The atomic weapons project was given the designation 'High Explosives Research'—abbreviated to HER—and Penney became CSHER. The work was located first at Fort Halstead in Kent and later, from 1950, at Aldermaston in Berkshire.

Reorganization under the Conservatives

When the Churchill government took office in October 1951, Lord Cherwell was appointed Paymaster General. Soon a Prime Minister's directive—a bizarre document, as Margaret Gowing calls it[20]—divided responsibility for atomic energy between the Paymaster General and the Minister of Supply (who was statutorily responsible under the 1946 Atomic Energy Act). The demarcation of functions was confused and the scope for misunderstanding and conflict almost limitless, especially with two such forceful characters as Cherwell and Duncan Sandys, who was the Minister of Supply from 1951 to late 1954. Morgan observed that when one (or both) was abroad there was peace, but when they returned to London warfare was resumed.

Cherwell was determined to reorganize the atomic project radically, and to remove it from the Ministry of Supply and indeed from the Civil Service. He was convinced that the dead hand of the Civil Service was responsible for the fact that the Soviet Union beat Britain by three years to its first bomb test[21]. He wanted an entirely new kind of body, an atomic energy commission funded by a Treasury grant-in-aid, but with the freedom and flexibility of private industry. Churchill was reluctant to agree to a change at least until after the first atomic test, but eventually in 1953 a committee was set up to make recommendations on the form of the new organization. It led to the United Kingdom Atomic Energy Authority Act of July 1954 and the creation of the Atomic Energy Authority—an upheaval that added to the burdens of the project leaders.

The new Authority took over the functions, staff, laboratories and plant of the old Ministry of Supply atomic project. On weapons there was a complicated demarcation system. The Ministry of Supply retained responsibility for development and production of all nuclear warheads and arranged contracts with the Authority for fissile material; it was also responsible for the overall planning, organization and conduct of major trials and arrangements for running the range in Australia. This allocation of responsibility for trials was laid down by the AE(O) in May 1954 and confirmed a year later. Coordination within Whitehall was effected by an atomic weapon tests executive committee (called variously according to the trial in hand—Mosex, Buffalex or Antex). As for policy on tests, this continued to be handled by committees much as before, and a high level official committee on nuclear test policy was not set up until 1957.

The scientific conduct of the trials, was the task of Aldermaston, where there was a small but effective trials planning staff with experience going back to *Hurricane* and *Totem*. The Service departments set up their own internal organization for dealing with trials; the Air Ministry needed an especially strong one. But after 1954 the Ministry of Supply, with overall responsibility for trials, had a minute staff to handle them. Under the CAW (later, the DGAW) the Director of Atomic Weapons (Trials) was a genial and hardworking retired naval officer, Captain F B (Frankie) Lloyd, RN. He had a total staff of two junior officials, neither of them a scientist. He pointed out the various weaknesses of the whole organization, and the inadequacy of his own tiny directorate, but little seems to have changed by the time he retired in 1960, when the Ministry of Supply was wound up and its atomic weapons functions passed to the Ministry of Aviation. By then the major trials had ceased, though the Maralinga range was still very much in use for minor trials.

The men

Of the United Kingdom politicians who made the nuclear decisions, and the officials and scientists who advised them on policy and implemented it, only a few can be mentioned here. Because of the central importance of nuclear policy all Prime Ministers from Attlee to Macmillan were deeply involved. Attlee initiated and fostered the programme, and also the arrangements with Menzies, the Prime Minister of Australia, for the first test in the Monte Bello Islands in 1952.

The *Hurricane* plans were carried through by the Churchill government, which took office in October 1951. Churchill, who retained from the war his powerful interest in atomic energy (and an obsession with the old Quebec and Hyde Park agreements), paid detailed attention to *Hurricane*, even taking the chair himself at planning meetings. The Australian connection was strengthened by the friendly relationship between Churchill and the conservative and anglophile Menzies. Until Churchill retired in April 1955 he dominated defence policy. Events developed rapidly, with the first and second weapon trials, the decision in 1954 to make a British hydrogen bomb, the launching of the first civil nuclear power programme in 1955, and the establishment of a permanent range in Australia. There was also the beginning of an intense debate on fallout and Churchill responded quickly to Parliamentary and public anxiety by setting up in 1955 a Medical Research Council enquiry into radiation hazards.

Anthony Eden, who followed Churchill in April 1955, bore the full brunt of the fallout debate, and during the first half of 1956 he agonized and temporized over the decision to approve the high yield nuclear explosions (the first *Grapple* series) in the Pacific in 1957. He also had to face growing national and international opposition to weapon tests, increasing Australian sensitivity, uncertainties about the future of testing, and the difficult stop-go international discussion that finally led to a test moratorium in late 1958. But before then he had resigned because of ill-health and had been succeeded, in January 1957, by Harold Macmillan.

Macmillan, who had briefly (1954–55) been Minister of Defence, was perhaps the most deeply engaged of all in atomic affairs. His premiership of nearly five years began with a major change of defence policy, enunciated in the Defence White Paper of April 1957[22], and with the first series of weapon tests in the Pacific, which gave Britain a thermonuclear weapon capability. His period of office saw the continuation of the fallout controversy; the birth of the Campaign for Nuclear Disarmament (CND); and the beginning and end of a three-year moratorium on tests by the three nuclear powers.

His talks with Eisenhower in October 1957, and their joint Washington Declaration, opened a new era in Anglo-American atomic relations and led directly to the 1958 bilateral agreement on nuclear defence. Under Macmillan's administration interdependence flourished; strong practical links were forged, and the Polaris agreement was made in April 1963. At the same time, international negotiations progressed, even if slowly; the Partial Test Ban Treaty which banned atmospheric weapon tests was concluded, and came into force in October 1963, just as Macmillan resigned the premiership.

Of Churchill's Ministers, the most influential was Lord Cherwell, his friend and scientific adviser for many years, a member of his wartime Cabinet, and Paymaster General in his 1951–55 Cabinet. Cherwell was a distinguished scientist as well as a Conservative politician. His involvement with atomic energy went back to the Maud Committee and, through membership of a technical committee, he had retained an official position in atomic matters throughout the Attlee years. The connection continued, and until his death in 1957 he was a Board Member of the United Kingdom Atomic Energy Authority, which he had created almost single-handed.

Of the three Ministers of Supply who were statutorily responsible for atomic energy from 1946 to 1954 when the Atomic Energy Authority was set up, only Duncan Sandys left a lasting impression. Nor did successive Ministers of Defence—there were three between 1954 and 1957—until Sandys. He was an exceptionally forceful, energetic and hardworking Minister, abrasive in personality. His three years as

Minister of Supply were frustrated by the conditions imposed by the Prime Minister's directive and by conflicts with Cherwell. It was also a crucial period of action: *Hurricane, Totem,* plans for Maralinga—Sandys had doubts about the wisdom of a permanent range—and the formation of the Atomic Energy Authority which he strongly and openly opposed.

At the Ministry of Defence—January 1957 to October 1959—he was responsible for the 1957 Defence White Paper, written in a few weeks and largely by himself, which based defence policy more firmly than ever on nuclear deterrence and announced the end of conscription in 1960. It was elaborated by the 1958 and 1959 White Papers[23].

Of the administrators and scientists who advised Ministers and implemented the nuclear weapon policies, Portal and Makins have already been mentioned. The latter was influential especially in the Anglo-American context. So too was the first chairman and chief executive of the Authority, Sir Edwin (now Lord) Plowden. He was at the heart of policy-making in Whitehall and played a vital part in achieving the 1958 bilateral agreement.

The defence policy was dependent on the work of hundreds of scientists, engineers and technicians engaged in research, producing fissile material and other special materials, and designing, fabricating and testing nuclear devices and weapons. They came together from many sources, some returning from the Manhattan Project or from Canada, some from radar research, some from other defence research establishments, some from the universities.

The man who was recognized as indispensable to the weapon programme was William Penney. He had become assistant professor of mathematics at Imperial College at the early age of twenty-seven; during the war he worked for the Home Office on the effects of high explosives, and for the Admiralty on the effects of waves on the transportable Mulberry harbours used in the Allied invasion of Europe. In 1944 he went to Los Alamos, and became a key member of the staff. He was one of the two official Britons—the other was Group Captain Leonard Cheshire VC—in the observer plane in the Nagasaki bombing raid of 9 August 1945, and in 1946 was invited to take part in the United States bomb tests at Bikini; the Americans made several unsuccessful attempts to persuade him to work in the United States. 'He is our chief—indeed our only—real expert in the construction of the bomb and I do not know what we should do without him', Cherwell wrote to Churchill. 'He played an outstanding part in designing the original American bombs at Los Alamos in the war and participated in the first tests. The Americans admit frankly that they would give a great deal to get him back. But on an appeal to his patriotism he gave up the offer of a very attractive professorship and came into government service. He is not always tactful but his heart is in the right place. He now runs the bomb production establishment . . . and is responsible for the whole of the scientific side of the Australian test operation'[24].

'Penney's mathematical skill', Margaret Gowing writes, 'had the elegance, simplicity of approach and intuitive understanding that build a great reputation'[25]. His pre-war academic work had also given him an interdisciplinary approach, and he had an outstanding ability to find practical solutions to problems. He had, besides, a gift of communication, and of simple and lucid explanation of scientific matters to the uninitiated, whether politicians, Servicemen of all ranks, or radio audiences. He got on extremely well with the Americans and with the Australians, because they both found him entirely honest and unaffected.

Who were the men who worked with him?[26]. He had much greater difficulties of recruitment than did the already well known Cockcroft at Harwell. A top secret weapons establishment was less appealing. There had to be tight security restrictions; deadlines were inexorable; the work was often difficult and dangerous; the scientists could not publish their results as Harwell staff were comparatively free to do; some potential recruits had conscientious objections, or a strong distaste for weapons.

The weapons group was always short of staff, sometimes desperately so. Few of the returning Manhattan Project scientists, even those from Los Alamos, joined the weapons work. Most of Penney's men therefore were extracted from defence research establishments. His senior scientists were generally older than those in Cockcroft's or even Hinton's organizations, and were highly experienced in their various fields. They were joined by a few war time recruits, including some clever young academics. For reasons of space, only a few of the weaponeers can be mentioned here, but they included R Pilgrim, an expert in blast measurement who had been at the 1946 United States test with Penney and who played a central part in trials planning operations; G L Hopkin, metallurgist; L C Tyte, W J Challens, C A Adams and I Maddock, who were experts in electronics and instrumentation; E H Mott and W J Moyce, explosives experts; D E Barnes and G C Dale, health and safety specialists; chemist D T Lewis; mathematical physicist J Corner; and radiochemist Frank Morgan, the only Harwell scientist who agreed to transfer to Penney's staff. One other man, who was not a scientist, must be mentioned here. In 1950 Admiral P Brooking, a retired naval officer, was appointed as Penney's deputy to give him some relief from administration.

Later, in 1954, the Chief of the Royal Naval Scientific Service, W J (now Sir William) Cook was appointed as Penney's deputy, with special responsibility for managing the hydrogen bomb programme; the time schedule was very tight, and he was a highly efficient and hard-driving organizer. But in 1958 he was promoted and moved from the weapons post in a major Atomic Energy Authority reorganization.

Penney himself was more and more in demand to advise on disarmanent, test-limitation and test-ban negotiations, and by the time the major trials came to an end he was spending much of his time in Whitehall or Geneva. Then in 1959 he moved from Aldermaston to Harwell, as Authority Member for Scientific Research, and his responsibilities for nuclear weapons passed to a newly appointed Member for Weapons Research, Air Chief Marshal Sir Claude Pelly. In 1961 Penney became Deputy Chairman, and in 1964 Chairman, of the Atomic Energy Authority.

The British public

What about the British people, on whose behalf all this was done and who paid for it in their taxes? It is sometimes thought that there was from the beginning opposition to atomic weapons. But there was no controversy when the atomic bomb decision was disclosed in the House of Commons in May 1948. There was no opposition on party lines; the Labour Party (except briefly in 1960/61) officially supported the British defence policy, though Labour MPs attacked nuclear weapon tests from 1954 onwards when anxiety about fallout flared up all over the world; and later many individual Labour MPs were to become supporters of the Campaign for Nuclear Disarmament. CND was launched at the beginning of 1958, grew very rapidly and recruited many big names, including Bertrand Russell, who in 1961, at the age of 89, went to prison for demonstrating against nuclear weapons; yet in 1947, when the United States still had a nuclear monopoly, even he had advocated using the threat of preventive war to compel the Soviet Union to accept an American plan for international control of atomic energy[27]. Even when the nuclear issues, especially weapon tests, were being hotly debated, public opinion polls showed remarkably steady support for—or at least acquiescence in—government nuclear policy. It is against this background that the British weapon tests were planned and carried out.

Notes and references

1 The substance of this section is taken from Margaret Gowing *Britain, America and the Bomb* in *Retreat from Power* (Vol. 2) (ed. David Dilkes, Macmillan, 1981). For a full and detailed account see Gowing *Independence and Deterrence* (Vol. 1) (Macmillan, 1974).

2 Otto Frisch was responsible for the name of the Maud Committee. When Denmark was overrun by German forces, Niels Bohr in Copenhagen had sent a telegram to Otto Frisch ending 'Tell Cockcroft and Maud Ray Kent'. Maud Ray, who lived in Kent, had been the Bohr children's governess. Not knowing this, Frisch thought it was a cryptic message (perhaps an anagram of 'raydium taken' meaning that the Nazis had confiscated the Copenhagen stock of radium). The name came to his mind when a non-informative title was needed afterwards for the secret committee. Subsequent ingenuity produced the mythical interpretation—Military Applications of Uranium Detonation. [Alwyn McKay: *The Making of the Atomic Age* (OUP, 1984), p. 54, and Margaret Gowing: *Britain and Atomic Energy 1939–45* (Macmillan, 1964), p. 45.]

3 The text of the Quebec Agreement is published as Appendix 4 in Gowing: *Britain and Atomic Energy 1939–1945*.

4 See Gowing: *Britain and Atomic Energy 1939–1945*, Chapters 6 and 10.

5 Gowing: *Independence and Deterrence*, Vol. 2, p. 205.

6 Attlee said 'We had worked from the start for international control of the bomb. We wanted it completely under the United Nations. That was the best way. But it was obviously going to take a long time. Meanwhile we had to face the world as it was. We had to look to our defence—and to our industrial future. We could not agree that only America should have atomic energy'. [Francis Williams: *A Prime Minister Remembers* (Heinemann, 1961), p. 113, quoted by A J R Groom in *British Thinking about Nuclear Weapons* (Frances Pinter, 1974).]

7 H C Deb, Vol. 450, col. 2117, 12 May 1948:
Mr George Jeger asked the Minister of Defence whether he is satisfied that adequate progress is being made in the development of the most modern types of weapons.
The Minister of Defence (Mr A V Alexander): Yes, Sir. As was made clear in the Statement Relating to Defence 1948 (Command 7327), research and development continue to receive the highest priority in the defence field, and all types of weapons, including atomic weapons, are being developed.

8 Gowing: *Independence and Deterrence*, Vol. 1, p. 407.

9 Gowing: *Ibid.*, Vol. 1, p. 229.

10 Gowing: *Britain and Atomic Energy 1939–1945*, Appendix 8.

11 Gowing: *Independence and Deterrence*, Vol. 1, Appendix 4 (p. 82).
12 Gowing: *Ibid.*, Vol. 1, Chapter 6 and Appendix 9 (p. 241).
13 Gowing: *Ibid.*, Vol. 2, Chapter 16.
14 Gowing: *Ibid.*, Vol. 1, p. 450.
15 Cmnd 537 (HMSO 1958).
16 Cmnd 859 (HMSO 1959).
17 Gowing: *Independence and Deterrence*, Vol. 1, Chapters 2 and 12.
18 Later Lord Hinton of Bankside; a great engineer who has been called the Brunel of the twentieth century. Accounts of Cockcroft, Hinton and Penney are given in Gowing: *Independence and Deterrence*, Vol. 2 Chapter 13.
19 It was believed by senior people in the project that the Prime Minister had intended to appoint Sir William Morgan, who had impressed him as the Chiefs of Staff representative in Washington, but that he had confused the names and so the letter was sent to 'the wrong Morgan'. (Gowing: *Independence and Deterrence*, Vol. 1, p. 46).
20 Gowing: *Independence and Deterrence*, Vol. 1, p. 428.
21 This is not true. Gowing: *Ibid.*, Vol. 1, p. 434.
22 *Outline of Future Policy* Cmnd 124 (HMSO, 1957).
23 Cmnd 363 (HMSO, 1958) and Cmnd 662 (HMSO, 1959).
24 Gowing: *Independence and Deterrence*, Vol. 2, p. 18.
25 Gowing: *Ibid.*, Vol. 2, pp. 6–7.
26 Gowing: *Ibid.*, Vol. 2, p. 30.
27 C Driver: *The Disarmers* (Hodder and Stoughton, 1964), On the protest movement, see also A J R Groom: *British Thinking about Nuclear Weapons* (Frances Pinter, 1974), Chapters 9, 12, 19 and 21–25.

2 Why Australia?

Why not an American range?

With no wide open spaces like the arid regions of New Mexico and Nevada, the British had to look overseas for a test site. They needed a large uninhabited area, in a friendly country, where they would have logistical support and local facilities. Ideally they would have liked to use an established American range; the benefits and economies were obvious, though there would be some disadvantages. In the winter of 1949–50, high-level atomic negotiations in Washington offered the hope of renewed Anglo-American collaboration, including an integrated weapons programme, but in February, as we saw, they broke down after the arrest for espionage of the German-born Harwell physicist, Klaus Fuchs.

Nevertheless, it still seemed that weapon-testing facilities might be obtained through the United States military authorities, who were encouraging, and in the summer of 1950 an official request to use the range at Eniwetok in the Pacific was made to the United States Chiefs of Staff[1]. But no reply came, and in September the British Chiefs of Staff recommended to the Prime Minister a site suggested by the Admiralty—the Monte Bello Islands, a small uninhabited group of islands off the north west coast of Australia, 'the coast of coral and pearl'. Here a British ship, prophetically named the *Tryal*, had been wrecked in 1622—the first documented contact with Australia.

Attlee promptly sent a message to the Australian Premier, Robert Menzies. In it he explained about Eniwetok; a reply from the Americans was still awaited, but meanwhile he hoped that the Australian government would approve in principle a British weapon test on Australian territory and would agree to a survey of the Monte Bello Islands[2]. Menzies quickly assented and in November 1950, after a somewhat curt refusal from the United States Chiefs of Staff, a small survey party went out to Australia and reported on the Monte Bello site in January 1951[3].

Meanwhile, Penney had been looking at alternative possibilities in Canada[4]. Provisional plans for an integrated Anglo-Canadian effort were drawn up and the site requirements were defined. These included a detonation area, a temporary camp site at least 10 miles upwind and a base camp with laboratories, workshops, etc, at least 25 miles upwind. The site would have to be isolated, with no human habitation within 100 miles downwind. Prevailing winds should blow contamination over the sea, but clear of shipping. The site should be large enough to accommodate the detonation of about a dozen weapons over several years; since each explosion would cause severe contamination over about 500 yards' radius, each detonation would have to be at least 3 miles from the previous one.

Seven sites in Canada were investigated, and one, near Churchill on the west coast of Hudson Bay, seemed suitable from the technical point of view, except that the sea was too shallow for ships to be used near the shore.

Attlee and Menzies discussed the subject again when the latter visited London in January 1951. Then in March Attlee wrote to say that Britain would not wait any longer for the American test site, and would be most grateful both for permission to use the Monte Bello Islands in October 1952, and for Australian help in preparing and carrying out the trial. The explosion, he said, would contaminate at least some of the islands with radioactivity, and for about 3 years the area would be unfit for habitation or even for visits by the pearl fishers who occasionally went there. Menzies agreed to a detailed survey of the Islands.

An Australian general election was pending, but as soon as the Menzies government was re-elected in May 1951, formal agreement to the test was received from Canberra[5]. However British Ministers had decided to make one more approach to the Americans, while keeping the Australian option open, and June 1951 was set as the deadline for a final decision. But it was August when the American Secretary of State replied; though he refused the British request for Eniwetok because of the McMahon Act (see Chapter 1), he offered alternative proposals for a joint test in Nevada. Penney flew to Washington for urgent consultations, which convinced him that from his point of view a satisfactory test in Nevada was possible.

However the general opinion, including that of the Chiefs of Staff, was that the test should be in Australia (see Map 1). There would be considerable political advantage in showing, as Mr Shinwell, the Minister of Defence, said, that Britain was not merely a satellite of the United States. The Nevada conditions were very restrictive and would make all the British results available to the Americans without reciprocity,

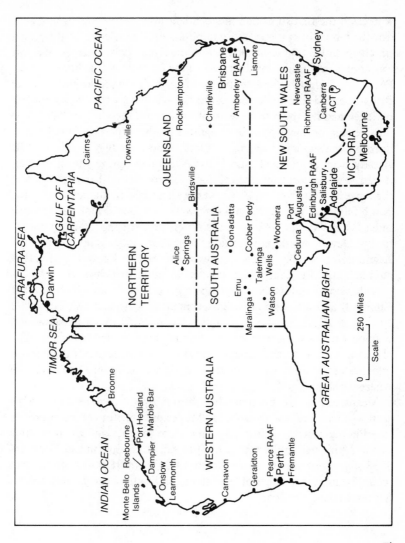

Map 1

whereas if the British had an independent programme they would control their own operations and would acquire knowledge of their own which could be used to negotiate with the Americans. Independence, it was argued, would be invaluable, and the costs would be little greater. Penney had already forecast the need for a dozen explosions and the British needed a test site that could be relied on; previous atomic experience had led them to be wary of reliance on the United States, and the Nevada option would be a gamble as the Americans might later 'turn off the tap and leave us helpless'. The Canadian possibility had already been abandoned, and if the Australian option was also abandoned it would probably be for good. There were other objections to the American site for Britain's first test. 'In the lamentable event of the bomb failing to detonate', said Cherwell, 'we should look very foolish indeed'—and in full view of all the American newspapers. Most importantly, Nevada would not provide the shallow underwater test that the Admiralty especially wanted; it was essential to know the effects if atomic bombs in enemy ships were exploded in British ports.

A decision was further delayed by a general election, which brought Churchill and a Conservative government to power in October 1951. Finally, in December 1951, Ministers confirmed the Australian site, with only ten months to go before the trial, code-named *Hurricane*. The choice was decisive; as Penney wrote three months later: 'If the Australians are not willing to let us do further trials in Australia, I do not know where we should go'[6].

Meanwhile active planning had begun over a year earlier[7], since stores—including, for instance, 150 miles of cable for communications (see Photograph 1)—would take months to procure and the first ships of the *Hurricane* flotilla would have to sail from England in February 1952 if the test was to be in October that year. If not, a whole year would be lost since favourable weather conditions seemed likely only in September and October.

Political pros and cons

Australia was chosen not only because of her uninhabited islands, which gave the opportunity of a shallow underwater explosion, and her vast empty regions of bush and desert. There were also strong political arguments for the choice.

Many people in Britain and Australia today cannot appreciate how close, indeed intimate, the two countries were in the 1950s[8]. It is true that Australia had necessarily become more independent of Britain after Pearl Harbour. With the Japanese thrust to the South, the fall of Singapore in February 1942 and the bombing of Darwin, Australia could not look to Britain for protection and Curtin, the Prime Minister, had made a historic appeal to the United States—an action deplored by Menzies, then Leader of the Opposition, among others.

Before the war most Australians had taken it for granted that only British migrants should be encouraged, or even allowed, to settle in Australia, and from 1946 British ex-Servicemen and their families had received free, and other Britons assisted, passages. This stream of British migrants reinforced the feeling of many Australians that Britain was their Motherland, even 'home'. However a shift was beginning as immigration from other countries increased dramatically: between 1947 and 1970 two-thirds of the 2½ million immigrants were from other European countries; they, too, could apply for assisted passages. The population nearly doubled to 13 millions, of whom fewer and fewer had British links or antecedents.

Trading patterns also changed. In the 1950s, Britain was still Australia's most important trading partner and British investment in Australia was higher than that of all the other countries of the world put together. But trade with the United States and Japan was growing, and by the 1960s Japan was far and away Australia's main trading partner. Nevertheless, the announcement in 1961 of Britain's intention to join the Common Market, heralding a major change in Britain's trading allegiance, shattered many Australians. The loosening of the Commonwealth bonds was signified in 1973 by the changes in British nationality laws. Hitherto British and Australian passports had been interchangeable. Now they were separate, and Australian passports no longer bore the words 'British subject'.

In 1950, the Cold War turned into a fighting war in the Far East, not Europe, and Australia was deeply involved as her forces fought again in Korea and Malaya. In 1949 Menzies had become Prime Minister; strongly pro-British, he had intense feelings of loyalty to the British Commonwealth. He firmly believed that Australia must play her part in the common defence of the free world and that, although in defence matters generally Australia had tended to turn to the United States, there was still scope for Anglo-Australian defence co-operation. This was already being demonstrated at Woomera, the range stretching

1250 miles across the coast of Western Australia which was used for testing and developing guided missiles and long-range weapons. This joint project (named after an Aboriginal weapon, a throwing-stick used to launch spears) began very soon after the end of the war, and was in operation by 1950. Britain was producing all the weapons for testing and supplying much of the equipment and scientific personnel, whereas Australia, at a cost of some £10 million a year, provided all the support as well as some scientists and engineers. A partnership in weapon testing was therefore not unprecedented, and use of her territory and resources to help the British nuclear deterrent was seen as part of Australia's defence contribution.

Australia was especially interested after the war in the industrial development of atomic energy, seemingly so important to a country thought to have no indigenous oil and little coal. (Exploration was to change this, as Australia proved to be very rich in coal and so far has not found a nuclear power programme worthwhile.) She was determined to keep abreast of atomic research and development and hoped for a Commonwealth collaborative project led by Britain. However at the Conference of Dominion Prime Ministers in May 1946 the only collaboration offered was limited to a few places for Australian research fellows at Harwell, and help in finding and developing uranium supplies. In 1947, Australia and New Zealand asked for information about Gleep, the low energy research reactor at Harwell, but no agreement was reached. One of the stumbling blocks was that the Americans were known to be dubious about Australian security, and in 1948 one unnamed critic was said to have alleged that 'no Australian, from the Prime Minister down, can be trusted not to be careless or worse'[9]. In fact, their security arrangements during the weapon tests were to be highly effective.

The British thought hard during 1947 about a coordinated Commonwealth programme, but because of the Quebec Agreement (see Chapter 1) could do nothing without consulting the United States. It was decided to seek Canada's views first, and then those of the United States, but the Canadian authorities were so emphatic that full cooperation with the United States must take priority over all other objectives that the idea of a Commonwealth programme was abandoned. As we saw, the *modus vivendi* of 1948 made special provision for information to be given to British Commonwealth countries (see Appendix B), but only in strictly defined areas.

By 1951, Australia was interested in beginning a nuclear power programme and naturally hoped for British help. The proposal was discussed when Menzies was in London in January 1951; he was told that under existing rules it would be a classified project, that American and Canadian agreement would be needed before Britain could help, and that they would be very exacting about security. After his visit, he and Attlee exchanged telegrams about the promising uranium prospects at Radium Hill in South Australia, and Attlee reaffirmed Britain's desire to help with the nuclear power project, but again pointed out the limitations imposed by the tripartite agreements.

The supply of uranium was in the early postwar years expected to be the limiting factor in atomic development. Then reserves were found at Radium Hill and at Rum Jungle in the Northern Territories, and by 1951 it was clear that Radium Hill would produce important supplies of ore. But Britain could not accept Australia's offer of joint development because the time did not seem opportune to seek American agreement to the sharing of classified information with her. So in 1952 Australia invited a United States mission to examine all their uranium occurrences; paradoxically it was then the Americans who brought the British into the negotiations, and successful deals were made between Australia and the Combined Development Agency (the tripartite body set up by the Quebec Agreement to obtain and allocate supplies of uranium ore).

British desire to cooperate with Australia was genuine but largely frustrated by existing commitments to the United States—in the Quebec Agreement and later the *modus vivendi*—and by American distrust of Australian security to which the British were hypersensitive[10]. The overwhelming desire for a renewed Anglo-American partnership, and the fear of spoiling chances of achieving it, inhibited all Britain's other relationships in the Commonwealth and Europe. The Americans themselves lacked these inhibitions and tended to be more forthcoming with the Australians than they would allow the British to be. Britain's inability to help the Australians, except to a quite minor extent, was the more open to criticism because of her dependence on Australia for a site for *Hurricane* and almost certainly for further trials.

In spite of the disappointments and frustrations over technical cooperation, the Australians showed great generosity over *Hurricane* even when the British were in an agony of indecision over whether to go ahead with the Monte Bello plan or accept the belated Nevada offer in September 1951. They collaborated whole-heartedly, and the Services gave indispensable, and free, assistance in support of the test.

The risks in these uninhabited islands seemed negligible; there was little or no hostile public opinion in Australia—rather, some pride in a historic occasion. However, the Australian government was well aware that it could not abrogate its sovereign rights and duties; if secret and hazardous operations were to be carried out in its territories by another nation—however close a friend—it had at least to know what was happening and to exert some real control. It was responsible for the safety of its own people and land; it had to decide how far it could accept general assurances of safety from the British, and what information it needed in order to examine them critically and in detail. It had to answer to its own Parliament and public opinion, and eventually to face a general election. It had too to answer for its expenditure in money and resources; not a large consideration for *Hurricane*, but more onerous later.

The British, constrained both by the agreements with the United States and by their unquenchable hopes of renewed Anglo-American partnership, were very inhibited in providing information to the Australians. They had, moreover, developed a general feeling that the fewer the people who knew Britain's weapon secrets the better— whether in the United States or the rest of the world. If the British felt they could not even give the Australians information about nuclear reactors, it was still more impossible to tell them anything about atomic bombs, and information about a test could reveal secret weapons data. What did the Australian authorities, who were not intending to develop atomic weapons themselves, need to know for their own purposes? How much could they be told without disclosing highly classified data and violating obligations to the United States?

For both countries there were administrative complications. Unlike the United States, which was carrying out huge test programmes in its own country or in American Trust territories in the Pacific, Britain would be operating on the soil of another sovereign state. This was bound to be complicated, even though the arrangements were surprisingly informal at first. Proposals for tests had to be approved by British Ministers and then submitted for Australian approval, and each one had to be processed through two government machines. The British had to work out with Australian colleagues 12 000 miles away the details of complex operations that involved several government departments and all the armed services of both nations. Nothing could be said officially in either country without coordination; every announcement, speech, or answer to a Parliamentary Question in either country had to be discussed, agreed and synchronized. Public relations involved the

Australian Press and public, as well as the British; Press stories in one country might be, and sometimes were, picked up instantly in the other.

The political relationship between Britain and Australia in the post-war decade-and-a-half is reflected in the fact that these curbs on the transmission of information to the Australians about explosions in their own country—equivalent to thousands of tons of TNT and releasing large quantities of radioactive fission products—were regarded as reasonable by the British government and acceptable by the Australian government.

Politicians and scientists

'The last of the Queen's Men'[11]

Menzies towered over Australian politics throughout the whole period of weapon tests. A most able and experienced politician—he had held many ministerial offices since entering Parliament in 1928 and had been Prime Minister from 1939 to 1941—he became Prime Minister again in 1949 at the head of a Liberal/Country Party coalition government and retained office for seventeen years, until he retired in 1966. To some he was an urbane far-seeing world statesman, to some he seemed an arrogant and unscrupulous reactionary[12], but all agreed on his ability. An extreme anglophile, he was the last of a long line of Australian Prime Ministers who felt that London was the centre of the world[13]. He was loaded with honours by 'the Motherland'; a Privy Councillor, a Companion of Honour and, in 1963, a knight of the exclusive Order of the Thistle, he succeeded Churchill in 1965 as Lord Warden of the Cinque Ports, an honorary office of immense prestige.

Menzies was the presiding genius of the very special relationship. His support, and that of his government, for the British atomic weapon test programme were crucial, as Australian public opinion became more and more restive. If he had lost power, it was probable that a Labour government under Dr Evatt would have put an end to the tests. The British were well aware of how much they owed to Menzies, and how much they depended on his personal support and his continuation in office. An Australian song of the time might have been written for them[14]:

But we might lose our Menzies; wherever would we be
If Menzies means as much to you as Menzies means to me?

The Australian Minister in charge of atomic energy matters, including the British weapon tests and the permanent proving ground at Maralinga, was, until 1958, Howard (later Sir Howard) Beale. He gave the British programme his enthusiastic support, in sometimes difficult circumstances. The major trials were over by the time he moved to Washington, where he achieved considerable success as Australian ambassador.

The scientists

The scientists in Australia with knowledge and experience of atomic energy nearly all had close links with Britain and British scientists, and at least two—E W Titterton and J P Baxter—came from England to posts in Australia after the war; Titterton to the Australian National University in Canberra (ANU) and Baxter to the University of New South Wales. There was, as we saw, no distinction at that time between British and Australian nationality and no separate passports. Three Australian-born scientists—Oliphant, Martin and Eddy—had been in the Cavendish Laboratory at Cambridge under the great Rutherford. Some—Oliphant, Baxter and Titterton—had worked in Tube Alloys and in the Manhattan Project.

Four scientists require special mention here; three because of their parts in the British atomic weapon test programme, and one because of his conspicuous absence from the stage. The missing actor was M L E (later Sir Mark) Oliphant, Director of the Research School of Physical Sciences in the Australian National University—which he helped to found—in Canberra. He was born and educated in Adelaide and went to Cambridge University in 1927. In 1935 he was Rutherford's assistant director of research at the Cavendish. In 1937 he became professor of physics at Birmingham University, England, where Frisch and Peierls wrote their famous memorandum showing that an atomic bomb was possible. Oliphant was a member of the Maud Committee and in 1943 joined the Manhattan Project. For his outstanding contribution, General Groves, the head of the Project, put forward his name, and his only, in 1946 for the Congressional Medal of Freedom with Gold Palm. This is the highest honour the United States can bestow on a foreigner[15]. However it was not then Australian government policy to permit foreign decorations for Australians, and Oliphant did not receive the award.

If he had, the subsequent story would have been very different. He did not know about it until 1980.

After returning in 1950 to Australia and the ANU, he was made chairman of an industrial atomic energy policy committee. Yet this most distinguished nuclear physicist was not invited to advise on the tests by the Australian government. The omission was due to an absurd event in 1951 when he was to attend a scientific conference in Chicago but was unable to obtain a United States visa. He was not accused of communist connections or subversive activities, and the security authorities, in the United States and Australia, had nothing against him. He had never, he said, knowingly transgressed security rules. If he had done so, the highly security-minded Groves would certainly not have recommended him for any honours. But the McCarthy era was in full swing in the United States, and Oliphant was a victim of innuendo and political smear, labelled 'inadmissible', 'a do-gooder', 'one of the boys who monkey around with pinkos'[16]. The visa affair, despite Oliphant's friendly personal relationship with Menzies, immediately and powerfully affected the attitude of both Australian and British governments, because of their sensitivity to American reactions. If his participation in atomic energy affairs might, however unreasonably, have unfortunate repercussions in Washington, he must be excluded.

The question of Australian observers at the first weapon test in October 1952 did not arise until early 1952. Canadian scientists were to participate; as we saw in Chapter 1, Canada, as a signatory of the tripartite agreements, was in a different position from other Commonwealth countries. The Australians asked about their own scientists. Penney wanted to invite two or three, and one from New Zealand, and he was anxious also to borrow Titterton from ANU, not as an observer but as a telemetry expert (see p. 31). Lord Cherwell, the British Minister responsible for atomic energy policy, was asked; his prime concern was that the presence of Australian scientists might give the Americans an unfavourable impression of British security arrangements. However if the problem was frankly explained to Menzies, and he felt that some Australian scientists should attend, Cherwell would be prepared to agree to Titterton. Two junior technicians might also be accepted.

The Australians were understandably dissatisfied; after all, the British were using their territory and were dependent on them. Eventually the British authorities invited the Australian Defence Scientific Adviser, Professor L H Martin, as well as Titterton; later W A S Butement was included. Accommodation was scarce and all of them would not only observe but make themselves useful. After the visa incident, Cherwell and the British government would never have agreed to invite Oliphant for fear of American reactions, and about the same time the Australian government itself reconstituted its Atomic Energy Policy Committee in order to exclude him from discussions even of peaceful applications of atomic energy[17]. So, contrary to public expectations, Oliphant was not invited to *Hurricane* or any of the subsequent tests, and the Australian government did not ask him to serve on its Atomic Weapons Tests Safety Committee (AWTSC). If asked he might well have refused; he hated scientific secrecy and, as he wrote to a friend, 'That is why I dropped right out of the military business when I came back to Australia'[18].

Thus the Australian scientists present at the 1952 trials were Martin, Butement and Titterton. In 1955 they all became members of the AWTSC, together with Eddy, Baxter and, later, L J Dwyer. Eddy, head of the Commonwealth X-Ray and Radium Laboratory, died suddenly shortly after the *Mosaic* trial in 1956, and the new head of CXRL, J E S Stevens, took his place on the committee. J P (later Sir Philip) Baxter was a British chemist from ICI who had worked in Tube Alloys and the Manhattan Project, took a chair in chemical engineering at the University of New South Wales in 1949 and later became chairman of the Australian Atomic Energy Commission; he played little or no part in the AWTSC. L J Dwyer, head of the Australian Commonwealth Bureau of Meteorology, was soon appointed to the AWTSC—wisely in view of the crucial importance of meteorology in the trials—and was a very active member.

L H (Sir Leslie) Martin—another Cavendish Laboratory man—was Professor of Physics at Melbourne University, and the government's Defence Scientific Adviser from 1948 to 1960. He was responsible for the setting up, none too soon, of the safety committee (AWTSC) which he chaired until 1957, and he was present at many of the trials. After 1957 he withdrew from the AWTSC and proposed its reorganization, but was active in advising the Department of Defence and the Australian government on the British minor trials at Maralinga (see Chapter 10).

Alan Butement, who was Chief Scientist at the Department for Supply, was born in New Zealand and educated first in Australia and then in England, where he worked for nearly twenty years in an Admiralty experimental establishment and in the British Ministry of Supply. During the war he was engaged in radar research. In 1947 he returned to

Australia to help set up the Long Range Weapons Establishment (LRWE) of which the Woomera Range is a part, and became its first chief superintendent. Then in 1949 he was appointed to the Department for Supply, which was responsible for atomic energy matters, including the tests. Besides being on the AWTSC, and present at most of the trials, he was very actively involved in exploration for weapon test sites, and in the business of getting them established. It was he who named the greater desert area chosen for the permanent range—Maralinga, an Aboriginal word meaning field of thunder.

Most influential was E W (later Sir Ernest) Titterton, though unlike Martin and Butement he did not have a departmental base; he was Professor of Physics at the ANU. He had been Oliphant's first research student at Birmingham University, had worked there with Otto Frisch, and then had been one of the group under Oliphant that developed the cavity magnetron, which revolutionized radar and changed the course of the war. In 1943 he went to the Manhattan Project and remained at Los Alamos until 1947, becoming head of the Electronics Division there. He was a senior member of the Timing Group at *Trinity*, the first atomic test at Alamogordo in July 1945, and was an adviser on instrumentation at the United States *Crossroads* trial at Bikini in 1946—where as the anonymous 'voice of Abraham' he gave the countdown and detonation orders[19]. After leaving Los Alamos, he spent the next three years at Harwell. Penney badly needed Titterton's experience and special scientific skills, and he tried hard but unsuccessfully to attract him to the weapons establishment. In 1950 Oliphant offered his old student a chair at ANU, and Titterton (though he had been tempted to return to the United States) accepted and migrated to Australia.

In view of Titterton's unique expertise, it was natural that Penney, who had so much wanted him on his staff, should be anxious at least to borrow him as a telemetry expert at *Hurricane*; it was in that capacity, rather than as an observer for the Australian government, that Titterton took part. He attended all the major trials—after 1955 as a member of the AWTSC—and when the AWTSC was reconstituted as a three-man committee he became chairman. He had a knowledge of atomic weapons, and an experience of weapon testing since 1945, such as few scientists in the world, and no other Australian scientist, had. But, as a very new Australian with close United Kingdom ties and a Los Alamos background, his position was bound to be seen by many as an ambiguous one.

Notes and references

1 Gowing: *Independence and Deterrence*, Vol. 1, p. 307.
2 Gowing: *Ibid.*, Vol. 1, pp. 336–37.
3 Gowing: *Ibid.*, Vol. 2, p. 478.
4 *Ibid.*
5 Gowing: *Ibid.*, Vol. 2, p. 479.
6 Gowing: *Ibid.*, Vol. 1, p. 337.
7 Gowing: *Ibid.*, Vol. 2, pp.478–9.
8 Much of the material for this section is drawn from Russel Ward: *The History of Australia in the Twentieth Century*.
9 Cockburn and Ellyard: *Oliphant*, p. 187.
10 However when the United States demanded the withdrawal of Australian scientists working on guided weapons in Britain the British refused. In this field, unlike atomic energy, they valued Commonwealth cooperation more than United States information (Barker: *The British between the Superpowers 1945–50*).
11 Russel Ward: *The History of Australia in the Twentieth century*, citing Kevin Perkins *The Last of the Queen's Men*.
12 Russel Ward: *Ibid.*, p. 337.
13 Russel Ward: *Ibid.*, p. 363.
14 Russel Ward: *Ibid.*, p. 245.
15 Cockburn and Ellyard: *Oliphant.*, Chapter 14.
16 Cockburn and Ellyard: *Ibid.*, p. 229.
17 Cockburn and Ellyard: *Ibid.*, p. 192.
18 Cockburn and Ellyard: *Ibid.*, p. 193.
19 Gowing: *Independence and Deterrence.*, Vol. 1, p. 113.

3   *Hurricane*—1952

Planning

Cross Roads, the American test at Bikini atoll in the Pacific in 1946, was a gigantic scientific experiment some 5000 miles from the United States mainland. 150 aircraft and over 200 ships had been employed, and 42000 men had taken part. It is difficult to carry out these complex operations at a great distance; *Hurricane* was such an operation, but British resources were scanty and plans modest. Dr L C Tyte, the technical director of *Hurricane*, and his small planning group in HER[1] at Fort Halstead in Kent—the main atomic weapons establishment before the Aldermaston site was developed—estimated the manpower requirements at 245 scientists and scientific assistants and 100 industrials, but the number of scientists who eventually carried out the trial was only 100.

Tyte's group prepared a 'trial book' on every aspect of the HER part of *Hurricane*. They ordered instruments and stores, planned the scientific operations and safety measures in meticulous detail, selected and trained people, organized teams and allocated duties.

Though the atomic explosion was the purpose of the enterprise, HER's plan was part of a bigger overall plan, involving several British and Australian government departments and all the armed services of both countries. A co-ordinating committee called the *Hurricane* Executive, representing all the United Kingdom interests under Admiralty chairmanship, was formed in March 1951 and soon afterwards Rear Admiral A D Torlesse was appointed as task force commander. In Australia a *Hurricane* Panel was set up in July 1951 to coordinate action there. It was chaired by the Deputy Chief of Naval Staff and comprised representatives of the three Services, the Department of Defence and the security authorities.

The British Navy, already overstretched, had a challenging task. Five suitable ships had to be designated and specially fitted out in complete secrecy and with no time to spare; ship conversions were done at Birkenhead and Chatham and on the Clyde. An aircraft carrier, HMS *Campania* (a Seond World War conversion from a banana trade merchantman), after completing her duties in the 1951 Festival of Britain, was to serve as flagship and headquarters of the whole expedition. Two landing ships (LS4), HMS *Zeebrugge* and *Narvik*, were to transport a detachment of Royal Engineers and their heavy civil engineering equipment, and on arrival in the Monte Bellos, *Zeebrugge* was to move south to act as a laboratory for the radiochemists. Another LS4, HMS *Tracker*, would be the health control ship and health physics laboratory. An old River Class frigate, HMS *Plym*, which would transport the unarmed test weapon, was secretly designated as the target vessel, destined to be destroyed in the explosion; *Plym* had to be fitted with an elaborately equipped weapon-room in which the device could be safely detonated by remote control.

This flotilla was to transport civilian scientists, Army personnel and large quantities of stores of all kinds; it would be a long voyage—up to eight weeks for *Campania* and *Plym*, which would have to go round the Cape, not through the Suez Canal. The Royal Navy was to take the opportunity of showing the flag, making formal calls at various ports en route. The length of the voyage would allow scientists more time to polish their plans, but most unfortunately the opportunity was not taken to organize joint planning meetings on board between the scientists and the Naval Staff.

Once arrived in the Monte Bellos (see Map 2), the flotilla would have to provide completely for all the *Hurricane* personnel, as well as its own crews, for some twelve weeks on a group of bare and inhospitable islands with no resources of any kind, not even fresh water. Besides food and shelter, transport would be needed. It would be much more complicated carrying out the test in these small scattered islands than on a single island or on the mainland, for scientists would have to commute from ship to shore and from island to island, in order to set up and maintain their equipment—batteries, cameras, blast gauges, seismographs, calorimeters, thermometers, ionisation chambers, air samplers and so on. This traffic meant constant boatwork, with a frequent boat service to take scientists to their scattered workplaces and return them at night to camp or ship so that no one was left marooned on an outlying island. The Royal Navy also had helicopters available.

Hurricane was primarily a naval operation, but the work of the other Services was of the greatest importance. By the time of *Hurricane* there were ten RAF officers attached to Penney's staff, led by Wing Commander J S Rowlands GC (now Air Vice Marshal Sir John Rowlands), who was closely involved in the design of the weapon. He and his

Map 2   Monte Bello Islands

carefully selected team collaborated most successfully with the scientists. The RAF also had an essential role in providing long-distance communications and transport. The Royal Australian Air Force (RAAF) was to carry out tasks involving radiological surveys, and providing security patrols. Under separate arrangements, the RAAF was to collect samples of airborne debris and to track the radioactive cloud. The Army was asked to assist with civil engineering and construction work on the islands, and a small planning staff was immediately attached to Fort Halstead. This, too, proved a very successful arrangement. The Royal Engineers were due to sail in February, four months ahead of the rest of the flotilla.

Apart from detailed logistic and scientific planning, there were endless political and administrative questions to be dealt with by Ministers and officials in London and Canberra. How could the secrecy of the operation be ensured? How could entry into an area around the islands be effectively, and legally, prohibited and for how long? (They were outside Australian territorial waters, and it was not even clear to whom they belonged, as no one had ever wanted them before). What information should be given, and when, to the British and Australian press? Should Australian and Canadian scientists be invited to participate?— They were. Should civilian staff on the expedition be given extra duty allowances or special insurance, in recognition of the long separation from home, rough living conditions, and hazards of working in small boats in a reputedly shark-infested sea?

Australian participation

Australia was asked for, and gave, generous logistic support. The Royal Australian Navy (RAN) and the Australian Weather Bureau began meteorological observations a year in advance of the trial. The Navy surveyed and charted the islands and surrounding waters, marked channels, laid buoys and moorings, ferried passengers and supplies, provided a weather ship, and patrolled the area before and after the trial. The Army provided equipment, vehicles and transit camp facilities. An airfield construction squadron of the Royal Australian Air Force (RAAF) made roads on the islands, and with Navy help—and with remarkable speed and efficiency—laid a vitally important pipeline from an inland river to a jetty on the coast, from where fresh water was shipped to the islands. As we saw, the RAAF undertook various flying tasks—courier services and passenger transport; security patrols and coastal monitoring by Dakotas; and air sampling by Lincoln aircraft.

A few Canadian scientists were to participate in the test, but the question of Australian scientists was apparently, but most surprisingly, not discussed until February 1952, when Penney suggested to the *Hurricane* Executive that two or three might be present as observers. In April, at Penney's personal request, as we saw, the Australian government was asked if E W Titterton, recently appointed Professor of Physics at the ANU, might take part as a telemetry expert. Two junior Australian scientists were also requested, one to join the health physics group, and at the same time laboratory facilities for the British radiochemists were asked for.

These arrangements did not please the Australian authorities, who thought they should have senior representatives present as observers. It was not until September that the question was resolved by an invitation to Professor L H Martin, the Defence Scientific Adviser, and W A S Butement, the Chief Scientist at the Department of Supply, as well as to Titterton (see Chapter 2).

Safety

Safety of the Australian mainland

By the time the flotilla was to sail, it was impossible to keep *Hurricane* secret any longer and in February 1952, after much discussion of the precise wording, a joint announcement was made by the two governments:

> In the course of this year the United Kingdom government intend to test an atomic weapon produced in the United Kingdom. In close cooperation with the government of the Commonwealth of Australia, the test will take place at a site in Australia. It will be conducted in conditions which will ensure that there will be no danger whatever from radioactivity to the health of people and animals in the Commonwealth.

Radiation safety had been a paramount consideration for Penney and his staff in planning the trial. Though this was the first British test, the scientists had available both theoretical knowledge and practical experience of atomic weapon tests and weapon effects. British scientists, including Penney, had participated in the United States trial in New Mexico in July 1945, and six had been present at Bikini in June 1946. They also had a substantial handbook that the Americans had published in 1950, *The Effects of Atomic Weapons*. It contained a mass of up-to-date information on the nature of atomic explosions; the characteristics of air, surface, underground and underwater bursts; the significance of local, or early, fallout and long-range fallout; blast, radiation and thermal damage; properties of radiation; the clinical syndrome of radiation sickness; genetic effects of radiation; radiation monitoring instruments; decontamination procedures; and methods of protection.

The British scientists knew that the shallow underwater explosion of a 'nominal' atomic bomb—i.e., about 20 kilotons—would create a fireball that would rise high into the atmosphere carrying a column of water and spray as well as fission products and other bomb constituents, with many tons of steel, some of which had been vaporized, and perhaps 1000–10 000 tons of sand and 10 000–100 000 tons of water. Because of the great weight of water drawn up in the plume, the fallout would be precipitated quickly and within a few thousand yards from the point of detonation; most of the radioactivity would be dispersed in the water around the islands and would not be intense except close to the explosion centre and for a short time after firing. The fallout hazard was therefore expected to be very localized, with little if any risk of contaminating the Australian mainland—47 miles to the south east at the nearest point—unless the wind was blowing from the Islands towards it. Meteorology was crucial to safety.

In the autumn of 1951 HER staff prepared a report on the meteorological and safety aspects of *Hurricane*, and especially the safety of communities on the mainland. The coastal region, it noted, was arid but subject to occasional tropical storms, and 100 to 150 miles inland a range of hills rose to 3000 feet. In this area, within 150 miles from the islands, were several townships, four airfields and about twenty homesteads.

The authors of *The Effects of Atomic Weapons* had recognized that serious radioactive hazards might be caused downwind of a surface explosion, but early fallout in inhabited areas had been little studied, and no relevant standards existed. The International Commission on Radiological Protection (ICRP)—an independent scientific body first set up in 1928, and reconstituted in 1950 to deal with post-war radiation protection matters—had recently recommended exposure limits for radiation workers, but had not yet dealt with non-occupational standards. (It did so in 1958.) It was also considering occupational limits for ingested and inhaled radioactive substances; the British Medical Research Council had tentatively suggested a limit 100 times lower for the general population.

The HER scientists argued that if the ICRP pronounced it safe—that is, involving a risk that was small compared to the other hazards of life—for a radiation worker to receive an exposure of 0.5 roentgen (r) a week for all his working life—perhaps for 40 years—then an integrated dose of 2r, equivalent to one months' occupational dose, was reasonable for other people as what was probably a once-for-all exposure. Calculating the fallout that, in the most unfavourable conditions, could reach the mainland, and the external and internal radiation doses it could give rise to, the HER report concluded that there was a risk of exceeding the safe levels if the wind was blowing from any direction between west and north east (through north), especially if the winds were fairly uniform at different heights.

To avoid this, firing criteria had to be correct and weather forecasting reliable. The meteorologists would have to work with the scientists responsible for theoretical predictions; the latter, knowing the design and estimated yield of the weapon, could calculate the probable height of the cloud, the probable size and distribution of fallout particles in different parts of the cloud and in its stem, and their rate of fall. From these data, combined with the meteorologists' forecasts of wind directions and speeds at various altitudes, it would be possible to predict fallout patterns and so to advise the trial director and task force commander when conditions were favourable or unfavourable for firing.

Wind directions and speed usually vary considerably at different altitudes, and two years' observation of wind frequency during October on the west coast of Australia showed that, at altitudes of 6000 ft and 10 000 ft, 83 per cent of the winds would carry the cloud over the mainland, but winds at 3000 ft would do so less frequently. Out of the 10 days in October when other conditions (such as tides) were suitable, there would probably not be more than 3 days when the wind would blow the cloud away from the mainland; in some years, perhaps 6 or 8 days; in some years, perhaps none. Firing opportunities might therefore be infrequent, but *Hurricane* was deemed to be of such vital importance that these odds were acceptable even though a long wait might be necessary.

Meteorological forecasting for *Hurricane* was to be based on routine weather forecasts from Canberra and special information from the

Australian weathership and the RAAF stations at Pearce, Onslow, and Port Hedland. Once all was ready and the standby period had begun, D−1 (the day before the firing) would be decided on the basis of regular and frequent forecasts. Detailed preparations would then be put in hand and, if forecasts continued favourable, D-day would be declared, and everyone would take up his allotted position. D-day itself could only be declared if meteorological conditions were right, the sea was calm enough for the boats, and the technical requirements could all be fulfilled; if the wind changed or some unforeseen hitch occurred the firing might have to be cancelled and a new date set for D−1. The firing criteria designed to protect the mainland, the ships and H1 (the main island site) defined acceptable speeds and directions of mean winds at surface level, at heights up to 5000 ft and at heights up to 30 000 ft. No air up to 5000 ft must reach the mainland from the site of the explosion within 10 hours; this would allow time for the comparatively heavy particles of fallout carried by low level winds to be deposited in the sea. After final meteorological observations, if the task force commander, jointly with the scientific director, decided that the firing should proceed, countdown would begin.

Post-firing precautions were to include high-level flights over the coast to measure atmospheric radioactivity, and a radiological survey of the Australian coastline from Onslow to Broome by Harwell scientists in low-flying RAAF aircraft fitted with sensitive detectors. If the low-level air survey indicated any need for it, a ground survey would also be carried out using jeeps. However, provided the firing took place in the meteorological conditions specified, the planners were confident that there was no risk of significant deposition of radioactivity on the mainland. On this the Australian authorities had to rely on the categorical assurances given by the British, as they did not have technical information about the test.

Safety of trial personnel

Safety distances were calculated that would give assurance that no one was in danger from the explosion itself—whether from blast, heat or initial radiation—and all the trials personnel would be upwind of the detonation and at least 6 miles (10 km) away. The main hazard would be immediately after the explosion; especially to those who, during the so-called 're-entry phase', were to make sorties to the contaminated lagoon and islands to collect instruments and samples.

The ICRP had, as we saw, recommended a weekly limit of 0.5 r, which it considered adequate to protect radiation workers routinely exposed to radiation, but had not yet considered infrequent, 'one-off', or emergency exposures. (It did so later). Penney approached the Medical Research Council for advice, and for its approval of suggested radiation standards which his staff had discussed with J F Loutit, the Australian-born MRC radiobiologist, and with W G Marley, Harwell's chief radiological expert, who had been at Los Alamos. An MRC panel—after studying the proposals in the light of ICRP recommendations, clinical experience and American published data—endorsed three maximum permissible levels (MPL) of external gamma radiation for the trial[2].

The first limit was the 'normal working rate', a low rate for continuous exposure over a period of normal working; this was 0.1 r a day of gamma radiation (equivalent to 0.06 r to important organs). The second, the 'lower integrated dose' of 3 r (gamma), was allowed only if necessary to ensure smooth working, and with the radiological safety officer's permission. Anyone receiving a dose at this limit would not be exposed to radiation again during the operation. The third, the 'higher integrated dose' of 10 r (gamma), was for use in cases of extreme urgency in order to recover vital records that might otherwise be lost; it required the express approval of the task force commander (who would of course be advised by the scientific director and the health physics adviser). Anyone exposed at this limit would be withdrawn from radiation work for a year.

The 0.1 r exposure level for a working day was the same as the existing ICRP occupational limit, and though a 3 r integrated limit was not in the 1950 ICRP recommendations, it was adopted by the ICRP in 1958 (when 3 r in 13 weeks replaced the weekly limit for radiation workers).

These levels, which the MRC panel considered to be innocuous—or at the worst to carry negligible risks—were then authorized by the Chief Medical Officer of the Ministry of Supply; he added certain requirements about film badges, exposure records, respirators, and protective clothing. The Ministry passed the information to the Admiralty, War Office and Air Ministry for agreement, and the radiation standards were embodied in *Hurricane* plans and *Hurricane* trial orders, together with detailed safety rules and procedures. These MPLs referred to external, not internal, radiation; the latter was not considered a hazard for *Hurricane* personnel, as respirators and protective clothing would be worn for operations such as sorties into areas where radioactive material might be inhaled.

The British scientists were aware that these standards were similar to those used in United States trials (see Appendix G). The United States limit in 1950 was 0.1 r in one day, or in special cases up to 3 r in one day if approved by the top radiological officer; the person exposed then received no more radiation for 30 days. Exposures above 3 r required permission from the task force commander, but no upper limit was specified. In 1952 and again in 1953 the Americans altered their rules somewhat, limiting exposures whenever possible to 3 r in 10 weeks and 3.9 r in 13 weeks (the length of the respective test periods).

The *Hurricane* scientists gave much thought to safety. Their calculations were based on 'worst case' assumptions and allowed, they felt, ample safety margins; they were confident that, given reliable forecasting by the meteorologists, no public hazard would arise. They also had grounds for confidence in the safety of *Hurricane* personnel, and in the event no doses over 5 r were recorded.

The prohibited area

With *Hurricane* in view, the Australian Parliament rapidly passed the Defence (Special Undertakings) Act 1952, which went through all its stages between 4 and 6 June; it declared that, for reasons of security and the safety of shipping, an area within a radius of 40 miles of the Monte Bello Islands was a prohibited area. There were some doubts in Britain about the Act, because it implied Australian sovereignty over a considerable extent of the high seas outside territorial waters, and so might create an unfortunate precedent. The British proposed that, following the American example, the two governments should issue a joint warning nearer the date of the test; the declaration of a danger area would be based purely on safety considerations and would not imply sovereignty. To seaward, a safe distance of 100 miles was necessary, but this distance was reduced in sectors south of Monte Bello to avoid including a part of the Australian mainland, since firing would not be permitted in conditions that might allow fallout to contaminate it. The terms of the warning were agreed; it was promulgated on 8 August through the usual channels used for warning shipping and aircraft of all nations, and safety patrols by Australian ships and aircraft were arranged.

The expedition

The voyage out to Australia was not the prolonged rest-cure that the British scientists had been promised by one senior official in Whitehall. There was much practical work to be done—checking, re-packing and stowing stores, calibrating pressure gauges, building and testing electronic equipment and so on—and much further planning, for there would be little spare time after reaching the islands. Regular meetings of the team leaders were held on board, but without some of the senior scientists (who were coming later by air) and without the Naval staff. Also unfortunate, though inevitable, was the absence of Australian scientists and Service staffs, who did not meet the *Hurricane* party until it reached Fremantle.

For some, the voyage was nightmarish. Conditions on board were overcrowded and extremely uncomfortable, especially in hot weather. In certain winds the *Campania's* ventilation system distributed fumes from the engine-room into some of the cabins, making them almost uninhabitable. Seasickness afflicted most of the scientists at some time. Tensions frequently arose, especially on board the *Campania*, between the Naval officers, with their formal and disciplined tradition, and the boffins, with their easy going manners and unconventional dress and their habit of discarding jackets and ties in tropical heat. The 'passengers' were often in the way while shipboard routines went on around them. Where *were* they to go while the ship was scrubbed over? Where *should* they sun-bathe if not on the quarter deck or the gun platforms?

With professional Naval precision, *Campania* anchored on 8 August, exactly on schedule, in the so called 'parting pool' east of the Monte Bello lagoon. The lagoon was encircled by numerous tiny islands—with such nostalgic names as Crocus, Primrose, Gardenia and Bluebell—and four larger ones, North West Island, Hermite, Trimouille and Alpha. The scientific party found good roads and jetties and excellent buildings prepared for them by the Army, assisted by the Royal Australian Air Force. 'Truly the RE are magnificent', Tyte enthused and so too were the Australians. On-site preparations began with all speed. Probably the busiest team was the telemetry and communications group—responsible for the electronic firing system and for the network of communications and controls linking the ships and field sites—under Ieuan (now Sir Ieuan) Maddock.

The main site—the only one that would be occupied at the time of the explosion—was H1, on Hermite Island (see Map 2). Here there were excellent laboratories containing the control room from which the weapon in *Plym* would be fired, and all the apparatus that would monitor the firing circuit, inspect the state of the telemetry equipment throughout the islands, and receive and record multiplication-rate observations. Here too were the generators, and the area for charging the all-important batteries that would provide power for field equipment.

The main photographic stations were to be on Hermite, Alpha Island and North West Island. The remotely controlled high-speed cameras would operate at speeds up to 8000 frames per second, to show the development of the fireball, the water column, the cloud and other visual effects; ultra-high-speed cameras at H1 would photograph the early self-luminous stages of the explosion.

On Trimouille were most of the sites to be used for investigating blast and thermal effects. At hundreds of points on Trimouille and adjacent islands, gauges of many different types were placed—blast gauges, diaphragm gauges, seismographic gauges, and hollow containers (including 200 empty petrol cans, as used effectively by Penney at the 1946 Bikini test). Air-sampling equipment, made from modified vacuum cleaner units, was set up. Thermometers and calorimeters, and samples of special paints and clothing materials to show the effects of heat from the explosion, were placed at selected points.

At many points on the four main islands, the Radiations Hazards Division sited ionization chambers, of high and low sensitivity, complete with amplifiers and pen recorders and protected in shock-proof cylindrical structures. Some were connected by telemetry to the health ship, HMS *Tracker*.

A small MRC team under Dr W J H Butterfield[3] was to study the effects of radioactive deposition on plants and to measure the uptake of fission products, especially iodine and strontium. Other investigations included the effect of blast on structures and on aircraft, the protection of food from contamination, the decontamination of ships under service conditions and the radioactive hazard to ships from a 'base surge' should it occur—in the event it did not (see note on fallout in Appendix I).

Two serious problems soon appeared. It had been intended that most of the scientists would live in the base ship, *Campania*, going to and from the islands at morning and night, with only a few men having to camp ashore occasionally. However, the survey party had underestimated the effects of weather and tides. *Campania* could not enter the shallow waters of the lagoon and had to be anchored in the parting pool, but the pinnaces could not tie up alongside her at night there and had to be moored many miles away. For the scientists, this placed impossible restrictions on the length of the working day. Worse still, the small boats could not work in the parting pool in rough weather; soon after arriving the scientists were confined to the base ship for three days. Even in good weather the swell in the parting pool made it a hazardous business to transfer between *Campania* and small craft tied up alongside, especially for landlubbers wearing the Army boots issued for the rough terrain of the Islands. Most of the scientists therefore had to live ashore during the week, and the Navy quickly improvised two big tented camps, on Hermite and Trimouille. Despite complaints about the food, and the trouble with flies and termites, the arrangement was reasonably successful, and the naval officers were no doubt as glad to have the scientists out of their way as the scientists were to be free from shipboard constraints.

The second big problem was the boat service. Travelling times turned out to be nearly twice those estimated in the boat plans, and even the journeys between *Campania* and *Plym* often took 2½ to 3 hours. The transport craft were too few, and often broke down. The crews were perhaps the most overworked members of the expedition, but for all their efforts the scientists lost much valuable working time waiting about for long overdue boats. Incredibly, Tyte said, the success of the whole expensive operation hung on the 'thin red line of 3 or 4 LCMs'.

There were other thin red lines. The operation was hampered by many shortages and deficiencies—electric generators, VHF radio-telephone links which proved defective (taxi sets had fortunately been brought and they saved the situation), vehicles, duplicating equipment used for promulgating instructions, and staff. The expedition carried no spare men, and it was lucky that there were no serious accidents or illness. One junior assistant was responsible for maintaining all the batteries on which much of the field equipment on the islands depended—'no batteries, no trial'—and when he proved unsuitable, a replacement was hard to find.

All was ready for scientific rehearsals on 12 and 13 September and a full rehearsal on 18 September. Staff movements were planned in detail, boat schedules drafted, and mustering lists prepared, for everyone and everything must be in exactly the right place at the right time. From the time when assembly of the weapon began, all non-essential staff must be at least 5 miles from ground zero; by H hour all ships, and nearly all personnel, must be at least 10 miles south (i.e., upwind) of the target vessel. A few key staff would be stationed at H1 on Hermite Island, about 7 miles SSW of the explosion.

The radioactive core of the device arrived in a Sunderland flying boat on 18 September, in time for the rehearsal. On 22 September, Penney arrived, relaxed and confident, a powerful boost to morale (see Photographs 2 and 3). After reviewing the situation he hoped that 1 October might be D−1 day, but cancellations were always possible because of weather and there might be several successive D−1 days, with all the attendant problems of maintaining equipment and fully charged batteries in a state of readiness in the many scattered sites.

On the morning of 2 October, D−1 was announced. Scientists were busy inspecting and testing their equipment until they were evacuated from all the islands except Hermite. There they passed a cold and windy night in the camp at H1, tired and tense after five years of strain and stress and gruelling hard work. Just after midnight, work began in the weapon room in HMS *Plym*, berthed off the western shore of Trimouille; after finally setting the arming switch, the last two men made the rough return journey from *Plym* to H1 before dawn. Soon the camp was aroused, and D-day had begun.

After final meteorological observations, the task force commander and scientific director decided that the trial should proceed. The wind was from the south, so that all the early fallout would be carried north over the Indian Ocean. At 0915 hrs (local time) Maddock began the countdown to zero. Three seconds after zero, men running out of the buildings at H1 saw a huge water column rising rapidly, in complete symmetry and utter silence. Nothing visible remained of *Plym*. Thirty seconds after zero, a faint tremor appeared to emerge from the ground, followed almost instantaneously by the crash of the blast wave.

Soon after the detonation, Penney sent a personal cable to Lord Cherwell and Mr Sandys, the two atomic energy Ministers:

We have records in all important scientific experiments. We have fully met our guarantee to the Australians that no harmful contamination will be deposited on the mainland. All contamination went northwards and will stay there for at least another 10 hours. It is possible that no contamination whatever will reach mainland. The dispersion is already sufficient to eliminate all danger from fallout now taking place.

The meteorological conditions were extraordinarily fortunate for us and I am sure that no estimate of the power of the bomb can be made from photographs from the mainland. I think that we can rest assured that no significant dust samples can be collected by foreigners. We alone will know the power and efficiency of our weapon.

The reasons why the top of the cloud did not go above 15 000 ft were first that the air was very dry and second that there was a strong inversion at 15 000 ft. The ball of fire evaporated the water spout but even so the cloud was not saturated. Consequently there was no regaining of latent heat from condensation as the cloud lifted and the cloud stopped at the inversion[4].

The blast wind raised a great sandstorm and this observation alone in my opinion justifies the expectation that the weapon efficiency was up to my predictions.

The heat flash was intense but of short duration. It caused widespread fires in the vegetation over Trimouille. These fires are now dying away 8 hours after the burst. The contamination is intense on land north of Point Zero but is slight south of Point Zero. Our telemetry safety monitors are giving 100 r per hour 5 hours after burst at 1 mile due north. Our monitor further north is reading 3000, but we distrust this. All scientific work is proceeding smoothly and everybody is in good heart.

Twenty minutes after detonation, the men who had been at H1 left for much-needed rest and sleep on board *Campania*.

Meanwhile aboard *Tracker* preparations were being made for controlling re-entry into the radioactive areas to take samples and collect records and instruments. All the men entering contaminated areas had to pass through the health control in HMS *Tracker*, to be briefed and issued with film badges and protective clothing, and each party was accompanied by a health escort. On return they were undressed, monitored, and where necessary decontaminated; on a few occasions up to five showers were needed. The sorties were very exhausting in the hot weather, especially in the brown protective clothing (white was worn for later trials) (see Photograph 4). The resulting thermal stress was near the limits of tolerance for some men, who lost 2–4 litres of sweat in four hours, and up to 16 lb in weight; one of the effects of dehydration was extreme nervous irritability.

In certain cases where respirators had been thought unnecessary, urine analysis revealed minute traces of radioactivity which were soon eliminated. As the radioactivity must have been inhaled, the need for respirators, and their effectiveness, were both demonstrated. On some of the later sorties, after the levels of contamination had been reduced by radioactive decay, protective clothing and respirators were dispensed with, since thermal stress had become a greater hazard than radioactivity.

Re-entry sorties and recovery of the records continued, interrupted by some very bad weather and gale force winds, until 23 October. After the hardships and difficulties of the past three months, and the stress of the past two or three years, tensions found release in some splendid parties in the wardroom of *Campania*, where much liquor was drunk and some unprintable songs were sung by scientists and naval officers in hearty unison.

The flotilla sailed from the Islands on 31 October, and most of the scientists left the ship at Fremantle and were flown home by the RAF. Meanwhile an Australian unit of 18 men from the three Services, under an RAAF squadron leader who had taken part in *Hurricane*, was established on Trimouille, to carry out training in radiological health and safety and to undertake security duties after the task force departed. The British health team provided radiation detection equipment and other stores, and a detailed brief on residual radiation hazards, for the unit, which remained in the Monte Bellos until 16 December. Then, apart from periodic inspection and security patrols by HMAS *Hawkesbury*, and a British scientific survey in November 1953, the islands were deserted again until preparations began for Operation *Mosaic* in 1956.

'This important experiment'

Churchill sent Menzies a message of thanks and a report on the operation, and made a statement to the House of Commons, on 22 October:

> The object of the test was to investigate the effects of an atomic explosion in a harbour. The weapon was accordingly placed in HMS *Plym*, a frigate of 1450 tons which was anchored in the Monte Bello Islands. Conditions were favourable and care was taken to wait for southerly winds so as to avoid the possibility of any significant concentration of radioactive particles spreading over the Australian mainland. Specimen studies of importance to Civil Defence and to the armed services were erected at various distances. Instruments were set up to record the effect of contamination, blast, heat flash, gamma-ray flash and other factors of interest.
>
> The weapon was exploded in the morning of 3 October. Thousands of tons of water and of mud and rock from the sea bottom were thrown many thousands of feet into the air and a high tidal wave was caused. The effects of blast and radioactive contamination extended over a wide area . . .
>
> Very soon after the explosion, two naval officers undertook the dangerous task of flying helicopters over the heavily contaminated lagoon where *Plym* had lain. This was in order to take samples of the water so that its radioactivity could be measured. After a longer interval, scientists and service personnel in protective clothing entered the contaminated areas to examine the effects and to recover records.
>
> Technical descriptions of the performance of the bomb cannot of course be given. It may however be said that the weapon behaved exactly as ex-

pected and forecast in many precise details by Dr W G Penney, whose services were of the highest order. Scientific observations and measurements show that the weapon does not contradict the natural expectation that progress in this sphere would be continued . . .

The explosion caused no casualties to the personnel of the expedition. No animals were used in the test. Apart from some local rats which were killed, no mammals were seen in the affected area and such birds as there were had mostly been frightened away by the earlier preparations.

Churchill emphasized the British Government's great indebtedness to Australia; not only had the Australian Commonwealth allowed the use of their territory for the test but all branches of their government—and particularly the Navy, Army and Air Force—had given most valuable help in the preparation and execution of 'this important experiment'. He warmly congratulated all concerned in producing the first British atomic weapon on 'the successful outcome of this historic episode', and in conclusion complimented Attlee and the Opposition on initiating it.

How safe was *Hurricane*?

Safety of the mainland

How well did the *Hurricane* safety measures work? The islands themselves were, as expected, heavily contaminated at some points and would remain so for a time. The survey in November 1953 found them still highly radioactive in places, but it was possible to use certain areas again in 1956. There seems to have been negligible radioactivity on the Australian mainland. Twenty-four hours after the explosion, the coastline was surveyed by Harwell scientists using very sensitive detectors fitted in a Dakota aircraft, which flew along the coast from Broome to Onslow at a height of 500 feet—a very bumpy airsick flight of 4–5 hours in turbulent conditions. As no radioactivity was detected, it was decided that no ground survey was necessary. Eight hours later, high-level flights detected a localized concentration of radioactivity in the atmosphere at an altitude of 10 000 ft but hardly any at 8000 ft.

Air samples were taken, 200 miles from ground zero, at a height of 8–10 000 ft, by Lincoln aircraft of the RAAF, about 6 hours after the explosion. Some of the samples were analysed in a Melbourne University laboratory by a team of four Harwell radiochemists. Others were flown back to England for analysis.

Later there would be a network of over 80 fixed monitoring stations to detect and measure fallout on the Australian continent; there was no such monitoring in 1952. It was an essential part of the *Hurricane* plan that there should be no fallout on the mainland. But though the cloud containing the radioactive debris went safely out to sea after the explosion, hours later light evening breezes blowing onshore brought back some radioactivity and a secondary cloud crossed Australia from west to east. In the next week, very low levels of radioactivity were detected, by two of the scientists from Harwell, in rainwater samples from three places, one of them Brisbane.

The public health impact on the Australian population of fallout from all the major trials was recently estimated by two Australian scientists[5] using all the available data and considering all the pathways to man—by external radiation, and by internal radiation from ingesting radioactivity in food or water or inhaling air-borne radioactivity. Since monitoring results were not available for *Hurricane*, they used data from the 1956 and 1957 trials, taking account of wind trajectories and such factors as the comparative yields of the various detonations. Their resulting estimate of the collective dose equivalent (see Appendix G) to the Australian population from *Hurricane* was 110 man-sieverts (11000 man-rems) a figure that, they said, might be too low by a factor of 2 or might be 10 times too high. The possible public health impact of *Hurricane* and all other trials is discussed in Chapter 12.

Safety of test personnel

Of the 1518 *Hurricane* personnel issued with film badges, 1263 received no exposure above the measurable threshold, and only 148 received more than 0.5 r during the whole operation; 0.5 r, it will be remembered, was the normal *weekly* limit. No doses over 5 r were recorded (see Appendix H). These figures compare favourably with the exposures of radiation workers at the time, for whom the ICRP limit was then 0.5 r a week (i.e., 25 r a year) continuously for a working lifetime.

The RAAF had not issued radiation dosimeters and film badges to its Lincoln aircrews and no special precautions had been taken. When the Air Ministry had made enquiries two years previously, Harwell's chief radiological officer, W G Marley, had advised them that aircraft should avoid flying through the visible cloud after an atomic explosion, but that once the visible cloud had dispersed there would be no danger. (This view seems to be in line with American conclusions in the 1950 edition of *The Effects of Atomic Weapons*, though these relate to an airburst, not an underwater burst.) The *Hurricane* Executive had informed the Australian authorities that the radioactive hazard to aircrews in flying through the cloud would be negligible and that there would be no fear of the aircraft becoming contaminated. Later experience (see Chapter 4) showed this view to be mistaken, but calculations made after *Totem* indicated that the radioactivity levels at *Hurricane* and the radiation doses to Lincoln aircraft and crews were only a fraction of those at *Totem*, and were considered to be of no medical significance.

What did *Hurricane* achieve?

Hurricane had been a close-run thing, and could easily have failed. The plutonium was ready only just in time. The boats and vehicles were only just sufficient. There was no margin for illness or injuries, and if a few men had gone sick, the trial could have been seriously hampered. If the weather had been unfavourable on 3 October, there would only have been one other opportunity, on 23 October, before the task force was due to sail for home. Thanks to immensely hard work in Britain and in Australia—by scientists, engineers, Servicemen, boat crews and all concerned—and also thanks to a fair share of luck with the weather, *Hurricane* was a success.

For the scientists, it was the climax of a period of intense work; 'our first eruption', as one of them, well read in Milton, called it. It was also the beginning of a new period of research and development. It confirmed that their design worked, and that they had the makings of a nominal—i.e., about 20 kiloton—plutonium bomb, similar to the Nagasaki bomb, but with many advantages over the bombs which the Americans were making in 1946 when collaboration had ceased[6].

The scientists learnt a great deal from *Hurricane*, and the next two years saw dozen of scientific reports on all aspects of the trial. There were new data on shallow underwater nuclear explosions and hence on the possible effect of shipborne nuclear bombs in ports and harbours, a defence problem that had much exercised the British authorities. Data were provided for military and civil defence authorities on the effects of blast on various types of buildings, equipment and materials. Useful biological information was gained—though no animal experiments were done—by catching and examining local fish and animals and collecting vegetation for analysis. Much was learnt about radioactivity from local fallout, about protective clothing and about decontamination methods. The operation also yielded valuable administrative lessons (not always applied in later tests) about the need for sufficient time and staff for planning, and for closer coordination between the various elements involved; about the dangers of underestimating the resources required; about the inadvisability of sending the main scientific party by sea; and about public relations. All these lessons were summed up in a report by Captain Pat Cooper, a retired naval officer who acted as a liaison officer and technical aide to Penney.

To the world, *Hurricane* marked Britain's entry into the ranks of atomic powers alongside the United States and Russia. It did not however mean that Britain yet had a nuclear operational capacity. The device tested at Monte Bello was by no means a Service weapon; one scientist described it as a 'lash-up'. Even when 'weaponized', significant numbers could not be available for several years, and the V-bombers, the intended delivery vehicles, were not yet in production. The triumphant announcement that the test had been successfully carried out did not mean what the public perhaps thought. The British press generally reacted with chauvinistic pride but considerable inaccuracy, making flattering assumptions that the bomb could have been tested earlier but had been delayed for the sake of major improvements; that it was much more powerful than any American bomb; that it was much smaller; that it had been tested in a guided missile. In some quarters, however, the Press greeted the test with modified rapture; if not a waste of resources, it was a regrettable necessity due to the failure to integrate Anglo-American defence, or was an expensive demonstration designed to secure American cooperation[7].

Before *Hurricane*, in March 1952, Churchill had expressed the opinion that the outcome of the test was of supreme importance, because it would put Britain in a far better position to secure the full cooperation of the United States, which was essential to the success of a strategic air plan in war. He saw the test as establishing 'equality', thus enabling Britain not only to exchange scientific and technical information more freely with the Americans but also to initiate joint consultations on targets and methods of attack. But the United States—with their first thermonuclear test only a month away—were not particularly impressed. Dr Solandt, of the Canadian Defence Research Board, who was in Washington just after *Hurricane*, found there a feeling that the British weapon programme was merely a propaganda effort to interest the

United States authorities. By 1958 the position was to be very different.

Notes and references

Much of the material for this chapter comes from Gowing: *Independence and Deterrence*, Vol. 2, Chapter 24.

1 HER—High Explosives Research—the code name for the atomic bomb project in the Ministry of Supply (see Chapter 1).
2 The three limits also dealt with beta radiation, but details are omitted here for the sake of simplicity, since gamma radiation was the significant hazard. See Appendix G.
3 Sir John Butterfield, Regius Professor of Medicine in the University of Cambridge, was present as a Medical Research Council scientist at *Hurricane* and later at *Buffalo*. In his view, the HER (later AWRE) scientists were very impressive and the tests were excellently conducted, though he criticizes the protective clothing used at *Hurricane* as ill designed for hot conditions.
4 For the significance of inversions, see Appendix I.
5 Keith N Wise and John R Moroney of the Australian Radiation Laboratory (ARL), see Bibliography.
6 Gowing: *Independence and Deterrence*, Vol. 2, p. 473.
7 Gowing: *Ibid.*, Vol. 1, p. 54.

4 Totem—1953

The plan for Totem

Before *Hurricane* it was already clear that more tests would be needed later, but none was expected before 1954. However, after *Hurricane* Sir William Penney—he had been knighted after *Hurricane*—decided that another test was urgently necessary to answer some important questions.

As part of their 1952 appraisal of global strategy, the Chiefs of Staff had asked for a doubling of plutonium output for the nuclear weapons programme. It had been approved by the government, and two new reactors were to be built for the purpose at Calder Hall, adjacent to Windscale. These were called PIPPA reactors because, unlike the two original Windscale piles, they would produce power as well as plutonium, and would be net producers of electricity. Like the Windscale piles, they were to be graphite moderated, but they were to be cooled, and the heat extracted, by carbon dioxide gas in a closed circuit, instead of by air in an open-ended current. This change made an enormous difference to safety, besides utilizing the heat from the reactor core.

A major problem was the irradiation time—how long the uranium fuel cartridges could be left in the reactor. The longer they remained, the greater the burn-up of uranium, the fewer the fuel changes, the less the chemical processing workload, and the cheaper the product. Longer irradiation would transform more plutonium-239 to plutonium-240, and an increasing proportion of the latter must reduce the average explosive efficiency, because the neutrons produced by the spontaneous fission of plutonium-240 could start the chain reaction too soon. The weapon scientists had set the proportion conservatively, on the basis of an unproven theory. The *Hurricane* device had given about the expected nominal yield—it was approximately 25 kilotons—but gave no information about the statistics of plutonium-240 in reducing yields. Nor did the weapon scientists have complete confidence in their theory of yield versus quantity of plutonium.

The Calder Hall reactors, because of the higher neutron flux and higher temperatures, would produce plutonium-240 faster than the

Windscale piles. For the same plutonium-240 content, the irradiation period would have to be shorter. The consequent need for more fuel changes, and so more chemical processing, would mean delay and would increase the overload on the Ministry of Supply's atomic energy production organization, which was already seriously short of engineers and technicians. It would also mean considerable expenditure on additional plant at Windscale, at a time when the government was engaged in a severe reappraisal of public expenditure, and of defence expenditure in particular.

These problems required a better-informed re-optimization of the specification of the plutonium-240 content of the weapon material, on which the whole production plan depended. Practical experiments were urgently necessary. In December 1952, Penney sought and obtained Ministerial approval for two test explosions, in an operation later codenamed *Totem*. It was to be in October 1953 and once again, as for *Hurricane*, the planners would be pressed for time.

Monte Bello was out of the question; the Navy could not mount another naval expedition in the time available. Penney fully understood the difficulties and knew that the great distance to Australia was a serious logistical handicap. The *Totem* tests would be smaller and simpler than *Hurricane*, and what was needed was a test site where the logistics would be much easier. But the use of a United States range was still impossible, the timescale did not permit another worldwide search, and nowhere nearer than Australia seemed possible.

On his way to *Hurricane* in October 1952, Penney had called secretly at the Woomera Range in South Australia, and he and Butement had visited a potential test site—identified as X200 but soon given the name Emu Field—which the Australians had found in the desert 300 miles north-west of Woomera (see Map 3). Penney proposed that the new trial should be mounted there, and in December 1952 Churchill asked Menzies to approve the use of this site. The safety problem, his note said, had been carefully investigated; full assurances could be given to the Australian government, and the United Kingdom government would be glad to arrange for Penney to go through the calculations with Professors Martin and Titterton. Further, the test would only be carried out when the Australian authorities were satisfied that the necessary weather conditions were met.

Penney told the high-level Atomic Energy Official Committee that in his opinion the Australians had been 'reasonably content' with the way in which the British had carried out *Hurricane* without telling them very

Map 3 The Emu/
Maralinga area

much about it. They would want to know much more about the 1953 test, which would be on the mainland. Besides the details to be supplied to Martin and Titterton about contamination, he suggested that he should, orally, tell them and one or two specially cleared high-ranking officials to be nominated by the Australian government about certain general principles of the weapon. This information would probably have to be disclosed to Butement, who was in charge of the Woomera Rocket Range. It was intended, Penney said, to ask for some Australian Army officers to help in the radiological survey teams; this would give them valuable military experience and would reduce the number of men who would have to be sent out from the United Kingdom. They would obtain information about radioactive contamination, but only from low-yield weapons, and to prevent them from under-rating the British military weapon they should be told that the object of *Totem* was to determine how the yield of the weapon varied with the weight of plutonium. These views were passed on to Lord Cherwell. Only the last of these three suggestions was accepted, and the information was confined to radiological safety.

Menzies quickly approved the Emu Field proposal. The Australian Department of Supply assumed responsibility and set up a *Totem* Panel. Australian troops immediately began construction work on the site. Meanwhile the British had set up an interdepartmental committee, the *Totem* Executive (or Totex) and had appointed a trial planner, L C Tyte, who had been scientific superintendent at *Hurricane*, and a technical director, C A Adams (see Photograph 5); in May 1953, however, Tyte moved to a post at the National Coal Board. Staff lists were drawn up and the matters where Australian help was to be sought were itemized. Instructor Commander Westwater RN was to be responsible for weather-forecasting, as at *Hurricane*, but Australia was to be asked for major meteorological support in personnel and equipment. Construction work was to be kept to the minimum by shipping large trailers ready equipped to serve as laboratories, offices, and a health centre. Plans for air sampling would be much the same as for *Hurricane* and the assistance of the RAAF would again be requested.

An Australian liaison mission headed by Brigadier C L Lucas, the X200 site commander designate, arrived in England early in February for discussions on the site plan, buildings, water supplies, communications, meteorology, safety, contaminated waste and security. It was soon clear to the British that the worst difficulties would be overland transport and water. The nearest track was 100 miles away and the terrain was difficult; only vehicles with tracks or special wheels could cross the sandy ridges, and 30 miles a day would be good going. Most stores would have to be air-freighted to the site. The plan for a village of trailers was out of the question, as they could not be towed to the site and were too big to airlift; Nissen huts would have to be erected, and the men would have to live in tents. Water supplies were insufficient for more than 300 people; the shortage of water suitable for decontamination and for processing film badges would strictly limit the numbers who could work in contaminated areas. This meant that no experiments ancillary to the weapon trial itself could be included unless they were exceptionally important.

It was agreed that 45 Australian Servicemen, including some of the naval personnel who had been at *Hurricane*, would take part; twenty of them would have a course of radiological training to ensure that they took proper precautions, and this training might be considerably extended. Squadron Leader Thomas, who had been at *Hurricane* and in the post-trial unit at Monte Bello, would be available and would play a key role.

Though the nearest inhabited area was about 110 miles from Emu Field, a region to the north that was used by Aboriginals for hunting was only about 50 miles away. An Australian official had been specially appointed by the Australian authorities to deal with native affairs and to look after the interests of the neighbouring Aboriginals, and nine (later seven) Commonwealth Government 'peace officers' were given the task of ensuring that none strayed into the prohibited area. It was emphasized by Totex that contaminated materials on the range must be disposed of in such a way that the Aboriginals would not be endangered by their characteristic ingenuity in salvaging and using material thrown away by white people.

The basic timetable for the trial was agreed with the Lucas mission. All equipment, except the weapons, was to be shipped early in June, to reach Adelaide by late July. *Totem* staff were to arrive in Australia by the first week in September, the weapons would follow later in the month, and the trial, consisting of two firings about 10 days apart, would take place in October/November.

In March 1953 a British mission led by C A Adams, the *Totem* technical director, paid a two-week return visit to Australia. The prospect they found was daunting. The area was flat, with clumps of saltbush and occasional mulga and she oaks, and dead wood (see Photograph 7). The land surface was a compact mixture of sand and stone, with an underlying fine red dust that impregnated their clothes. There was little water. The weather was hot—105°F during a large part of the day—but chilly at night. Clothing to cover the whole body, including a bush hat and a veil, were said to be necessary for protection; bush flies, unless constantly brushed away, settled on hands, face, arms and shirt in a thick black mass. Bush fires might be troublesome. The airlift problem would be extremely difficult (in the event some 2500 tons of supplies and equipment were flown in to Emu Field and only 500 tons transported overland). They noted that the question of possible long-term effects of radioactive contamination, which might be carried long distances and precipitated by rainfall, had not been resolved.

The British government sent the Australian government an invitation for Australian scientists—expected to be Martin, Titterton and Butement—to be present at *Totem*. Meanwhile Penney's staff was preparing a safety brief, and in May they completed and despatched to Australia an appreciation of the *Totem* airborne hazard. This report (numbered A32) predicted the fallout for a 5-kiloton device but was capable of adjustment to the higher figure of probable maximum yield, for both shots, of 10 kilotons. The mechanism of the rise of the mushroom cloud and the distribution of contamination at various levels was not yet understood in detail, but it was certain that a large amount of material would be thrown up into the air—the vaporized 'gadget', the 100 ft steel tower it was to be mounted on, fission products from the explosion, and sand from the ground. As the fireball cooled, the vaporized material would condense into small particles together with some of the fission products. Other fission products would adhere to, and contaminate, the particles drawn up from the ground as the mushroom cloud rose. Once in the air, the particles would be dispersed by the wind and eventually fall to earth. If the contamination they caused was severe enough, it could be a health hazard—from external radiation (by fission products deposited on the ground or on the person), or from internal radiation (due to contaminated air, food or water). The body could tolerate some radiation, said A32, but above a certain level there would be a threat to health. Permissible contamination levels, the paper continued, had already been laid down for *Hurricane* by the Medical Research Council, on the basis of ICRP recommendations. To determine safe distances and safe firing conditions, these permissible levels had to be related to the expected contamination on the ground, and this depended on wind conditions. The fallout deposited downwind would steadily decrease with distance; moreover, the further the particles were carried before they fell to the ground the less dangerous the contamination would be because of dispersion and radioactive decay.

If the wind blew steadily at twenty miles an hour and in the same direction at all levels, the fallout would be along the line of the wind, spreading sideways by atmospheric turbulence as the distance increased; to either side of the central line, the intensity would fall off rapidly. In such conditions, from a 5-kiloton explosion, contamination outside a 50 mile radius could exceed a 'zero risk level' only in a very narrow sector, extending 120 miles from ground zero. This sector would be an area of 'slight risk'; for a 10-kiloton burst the corresponding distances would be 70 miles and 170 miles.

Neither a 'zero risk level' nor a 'slight risk level' was mentioned in recommendations of the International Commission on Radiological Protection (ICRP). They were proposed by Aldermaston, and were derived secondary limits that referred to levels of deposited radioactivity, not to maximum permissible doses of radiation. The Aldermaston health physicists defined the 'slight risk level' as 'that quantity of fission products which may cause some slight temporary sickness to a small number of people who have a low threshold sensitivity to radiation'. This level was derived from the maximum amount of external gamma radiation that could be tolerated with a slight risk, as defined; at that time, this was taken by most scientists as 25 r, and therefore 25 r was the standard adopted for the 'slight risk level'.

'Zero risk level' they defined as 'that quantity of fission products which will cause no measurable effect on the body'. ICRP gave 0.3 r as the maximum permissible dose (MPD) of external gamma radiation that might be received weekly over a lifetime; from this the authors of A32 argued that—for zero risk—3 r (ten times the weekly limit) ought not to be exceeded in any 10-week period.

These basic limits of 3 r and 25 r continued to be used almost throughout the Australian atomic weapon trials, though the secondary limits were revised at intervals. Corresponding limits were also set for beta radiation, and for internal radiation by the different exposure pathways. The variations in levels of surface radioactivity set for later trials were not variations in the MPD but in the quantity of radioactivity that it was calculated could give rise to such exposures (see Appendix G).

The conditions for firing set out in A32 were intended to be such that there was nobody in a fallout area where the surface radioactivity was above 'zero risk' level. These conditions were comparable to those derived from the published results of test firings in the United States, where over twenty atomic weapons or devices had by this time been exploded at the proving ground in Nevada, but the British calculations were more conservative. A32 recommended two practical limitations on firing the *Totem* rounds. First, to protect the base camp, firing should not take place if the mean wind up to a height of 10 000 ft was between 100° and 130°. Secondly, if—improbably—wind direction was constant with height the zero risk zone for a 5-kiloton detonation might be as far as 120 miles from ground zero (GZ); in that case, to safeguard the nearest homesteads and Aboriginal hunting grounds 100 or so miles away, firing should not take place if the predicted wind was 190° or between 218° and 246°.

The Australian scientists had several questions on A32, especially about the predicted height of the cloud. In June Titterton had an opportunity to visit England and was able to discuss A32, and the trial generally, with Penney and his staff. After this, and some correspondence with Aldermaston, Martin and Titterton informed the Australian Prime Minister in June that they were satisfied that no injury to health would result from the effects of the proposed explosions.

In July 1953 Totex—the *Totem* Executive in London—issued the following instructions to the trials staff:

Firing will occur only if
(a) the mean wind from surface to any level below 10 000 ft does not lie between 330° to 130° through north
(b) it is forecast that no rain will fall within 12 hours, nearer than 200 miles downwind.

Firing conditions for *Totem* 2, if necessary, can be slightly less stringent because we do not this time have to preserve a clean firing site for an immediately following trial . . ..

Operation *Totem*—Round 1

The main scientific party flew to Australia on 17 August and began preparations both for firing the first *Totem* round at T1 and for a series of minor component trials—code named *Kittens*—which was also to be conducted at Emu Field (see Chapter 10). Preliminary *Totem* rehearsals took place on 24 and 27 September, and the first weapon, or 'device', arrived by air on 26 September.

When Penney flew in on 29 September the first *Kitten* test had already been successfully carried out and the *Totem* teams were nearly ready for a full-scale rehearsal. There were 158 British staff there, and 17 Australians. Five Australian officers were in the radiation hazards group, which totalled 35 and was much the largest group; six Australians were in the meteorological team; Titterton and four others made up a neutron-detection group; one Australian officer took part in the small 'target response' programme for the investigation of weapon effects. In addition, the air-sampling and cloud-tracking programme was a major RAAF contribution (see below). Logistically, the whole operation was entirely dependent on the RAF and the Bristol and York aircraft that provided a freight and passenger service between Woomera and Emu Field.

On 30 September a party of VIPs, including Lord Cherwell and Mr Butement, visited the site, and Butement remained for some days after the rest had left. After a full-scale rehearsal on 1 October, standby began on 7 October, but was cancelled almost immediately because of bad weather. Captain Frank Lloyd RN, a senior Ministry of Supply officer, described conditions in a letter home:

> 'Life here is fun provided always one has a return ticket. A temperature range of 50° to 60° per 24 hours plus a very dry air is most bracing. The food is good, the beer is plentiful and the only thing we really lack is fresh water. The only other trial is when the wind gets over 15 to 20 knots. The dust is the devil . . .. The Australians under Lucas have done a first class job here . . .. All Bill's staff are in great heart . . ..

The weather had been hot and blustery, but on 8 October the rain began. D−1 was declared on Monday 12 October, but had to be cancelled. Penney cabled to London:

> Rain stopped play. Unseasonable weather continues to provide easterly winds which endanger camp and have given us dark clouds and considerable rain. We are doing everything possible to reduce time between the two explosions and will certainly regain a few of the lost days. My policy is to wait until conditions are entirely satisfactory, Press and VIPs notwithstanding, and not to fire on a Sunday.

D−1 was declared again on 14 October, a party of Press representatives and VIPs flew in from Adelaide, and this time conditions held good. The first round at T1 was fired at 7 am on 15 October (local time), about an hour after sunrise. The cloud rose to 10 000 ft, extending upwards to 15 000 ft; the explosion was more powerful than expected, and at 10 kilotons was the maximum adopted for fallout and safety calculations.

The cloud was tracked for two-and-a-half days. It preserved its identity to a remarkable extent and was clearly visible as a cloud even after 24 hours; it was reported later that owing to the very stable atmospheric conditions the cloud did not diffuse rapidly but was stretched in the direction of motion. It therefore produced a narrow band of radioactivity on the ground underneath its path.

Preliminary reports of the fallout pattern on the ground, from airborne surveys extending to a distance of 400 miles, were passed to Penney over the next few days. The reports showed that the sideways dispersion effects of windshear and turbulence on the radioactive dust in the cloud and stem were less than expected. However, the level of radiation off-range was said to be within the 'no risk' specification. Two years later, however, the calibration of the instruments used for the airborne radiological survey was reviewed, and the contamination levels were re-assessed; the fallout at Wallatinna, a homestead to the north-east, was corrected to a level about half-way between 'zero risk' and 'slight risk'.

The firing of T1, with winds blowing from between 211° and 240°, complied with the Totex directive. It can be argued however that it did not meet the A32 criteria. A32, it will be remembered, advised against firing when the wind was at 190° or between 218° and 246° if the wind direct was 'constant with height', but did not define the term. Is a wind structure varying over an arc of 23°—or at most 29°—to be considered 'constant with height' or not? If it is, T1 did not conform to A32; if not, it did.

Should T1 have been fired when it was? The first question is on what information the decision to fire was taken. Was it knowingly made in conditions that were unsatisfactory? Some nuclear weapons scientists, as well as others, have since said that it was a mistake to fire at the time—a judgment made by hindsight. Information available to the trials staff after the explosion should not be confused with information available to them beforehand. Predictions of the movement of the cloud in the hours following the explosion were made by the *Totem* meteorologists on the basis of information, from a network of weather stations, that was several hours old by the time the firing decision was made. At the pre-firing conference the senior British meteorologist, Commander Westwater RN, was apparently satisfied that conditions were suitable, but there is no documentation (pre-firing conferences were not usually minuted). The scientists who had to carry out the downwind monitoring of the fallout were expecting a much wider plume, and were astonished by the narrowness of the plume as their surveys developed.

Penney, as we saw, was determined to wait for entirely satisfactory predicted conditions. It was his firm policy never to proceed if anyone at the pre-firing conference had the slightest reservation, and it must have been the case that everyone present, including the Australian scientists and the meteorologists, was satisfied. Possibly the meteorologists overestimated the effect of windshear and atmospheric turbulence. Possibly the forecasts of the windshear acting on the cloud as it moved during the first few hours indicated greater deviation than was actually measured at the site, within minutes of the explosion, and reported in Westwater's report. I have found no complete and convincing explanation of the T1 firing, but nothing to suggest that the decision was taken in conditions on which anyone had any reason for doubts at the time.

Other questions about the fallout from the *Totem* shots and its possible health effects are discussed later in this chapter.

Operation *Totem*—Round 2

Immediately after the first round, Butement went off with a small reconnaissance party, which was joined by Penney and J T Tomblin, Adams' deputy, to look at another possible test site in the South Australian bush. They returned to Emu Field a few days later, in readiness for the second *Totem* round, T2. Meanwhile the *Kittens* series proceeded without a hitch, until the fifth and final experiment on 17 October (see Chapter 10).

At T2, as at T1, the device was mounted on a steel tower. Preparations were delayed by more bad weather, an unpleasant combination of rain, gusty winds and sandstorms. The weather improved on 24 October, and the next day standby was declared. Penney called a technical meeting of scientists in the evening to review the predictions of fallout patterns and to make certain that favourable conditions would hold good for firing early next day. He was joined by Titterton, two Australian meteorologists, two British meteorologists and three other British scientists. Penney and his staff estimated the probable maximum yield at 10 kilotons, the most likely yield at 2–3 kilotons, and the absolute minimum at ¼ kiloton. Westwater, the senior British meteorologist, estimated the cloud heights for these yields at 14 000 ft, 12 000 ft and 5000 ft, respectively. Corner, the scientist in charge of theoretical predictions, calculated that for a 10-kiloton burst, even with winds of 100 miles an hour, the zero risk level would be 100 miles from ground zero; winds of this speed were not expected, and the distance would be less with lower wind speeds. Results of air surveys appeared to indicate that the ground contamination levels from the T1 shot were about four times lower than had been predicted, and to confirm that the theoretical predictions had (as intended) been based on very pessimistic, worst case, assumptions. This view was in fact erroneous, since, as we saw, it was later found that the method used to interpret the air survey data gave ground contamination levels lower than they actually were by a factor of three.

At the meeting on 24 October, the meteorologists said that the wind was likely to carry the cloud from T2 to the south east. The nearest populations were at Tarcoola and Woomera, 200 and 300 miles away, respectively; there seemed to be a wide safety margin. Asked whether rain might fall through the cloud and bring down fallout before it left the mainland, one of the Australian meteorologists assured the meeting that there was no risk of rainfall. The cloud would go up into a hot dry mass of air which could not produce rain; then it would take some 50 hours to leave the mainland, and before it could be overtaken by a moist westerly airstream it would be too dispersed to present any hazard. It was agreed that the meteorological conditions likely to prevail for T2 satisfied the criteria accepted by Martin and Titterton, and that the safety factor was probably four times greater than previously believed.

The meeting then discussed possible reactions if the cloud was seen by members of the public. Apparently the cloud from T1 had been seen from Oodnadatta, probably from an aircraft. It was agreed that if there were any press questions about the cloud, the answer could be that it might have been a rain cloud. This ad hoc meeting was 'off side' in making such a suggestion, as the responsibility for dealing with the press lay with Captain Lloyd, who was present at *Totem* but who was not at the meeting. However nothing more was heard of a *Totem* cloud until the 'black mist' stories of 1980 (see below).

On the morning of 27 October, weather conditions held good and T2 was fired at 7 am (local time). Penney reported to Ministers—that is, to Cherwell and Sandys:

> T2 gave us a miserable night but went off on time with highly satisfactory wind conditions. My estimate from seeing explosions and comparing ground fused areas of two bursts from the air is that the yield of T2 was between 12 and 18 kilotons. [It was in fact 8 kilotons.] This high yield proved superior-

ity of intuition over maths, since our calculated yield was 2 or 3 kilotons. Extremely important consequences to our whole atomic energy programme . . . .. Top of cloud about 25 000 ft and bottom at 20 000. Stem torn to shreds before our eyes, and fanned out into quadrant between south and east. Cloud rapidly dispersing. Started moving towards point 60 miles north of Woomera but will swing towards east and then north of east.

The weather turned hot and sultry and by the evening of 27 October a heavy storm broke that continued intermittently all night. It did not however affect the *Totem* 2 cloud, which by this time was far away and well dispersed. Dismantling and packing began next day, 28 October, in cold damp weather, and the site was practically closed down by 2 November. A force of Australian peace officers and range security officers arrived, to be given a course in health control and guarding contaminated areas; on 6 November responsibility for the site was transferred from *Totem* staff to the Australian authorities in the person of Squadron Leader Thomas RAAF, who had taken over after *Hurricane* in 1952. By 12 November, all the *Totem* staff had left Emu Field.

After the *Totem* shots, the ground contamination by fission products seemed slight, apart from a narrow corridor downwind of the tower sites. This fallout, however, proved to be very different from what was expected, consisting of quite large particles that were not readily picked up by passing vehicles or blown about by the wind. On windy days, columns of dust extended several hundred feet into the air, but the radioactivity of the dust did not appear to be very high. Fallout had contaminated an unmanned photographic site on the eastern side of Emu Field, and this fact may have started the rumour that the camp was abandoned and never used again because of contamination. *Totem* was indeed the only major trial to take place there, but as we saw Butement and Penney were reconnoitring another site even before the second shot. Emu Field would have been quite unsuitable for a permanent test site; its disadvantages were so daunting that it is surprising it was used at all. But then the *Totem* operation had been considered especially urgent.

Two experiments

The Centurion tank

The timetable and the difficult conditions at Emu Field limited ancillary investigations very severely. Two experiments, however, were carried out. One was on the effects of the explosion on a Centurion tank and a simulated tank crew. The tank, provided by the Australian Army, was placed at about 250 yards from ground zero. Two hours before the explosion, it was left with its hatch closed, its engines running and the brakes off; the crew was represented by roughly fashioned dummies, each with two film badges. The damage was much less than expected; immediately after the explosion the tank's main engine was still running. But the prompt radiation dose to the crew would have been sufficient to cause radiation sickness in a few hours and death within a day or so.

Operation *Hot Box*

A second experiment was an Air Ministry operation codenamed *Hot Box*. In February the *Totem* Executive had approved a proposal that an RAF aircraft should fly into the mushroom cloud within a few minutes of the detonation. This flight was not part of the trial proper, nor part of the air-sampling or radiological-survey programmes, but was a separate experiment planned by the Air Ministry. They wanted to take advantage of *Totem* to investigate aircrew safety, behaviour of aircraft, and aircraft contamination in conditions of nuclear warfare.

The origin of Operation *Hot Box* goes back to 1948, when Squadron Leader D A Wilson, a consultant in radiology to the RAF, was attached to the Health Physics Division at Harwell. There, in 1949, he was shown some papers written by Fuchs, the Harwell physicist, which concluded that aircraft would be unable to operate anywhere in the vicinity of a nuclear explosion for some days. These papers had apparently been influential in the United States as well as in the British Air Ministry. Wilson was not convinced, and found errors in the calculations. He proposed to the Chief of the Air Staff and the RAF medical authorities that when British atomic tests began the opportunity should be taken of exploring the potential hazards to flying personnel. As *Hurricane* was unsuitable for this experiment, it was postponed until *Totem*. A specially prepared Canberra, equipped with precise instrumentation, was loaned to Group Captain Wilson at the beginning of 1953 and the aircrew (see Photograph 8) was assembled—Wilson himself as observer, a young RAF medical officer, Squadron Leader Geoffrey Dhenin GM, as pilot, and a volunteer (ex-Pathfinder) navigator, Wing Commander E W Anderson. At least two of the aircrew were well versed in radiation hazards, and they had planned *Hot Box* for months.

'It was', Wilson said, 'in no sense a Boys' Own paper type of exercise. It was a serious scientific experiment'. *Hot Box* was the first experiment of its kind, and produced results which were of value to the United States Air Force as well as the RAF. In fact, *Hot Box* would set operational parameters for a sortie by Canberra aircraft using atomic bombs. The *Hot Box* Canberra, incidentally, collected air samples for Frank Morgan, the radiochemist responsible for weapons diagnostics—the study of the performance of the weapon by radiochemical methods.

The aircraft entered the cloud 6 minutes after the detonation; passed through the cloud, by this time 2000 yards wide; and then made further short runs above and below the cloud. It was very thick, like a dense old-fashioned London fog, so that the pilot had to switch the aircraft lights on, and there was much turbulence. After landing the three officers showered, changed their clothing, and were monitored and medically examined. Analysis of blood and urine samples showed no trace of fission products. Their film badges and dosimeters—two films and two dosimeters to each man—gave high readings. The films indicated exposures of about 10r to about 15r and the dosimeters gave readings of about 20r; however film badges are generally more reliable, as quartz fibre dosimeters behave erratically in rough conditions, and altitude and turbulence could have accounted for the discrepancy. Because of the levels of the recorded doses and because the Air Ministry's essential requirements had been fulfilled, the second sortie, after T2, was cancelled at the insistence of Penney and Adams, although the three RAF officers were ready and keen to go again. These were the largest exposures recorded at *Totem*. Most (83 per cent) of the recorded exposures were less than 0.3r in a week.

Contaminated aircraft

Besides their routine transport, communications and patrol duties British and Australian aircraft had several different air survey and air sampling tasks. The radiological surveys were for safety purposes: to detect and chart fallout more rapidly and extensively than ground surveys could do alone, and to track the radioactive cloud—by instruments when it was no longer visible—until it had dispersed or had left the Australian Continent. Other flights were for weapons diagnostic purposes: aircraft were required to collect air samples early, but at some distance from ground zero; radiochemical analysis of the samples was used to provide essential data on the performance and yield of the weapon.

Yet other aircraft collected later air samples, at varying distances up to 2000 miles from ground zero, for scientific intelligence purposes. This was an independent and especially secret programme directed by Harwell and was based on their experience of monitoring foreign weapon tests by collecting long-distance samples. It was hoped to improve the efficiency of these monitoring methods by studying the results from British tests where the weapon information was known instead of unknown. The RAAF undertook these flights and made a very substantial contribution to this programme; at *Totem*, two squadrons of Lincoln aircraft and over 160 ground and air staff were involved.

Two days after *Totem* 1 a radiation hazards officer from Emu Field, who was visiting Woomera, checked the exterior of the *Hot Box* Canberra, which had been washed and scrubbed sufficiently to reduce the surface radioactivity to 'Active Service' standards. He found it still very contaminated in places, and when the *Totem* 2 flight was cancelled he began further work on it. He also advised the RAAF to suspend work on the Lincolns which had been on long-distance air-sampling sorties. Aircrews returning from their sorties had reported that their cloud-tracking instruments had gone off scale, and the station had called on Group Captain Wilson, of the *Hot Box* crew, for help. He, in fact, knew nothing about this intelligence programme, which was being controlled by a Harwell scientist based at Salisbury, near Adelaide. Wilson checked the aircraft interiors, and estimated the radiation exposures of the aircrews—who had no film badges although one pilot happened to have a dosimeter. As a medical radiologist Wilson was able to assure the station commander that no one had received a significant exposure. Nevertheless the RAAF were understandably annoyed and worried because they had had no warning of radioactive hazards on these operations. This was because the British, from their previous experience of intelligence flights, had expected none. There was a flurry of activity and some strong feelings, and Wilson immediately took an opportunity to visit Melbourne and call on the Director-General of Medical Services, RAAF, to explain the situation to him.

Meanwhile another radiation safety officer arrived at Woomera equipped to set up a health control system. A laboratory-style 'active area' with physical barriers was not feasible, but the precautions were explained to everyone, and Service discipline and supervision, he reported, ensured that they were strictly observed. Two of the Lincolns were found to be substantially contaminated and three slightly; unlike the more stream-lined Canberras, their exterior seemed almost designed to trap contamination.

A similar control was set up at Amberley. Nine Lincolns there were contaminated. The only significant risk was to the ground crews; one man was reported to have spent three hours climbing over the wings of a recently landed aircraft, and he had worn the same overalls for two more days before the contamination was realized. Measurements made on the overalls suggested at the time a total dose of 3 to 5 r, but it was later assessed to be much lower.

Other RAAF Lincolns operating from Richmond, near Sydney, also became contaminated, but full precautions were taken promptly, thanks to the United States Air Force. There were USAF aircraft based at Richmond and it had been agreed long before *Totem* that two B29s should take part in the long-distance sampling after T1 and T2. The B29s were 'flying met labs' and the crews were well protected against radiation hazards. They were surprised and shocked by the extent of contamination of the Lincolns and by the lack of safety measures, and they lent the RAAF monitoring instruments and instructed them fully on what to do.

The lack of foresight about the radiological protection of aircraft and men involved in the air-sampling programme was undoubtedly a serious deficiency. Separate control of the programme by Harwell, the failure to coordinate in the planning stages, the inadequate Harwell presence on the spot, and the extreme secrecy, all contributed to it. So did the belief that conditions would be like those of the British aircraft collecting samples over the Atlantic, and the misleading advice given to the Air Ministry in 1950 (see Chapter 3). Fortunately no one is assessed as having had a severe radiation dose. Moreover the position was put right before T2, thanks to the USAF and *Hot Box*.

Some *Totem* lessons

The two *Totem* shots, besides giving information on the plutonium-240 question, taught the scientists a great deal in the next two or three years about the conduct of trials and, in particular, about early fallout. The data were derived from two sources, ground and airborne surveys; the monitoring stations that were later set up all over the Australian continent did not exist at the time of *Totem*. After *Totem* 1, ground surveys had been carried out up to 10 miles from ground zero; after *Totem* 2, up to four miles. Altogether 4400 measurements had been recorded. Aerial surveys had been made by aircraft fitted with sensitive radiation-detecting instruments and flying at 500 feet over the fallout area. They had made over 80 traverses, up to 400 miles from ground zero. Aerial surveys were valuable because they could cover large distances very quickly; ground surveys were more limited in their range, and exposed the surveyors to radiation above the normal working limit. However there were problems with using data from airborne surveys: partly because of errors and uncertainties in the interpretation of aerial readings in terms of actual ground contamination: partly because of navigational problems and difficulties of maintaining a constant altitude when flying low in turbulent conditions.

After extensive analysis and re-analysis of the *Totem* data, it had become clear by 1956 that, because of the very unusual meteorological conditions, the early fallout from the first shot had been about twice that from the second and had provided an ideal demonstration of the validity of a 'no-shear' dispersion model. It was clear too that post-event analysis did not support the belief that the A32 method of predicting contamination were safely pessimistic, partly because it had underestimated the proportion of the radioactive content of the cloud that would remain in the stem. Nevertheless, because the conversions from radiation exposure values to 'zero risk' and 'slight risk' levels of surface radioactivity contained very conservative assumptions, A32 allowed for a considerable margin of error. Detailed studies of the *Totem* data were put to good use in the development of new and improved predictive methods to succeed A32.

Totem experience also provided administrative and organizational lessons, summed up by Captain Pat Cooper, who had commented on Operation *Hurricane*. Generally the operations, he said, had proceeded smoothly, but in future the air sampling operations should be integrated more fully into the trial plan and controlled more closely by the headquarters organization. The main difference in organization between *Hurricane* and *Totem* was that the former was run like a military operation, with a naval task force commander in overall control, and a scientific director responsible for the scientific aspects. *Totem* had no task force commander, and the scientific director had a most demanding scientific job to do without having to coordinate and control so many disparate groups. (In any case a civilian could not have been placed in immediate command of the British and Australian military elements.) The scientific group had operated very successfully, but a more extensive headquarters control was needed, embracing both the scientific and supporting forces and providing communications, transport and all the technical services for the whole operation.

Once more, the timetable had been desperately tight, as the *Totem* Executive had realized, and in a trial so hurriedly prepared as *Totem*, and planned by different groups of people 12 000 miles apart, full mutual understanding was impossible. There had been occasional clashes of strong and sometimes discordant personalities, but cooperation had been admirable. The RAAF stations had made an outstanding contribution. Woomera had been invaluable as railhead, transit camp, rest station, control headquarters for the Lincolns and Dakotas, and home for *Totem* administrative and signals staff. Operation *Totem* had been a technical success, said Cooper, thanks to the excellent spirit of the scientific groups and to the effective Australian support 'given willingly and enthusiastically by all concerned from top to bottom'.

Enthusiasm for the joint partnership was expressed at greater length by the Australian Minister for Supply. Understandably, while paying tribute to British achievements, he found it desirable to emphasize or even over-emphasize the part played by Australia. All Australians, he said, had cause to feel proud of their country's contribution, especially the planning and construction work done at Emu Field in the face of incredible difficulties and the great skill and professional ability of the RAAF pilots and crews. 'Although only a small nation', he concluded, 'we have given eloquent proof of our ability and willingness to take a major part in the defence of the freedom of mankind'.

The Public Health impact of *Totem*

A network of fallout-monitoring stations was to be set up across Australia in 1955, but there was no such system at the time of *Totem*. The Australian scientists, Wise and Moroney, in their 1985 appraisal of the public health impact of fallout from the British atomic tests, made estimates for *Hurricane* (p. 50) and *Totem* based on all the available information, re-examined in the light of more recent knowledge on the behaviour of fallout and pathways of exposure. They calculated the total Australian population dose from T1 as 70 man-sieverts—7000 man-rems—that is, one-tenth of the total from all the atomic tests from 1952 to 1957 (see Chapter 12). That from T2 they calculated as 60 man-sieverts, 6000 man-rems.

The local impact is discussed immediately below.

'The black mist'

Twenty-seven years after *Totem*, the T1 cloud reappeared when a story about a 'black mist' became current in Australia. (An Australian anthropologist, Professor Annette Hamilton, had heard it 10 years earlier.) After a broadcast about the nuclear weapon tests, an Aboriginal named Mr Jim Lester told a member of the Central Australian Aboriginal Congress about an event during his boyhood at Wallatinna Station, near the opal mining town of Coober Peedy. The date was uncertain; Aboriginals have no systematic method of dating, but probably few people could exactly date incidents in their childhood after 30 years. About seven o'clock on this particular morning, Lester said, there was a big bang and everybody in the camp site woke up asking what it was. Some time later—perhaps next day—they saw a black, greasy, shiny smoke rolling up to them through the mulga. It had a very strong smell, and it stayed around for a while. Later, he said, people began to be ill, and some, he thought, might have died. The symptoms were sore eyes, sickness and diarrhoea. He himself became blind in one eye, and wholly blind a few years later; an eye specialist told him that his blindness was due to glaucoma and measles.

Other varying reports of 'a rolling black smoke or mist', 'a reddish cloud', 'blackish smoke settling all day on the trees . . . as an oily dust', and a 'big coiling cloud-like thing like a dust storm' came from other places in the region, in particular from Welbourn Hill station. There was much public and media interest in Australia, and an account appeared in 1982 in a book by Adrian Tame and F P J Robotham[1]. The Australian Ionising Radiation Advisory Council was asked to investigate, and in 1983 its conclusions were published in a general report on the atomic tests (AIRAC No. 9). AIRAC was somewhat sceptical, but concluded that if the black mist had been caused by any of the tests it must have been by *Totem*, as Wallatinna was much nearer to Emu Field than to the range at Maralinga where the 1956 and 1957 tests took place. T1 was more likely than T2 because of its unusual fallout pattern due to low windshear and low turbulence, and the trajectory of the T1 cloud must have passed fairly close to Wallatinna. However, measurements made by ground surveys as the time had shown that, even immediately under the centre of the plume and at a distance of only 10 miles from ground zero, the radiation dose would have been too small to cause acute illness. Wallatinna was 107 miles from ground zero, and there were no local features to cause a 'hot spot' there. Doses sufficient to cause radiation sickness therefore seemed most unlikely—AIRAC calculated the highest as in the range 0.1 to 1.0r—and the probability of long-term damage to health was extremely low.

Possibly the severe epidemics of measles, then prevalent among the Aboriginals, became associated in their minds with unusual and disturbing sights, sounds and experiences and with warnings from officials about the dangers of what Lester called 'white feller's magic'. There was no mention of a black mist in Native Patrol Officer's reports, but in early 1953 a report referred to a recent measles epidemic in which 30 members of an Aboriginal group had died.

In 1983 the story reached the British press. On 3 May an article in *The Observer* reported allegations that some Aboriginals had been exposed to airborne debris from the British atomic test at Emu Field on 15 October 1953, and had suffered short-term and long-term health damage. Scientists at Aldermaston decided that the black mist stories, even if they seemed unlikely, ought to be further investigated, and they asked the Meteorological Office to collaborate in a study based on all the meteorological and radiological data from *Totem* and employing the latest knowledge and computing techniques. The joint study, using twelve variants of a basic mathematical model, was completed in 1984. It concluded that the sites at Wallatinna and Welbourn Hill did receive fallout from the test on 15 October 1953; that debris drawn into the convective boundary layer (CBL)—the layer of air close to the earth's surface—could have been sufficiently concentrated to be visible to observers; and that it might have had an appearance similar to that described. (However, as we saw, the descriptions varied considerably, especially as to the colour of the cloud—black, grey, white, blue or reddish). Nevertheless the highest possible lifetime radiation doses that could be deduced from any of the mathematical models used in the study were 100 to 120 millisieverts (10 to 12 rems) or more realistically 10 to 15 millisieverts (1 to 1.5 rem). Neither could have had adverse health effects in the short term, and the long-term carcinogenic risk was insignificant—about 1 in 10 000 but probably lower. This view of the health impact of T1 was similar to AIRAC's, though reached by an entirely different method.

AIRAC reviewed its 1983 findings in 1985. It continued to prefer observed data, from corrected (or normalized) aerial survey results, to estimates based on hypothetical models. But it, too, was still satisfied that any radiation dose received at Wallatinna (where the highest fallout occurred) was most unlikely to have exceeded the annual limit then allowable, and certainly could not have caused acute radiation sickness. It also seemed improbable that a black mist attributable to a single test could have extended to all the sites, besides Wallatinna and Welbourn Hill, from which 'black mist' stories had come.

The Aldermaston chemists were puzzled by the description of the mist or cloud as black and oily, with a strong smell—by some accounts of diesel fuel, by others of liquid propane gas, or dead kangaroos. An explanation that has been suggested is that it came from spinifex bushes ignited by the heat of the explosion ('Away to our left a black cloud of smoke billowed skyward. One of the boys is signalling . . . when we want to call to each other in the bush, that's how we do it—set light to the spinifex. The turpentine in it gives off that oily black smoke'[2]). But after T1 there had been only two or three trivial bush fires which soon went out.

There seems little doubt that some unusual cloud or mist was seen by a number of people after T1. In the years between 1953 and 1980, or 1970 when Professor Hamilton first heard about it, the stories must have been told and retold many times. But the black mist remains something of a mystery, though not, it seems, a harmful one.

Notes and references

1 Adrian Tame and RF P J Robotham: *Maralinga—British A-Bomb Australian Legacy* (Fontana/Collins (Australia), 1982, pp. 143–144).
2 Hammond Innes: *Golden Soak* (Collins, London, 1973, pp. 28–29).

5 Interval: 1953–56

The British H bomb decision

After *Totem* there was a pregnant pause before the next major trial in the spring of 1956. In the intervening 2½ years, much happened in the nuclear world. The United States carried out 23 more tests, making 65 since the end of the war. These included their second thermonuclear explosion at Bikini on 1 March 1954; the first had been in October 1952[1]. During the same period Russia had exploded at least seven nuclear weapons, including one in the megaton range.

There was still no Anglo-American collaboration on nuclear weapons, and the Churchill government decided in June 1954, with almost no debate or dissension, that Britain, too, must have hydrogen bombs. This intention was announced in a White Paper[2] in February 1955. 'We must contribute to the deterrent and to our own defence', it said, 'by building up our own stock of nuclear weapons of all types and by developing the most up to date means of delivery'. It assigned even higher priority to the 'primary deterrent'. Not having her own deterrent force would, it was argued, weaken Britain's prestige and influence in the world, surrender her power to influence American policy, and perhaps imperil her safety. Having the hydrogen bomb would make Britain a world power again. The hydrogen bomb, unlike the atomic bomb, was 'a great leveller', cancelling out the disparity between small countries and large[3]. The entire foundation of human affairs, Churchill told Parliament, was revolutionized by the hydrogen bomb, and with this awesome weapon in their arsenals none of the major powers would dare resort to war. Safety, he predicted, would be 'the sturdy child of terror', and 'survival the twin brother of annihilation'[4].

Penney and the British weapon scientists now had a three-fold task. They had to build up a stock-pile for the RAF of *Blue Danube* bombs based on the device tested at *Hurricane* in 1952. They had to develop and design a range of new and more efficient atomic weapons, to meet Service requirements and to make the most economical use of costly fissile material (weapons-grade plutonium was valued at £40 000 a kilogram in 1956). They had to begin H bomb research and development and carry it through to completion with all speed.

The fallout debate

They were to find themselves working in a changing political climate, worldwide and in Britain. Nuclear weapon testing had not been a matter of controversy until early 1954, but then a tremendous debate was initiated by an accident at Bikini, during the American *Castle* series. The occasion was the *Bravo* shot, a megaton groundburst, on 1 March. The test site at Bikini was surrounded by a warning area of some 30 000 square miles of ocean within which there might be a hazard to shipping or aircraft at the time of a weapon test. Survey aircraft searching the area in preparation for *Bravo* reported no shipping present; the meteorologists forecast wind directions such that fallout would miss the small group of atolls to the east. When the shot was fired, the yield was nearly 15 megatons—about twice that expected, but the margin of error was said to be not incompatible with a totally new weapon. Moreover the winds did not conform to predictions, and fallout was blown over three little islands about 170 miles away in the Marshall Group. The 28 Americans stationed there were quickly evacuated, but the islanders were not rescued immediately; then it was found that they had been showered with radioactive coral-dust, and that most were suffering from radiation sickness and burns[5]. There was no rescue at all for the crew of a Japanese vessel, *Lucky Dragon*, fishing outside the warning area about 72 miles east of Bikini. The boat was heavily contaminated; all the crew became ill and one died after getting home to Japan[6].

A reassuring statement—'the 236 natives all appeared to me to be well and happy'—was made by Lewis Strauss, the chairman of the United States Atomic Energy Commission (USAEC), at a press conference on 31 March. What thoroughly alarmed the American public was a remark that he made during the question period, not about fallout but about the horrific potential of the H bomb which, he said, could be made 'as large as you wish . . . large enough to take out a city . . . any city', such as New York[7].

On 1 April, the Japanese government formally asked the United States government to suspend hydrogen bomb tests in the Pacific during the fishing season, November to March, and called for international control of atomic energy and nuclear tests. Next day Mr Nehru, the Prime Minister of India, urged a standstill agreement by the atomic powers while the United Nations sought a means to ban atomic weapons. The idea of a moratorium was discussed by the United States Secretary of State, J F Dulles, and British Foreign Secretary, Anthony Eden, between April and June 1954. At first they saw some merit in it, but then decided not to support it. It was unacceptable to the British government once it had taken the decision to develop and manufacture H bombs. In Britain there was a spate of Parliamentary Questions, over 100 Labour MPs signed a motion demanding that all nuclear tests should be stopped, and a full-dress debate was held in the House of Commons on 5 April. On 19 April, Pope Pius XII in his Easter message gave a solemn warning about the pollution of the atmosphere, the land and the oceans.

The debate continued in Britain, where it had first begun, but soon died down in the United States as other preoccupations appeared; American interest tended to be intense but sporadic. There was little or no official United States information for the rest of 1954, except for repeated assurances of the well-being of the Marshall Islanders. The first detailed accounts of global and local fallout, and the implications for civil defence, were given unofficially by Dr Ralph E Lapp[8] in the *Bulletin of Atomic Scientists* in October and November 1954. He revealed that a 15-megaton explosion close to the ground could contaminate an area of 4000 square miles with lethal radioactivity and that 50 super-bombs could 'blanket the entire NE USA in a serious to lethal radioactive fog'. For some months in late 1954 and early 1955 the United States government debated whether to release full information about fallout; it was urged to do so by the civil defence authorities but feared that it would only lead to a demand for the cessation of tests. It finally issued an official report in February 1955, but, a few days before it was published, a further article by Lapp appeared[9]. It estimated that debris from *Bravo* had covered an elliptical area nearly 200 miles long and 50 miles wide, some 8000 square miles in all; if such a bomb fell on Washington, it said, lethal fallout would cover the entire State of Maryland. The official report confirmed Lapp's analysis, and admitted that anyone living 160 miles downwind of the explosion would be killed. But the main subject of the official report was global fallout and the worldwide effects of nuclear testing (especially the effects of strontium-90) rather than the danger from nuclear weapons used in war. It stressed that the radiation exposure from all tests so far was only 0.1 r, about 1 per cent of the average radiation exposure per generation from natural background sources. Although testing admittedly created some risks to human health, including genetic health, they were minute compared with the advantages gained for 'the security of the nation and of the free world'—a cost-benefit equation that would not have been universally accepted.

Worldwide concern about fallout did not abate. In the United States, public anxiety focused on the hypothetical dangers to the American people of fallout in the event of war, but in March 1955 real fallout from explosions at the Nevada test site caused near panic in some areas. Outside the United States, people worried more about global fallout from actual and prospective H bomb tests than about fallout in a possible nuclear war, though in Britain a high-level study of the latter was quickly put in hand by the government.

Meanwhile, many scientists outside the United States had been puzzled by the huge amount of fallout from *Bravo*. From a thermonuclear bomb, deriving the main power of the explosion from the fusion of light elements, the only fallout should have been that from the small atomic bomb used to trigger the fusion reaction. Even allowing for the fact that *Bravo* was a surface burst—and thus sucked up a great quantity of contaminated ground particles—why should a small atomic bomb have produced so much fallout? An answer came from a Japanese scientist who analysed some radioactive dust from the *Lucky Dragon*. He found isotopes of uranium that showed that *Bravo* must have been a three-stage device, consisting of the atomic bomb trigger, lithium deuteride to produce the fusion reaction, and an outer layer of natural uranium that was fissioned by high-energy neutrons from the fusion reaction. A full, unofficial, analysis of a three-stage (fission–fusion–fission) bomb was published by a British physicist, Dr Joseph Rotblat[10], who had been at Los Alamos but who had left weapons work after the war. As natural uranium was cheap he concluded that hydrogen bombs could be made at low cost and with virtually no limitation on size. Detonating 75 such bombs could, he believed, double the background level of radiation, with disastrous genetic consequences. The correctness of his analysis of the bomb's composition was publicly confirmed soon afterwards by Dr William Libby, a member of the USAEC.

Scientific controversy about fallout and its effects proliferated. Some of the world's most eminent geneticists warned of the cumulative effects of mutations and urged the need to safeguard the genetic heritage. Two investigations were put in hand independently. In the United States, the President approved a wide-ranging study, funded by the Rockefeller Foundation, under Dr Detlev Bronk, President of the National Academy of Sciences. In Britain, in response to Parliamentary pressure and public concern, the Prime Minister promised a review of the existing scientific evidence on the medical aspects of nuclear and allied radiations, and the Medical Research Council set up a committee of distinguished scientists and medical men under its secretary, Sir Harold Himsworth. It included experts in radiology, radiobiology, genetics, epidemiology and physics as applied to medicine, and was very varied in outlook as well as in scientific disciplines. Only one member, Sir John Cockcroft, came from the Atomic Energy Authority.

International anxiety about fallout continued and non-atomic countries protested vehemently against being subjected to fallout without their consent. India and Japan were particularly concerned, the latter because of her geographical position between the Russian and American test areas and because she feared for her Pacific fishing grounds; besides, the *Bravo* test had angered her, and the bombs of 1945 were a hideous memory.

It seemed probable that sooner or later tests would have to be abandoned, but none of the three atomic powers wanted to stop unilaterally. If there was to be an agreement to end tests, each nation naturally wanted to secure conditions and timing that would be best—or least disadvantageous—for it. A nation could gain propaganda advantages from proposing a ban on testing when it had completed it own tests.

Britain as the latecomer was in the most difficult position of the three powers. Since the United States and Russia were several years ahead of her in developing both atomic and thermonuclear bombs, she did not want to be obliged to cease testing before she was ready to do so. But nor did she want an arms race that she could ill afford, or to incur international disapproval, especially from Commonwealth countries; besides, Parliamentary and public opinion was vociferous enough to worry the government. Then, too, she had to be careful not to show willingness to suspend tests just when the Americans were planning a series; she had to be prepared to 'share the odium'. At the same time the British government could not be sure that it might not find the rug pulled from under its feet by a sudden American test ban initiative. In April 1955 President Eisenhower wrote to Mr Krushchev proposing a test ban; if the two of them agreed to end tests before Britain had completed what she regarded as her essential programme, she could hardly continue alone. Yet if she had to stop too soon, she would be locked into a position of inferiority. Of course if radioactive fallout from the tests really was a worldwide danger to health—and on this the scientists were divided—Britain could not support the continuation of tests, but she was nevertheless desperately anxious not to be forced to cut them short before achieving her basic objectives.

Test ban talks began in July 1955[11], but tests continued; Russia's second thermonuclear test, with a yield of 15 megatons, took place in November 1955, and the Russians then announced on Moscow radio their willingness to cease further experimental explosions if the United States and Great Britain did the same. This had the effect of sharpening public awareness. Parliamentary pressure on the Eden government—Anthony Eden had just succeeded Churchill as Prime Minister—was increasing, led by former Labour Ministers. Eden argued that the Russian offer was not made officially and that it might have appeared in a better light if it had been made before Russia's recent megaton explosion. The British government was ready to discuss these matters at any time, he said, but in any such discussions regard would have to be paid to the number and nature of the tests that each country had already made[12].

On 3 December, the *Manchester Guardian* published an article that the government took very seriously.

'The Prime Minister has been strangely reserved about H bomb experiments . . . On Thursday . . . he said that Britain would not take the initiative in proposing such a meeting . . . why ever not?. . . How long will the competition go on? What may be its price in terms of more people with mental disabilities, more infants with malformed limbs, and more adults who are sterile?. . . The need is simply to limit large explosions, not to prohibit all nuclear weapons tests of whatever size . . . Why not propose a limit of one explosion each annually? . . . Sir Winston Churchill said, it may be recalled, that we must have a British bomb in order to make sure of our voice in shaping Western policy; and regrettable as it may be, one British explosion may be the price of impressing Congress and the Pentagon'.

The Prime Minister instructed the Ministry of Defence to consider these ideas urgently, and the reply was prompt. Single detonations were less efficient than a planned series, and limiting them to one a year would make them prohibitively expensive in money and resources. Without some comprehensive scheme of disarmament, which seemed highly unlikely, the preservation of peace depended on maintaining a continuously effective deterrent. The nuclear art was advancing extremely rapidly and it would be against British interests to accept any limitation of tests which would reduce the prospects of maintaining the deterrent and keeping (said the Ministry) ahead of the Russians.

The need for continued testing was argued by two of the most senior Ministers, Lord Salisbury (Lord President of the Council, with responsibility for atomic energy policy) and Selwyn Lloyd (Minister of Defence). After the war was ended by the two atomic bombs on Japan, their argument ran, it was clear that a few such bombs—at most of the order of hundreds—would suffice to destroy any country in war. Now, however—they were writing in December 1955—megaton weapons had entirely altered the situation, because of their immense destructive power and because of the ease and speed with which they could be delivered. To destroy Russia with a stock of a few hundred kiloton weapons would take a very great aircraft effort, over at least a number of days; in this time Russia, by virtue of possessing megaton weapons, could certainly destroy her attacker before she was herself put out of action by kiloton weapons. It was now perfectly clear that a very small number of megaton bombs, perhaps a few tens, would suffice to destroy in war, and a long time thereafter, the economy of any country. Kiloton weapons were no longer, by themselves, a major deterrent. Megaton weapons had become the primary deterrent; the possession of kiloton weapons would constitute a secondary deterrent.

Besides megaton weapons, the Ministers said, Britain needed two types of kiloton weapons; one of 10–100 kiloton yield and a tactical weapon of 1–15 kilotons. The second type was more problematical, and full-scale tests were essential. If kiloton tests were now to be prohibited, Britain would be limited to the first type, and to crude, uneconomical and unreliable designs of the second (tactical) type. If megaton tests were to be prohibited, then Britain could not make a megaton weapon. The supply of kiloton and megaton weapons to the Services, they concluded, rested heavily on Britain's ability to continue testing.

In January 1956 the Prime Minister broadcast to the nation:

> . . . You know we are making the H bomb in this country just as one of the previous governments made the A bomb. I don't think there's any party difference about that; but we are making it because we believe that the H bomb is the most powerful deterrent to war that exists in the world at the present time . . . and so we have to build up the deterrent power. And there I must tell you something else. You cannot prove a bomb until it has been exploded. Nobody can know whether it is effective or not until it has been tested. That is why I have said there should be tests; that is why I have said I couldn't put us in . . . the position of inferiority to other countries; but that doesn't mean that I wouldn't like an agreement to limit, or restrict, or regulate tests; I think it would be a very good thing if we could reach one.

The British government believed that political pressure to ban tests might be more manageable if it showed some readiness to consider plans for limitation and regulation of tests. Provided its own position was safeguarded, there would be great propaganda advantages in not leaving all the initiative to Russia and India. However the Ambassador in Washington, Sir Roger Makins, was much disturbed. 'Of the three States making nuclear weapons', he cabled, 'we alone have not tested the megaton weapon and we cannot do so before 1957 . . . we have the most to lose from any curtailment of our freedom to conduct nuclear tests, and therefore the most to lose from raising the question of limitation'.

The British at this time were planning two series of atomic tests in 1956, as well as their first H bomb test in 1957, while the Americans were planning a series in the Pacific in 1956. The British government was most anxious to ensure that the Americans understood the necessity of the 1957 trials, and did not change their attitude as soon as they had completed their own 1956 programme. At the end of January 1956, a British delegation led by the Prime Minister went to Washington for talks. The President and his advisers maintained the view that the regulation of tests was impracticable and that the tests were of the highest military and scientific value. Moreover high airbursts did not cause the same harmful fallout as groundbursts, because they did not suck large amounts of dirt and debris into the radioactive cloud[13]. It was agreed that if questioned the Prime Minister should say that the regulation of nuclear tests had been discussed during these meetings and that the two governments held the firm conviction that, if properly conducted, these tests were not harmful.

The British side continued to argue the advantage of showing some readiness to control or limit tests. They expected a steady build-up of public feeling, not only from the left but from middle-of-the-road opinion and from the churches, and the British public was inclined to believe there was a real health risk. The American officials disagreed and seemed confident that the two independent reports on biological effects of radiation, being prepared by the Bronk Committee in America and the Himsworth Committee in Britain, would be reassuring even if not conclusive. However Dulles, the United States Secretary of State, conceded that if it was shown that nuclear tests harmed the human race, the two governments would certainly do something to control them.

After the delegation returned to London, Sir Harold Himsworth warned Ministers that any statement to the House of Commons that nuclear explosions were harmless might well make his committee resign. It was at a critical stage in its task and had not yet reached firm conclusions on the safety or otherwise of the test explosions. In his statement on 13 February, the Prime Minister reminded the House of the forthcoming reports and concluded, 'I am bound to report that H M Government and the United States Government at present share the conviction that the radiation dose to human beings arising from the testing of megaton weapons at the present rate is insignificant compared with the radiation dose received from natural causes'. This was quite true, and the Himsworth Committee did not resign.

The Prime Minister had postponed an announcement of *Grapple*, the 1957 high-yield bomb trials in the Pacific, in spite of increasing practical difficulties caused by the delay, because he was anxious to include an authoritative assurance from the Himsworth report, and he wanted also to include an undertaking to try to secure international limitation of tests.

The Himsworth Committee agreed its report on 24 May except for one member who was abroad and who, it was thought, might be difficult, but all the members signed and the report was submitted to the government. Himsworth thought that the consensus of scientific opinion would agree with his committee but he was not sure what American reactions would be. The report was not, it should be emphasized, a report on nuclear weapon tests or fallout; nor was the committee, as Churchill habitually called it, the 'genetic committee'. It was concerned with both somatic and genetic hazards of nuclear and allied radiations from all sources—natural, medical, industrial and military. But it was its findings on nuclear weapon tests that Ministers so anxiously awaited; would the committee have good news for them, they asked Himsworth.

After much discussion in Cabinet and Cabinet committees, it was decided that the Prime Minister should make an announcement on 7 June about plans for *Grapple*, shortly before the publication of the Himsworth report on 12 June. Meanwhile the Washington Embassy was instructed to inform the United States authorities in advance, in strict confidence, of the announcement and to show them relevant extracts from the report. Admiral Strauss, the chairman of the USAEC, left the British Ambassador in no doubt of his displeasure with the British report, or at least its statement on strontium-90, which was identified as the most important hazard. (Strontium-90 is a fission product with a half-life of 28 years, which concentrates in bone if it enters the body.) It would be easy enough, Strauss said, on the basis of USAEC studies, to 'tear the MRC statement to shreds'; however he hoped publication could be deferred, because of the current American tests in the Pacific, and the Presidential election campaign in which the

Democrats would make nuclear test limitation a major issue. Edgar Hoover, head of the FBI, also told the Ambassador of his concern. Tests at the present level were not dangerous, he insisted, and were absolutely necessary. The United States authorities 'would have no difficulty in demolishing the MRC statement', but would be reluctant to make a public issue of it. The Americans felt that a British initiative on limitation would embarrass the United States in regard to their own tests, and pointed out that the British had asked them recently for considerable assistance with *Grapple* in 1957. Makins himself did not like the idea of a unilateral initiative before Anglo-American consultation in the light of the two scientific reports; if the roles were reversed, he suggested, the British would very much resent it.

Meanwhile, between March and May, the Japanese government was protesting vigorously about nuclear weapon tests generally, and about the British tests at Monte Bello; they were worried about the Japanese pearl divers and the tunny fishing fleet off the Australian coast, and they had heard rumours of future tests at Christmas Island. Resolutions were passed by the Japanese Diet, and the Japanese Ambassador visited the Foreign Office repeatedly, but without success, to discuss weapon tests and to urge suspension.

Meanwhile the Bronk and Himsworth reports, with impeccable timing, both appeared on 12 June 1956 and came to very similar conclusions. This is not the place to compare them, but a detailed comparison is of great interest[14]. To the immense relief of British Ministers, the Himsworth report[15] concluded that existing and foreseeable hazards from external radiation due to fallout from test explosions of nuclear weapons—fired at the existing rate and in the same proportion of different kinds—were negligible. Genetic effects would be insignificant. The Committee's greatest difficulty was in assessing the strontium-90 hazard; there was evidence of a marked increase in the amount of strontium-90 throughout the world, but at present levels no detectable ill effects were to be expected. 'Nevertheless', the committee warned, 'recognising all the inadequacy of our present knowledge, we cannot ignore the possibility that, if the rate of firing increases and particularly if greater numbers of thermonuclear weapons are used, we could, within the lifetime of some now living, be approaching levels at which ill effects might be produced in a small number of the population'.

The report estimated that the population dose from fallout from bombs so far exploded would in the next 50 years amount to 0.02 to 0.04 per cent of the radiation received in the same period from natural radiation sources. It would gradually increase to 1 per cent if firing continued indefinitely at the same rate. The contribution from medical diagnostic X-rays was estimated at perhaps 22 per cent of the natural background. Lord Cherwell read the report 'with much satisfaction', not to say amusement; he found it comic that a medical committee had discovered that medical X-rays caused far more genetic mutations than all the nuclear weapon tests.

Though the committee had originated in public fears about fallout, it had dealt with radiation hazards comprehensively for the first time. Only a few sections of the report were specifically on nuclear weapon tests and they were mainly concerned with global fallout from thermonuclear tests. So, although the report was highly relevant to plans for Britain's first thermonuclear tests in 1957 and to discussions of a possible international test ban, it had little bearing on the kiloton trials in Australia. It gave the British thermonuclear tests a green light, but with a grave warning to proceed with caution.

Both the United States and the British reports had a somewhat limited national perspective, but in December 1955 after much pressure from the non-atomic member states, and after months of argument and negotiation about its membership and scope, the United Nations set up a scientific committee on effects of atomic radiation (UNSCEAR). Its function was not to set standards or recommend what member countries should or should not do; it was to receive, collate, evaluate and publish information on radiation levels and on the effects of radiation on man and his environment. It fulfilled an invaluable role. It had a world outlook and its first report, in 1958, by scientists from 15 different countries, brought together comprehensive data on fallout that could have been collected and compiled by no other means. But this lies well beyond our 1953–56 period.

This then was the political background to Aldermaston's work from 1953 to 1956. Penney and his scientists were working in an atmosphere compounded equally of extreme urgency and extreme uncertainty. They were under pressure to complete their research and development programme as quickly as possible, to beat the ban on testing—and even perhaps a ban on fissile material production—that seemed inevitable sooner or later. This sense of urgency affected everyone in the project, and prompted the most strenuous efforts from scientists, engineers and industrial workers alike.

A new organization and a new test range

Soon after *Totem* in 1953, there were big organizational changes. As we saw in Chapter 1, the Atomic Energy Authority was set up in 1954, outside the civil service but wholly funded by the Treasury, managed by a chairman and chief executive and a board of full-time and part-time members. In this reorganization Penney became Board Member for Weapons Research and Development as well as Director of the Atomic Weapons Research Establishment (DAWRE). Responsibility for nuclear weapons and trials was divided between the new Authority and the Ministry of Supply. One of the first tasks was to establish a permanent proving ground. *Hurricane* and *Totem* had been ad hoc operations, but now the time for improvization was over and some more settled arrangements were needed. Emu Field was, as we saw, a very difficult and restrictive site; though the Monte Bello islands were to be used for one more trial, they were not suitable for general use. The search for a permanent proving ground first began in late 1952; that search, and the outcome, are the subject of the next chapter.

Notes and references

1 *Bravo* in the *Castle* series, with a yield of approximately 15 megatons. The first US thermonuclear explosion (*Ivy-Mike*) with a yield of 10.4 megatons, had been at Eniwetok in October 1952; it was not a weapon, but a huge cumbersome device the size of a house, using liquid deuterium, which had to be kept refrigerated. The first United States airdrop of a thermonuclear weapon was at Bikini in May 1956, in between the first and second shots of the British *Mosaic* trial at Monte Bello.
2 Cmd 9391, Feb 1955, HMSO.
3 See Andrew Pierre: *Nuclear Politics*, pp. 92–94.
4 H C Deb, Col. 1899, 1 March 1955.
5 They received external radiation doses estimated at up to 2 sieverts (200 rems). Seven of them eventually had to have operations for thyroid cancer.
6 Accounts of the *Lucky Dragon* incident can be found in *Bulletin of Atomic Scientists*, Vol. X, Nos 5 and 9 (May and Nov 1954); in Ralph Lapp: *The Voyage of the "Lucky Dragon"*; and in Robert A Divine: *Blowing on the Wind*.
7 Divine: *Blowing on the Wind*, p. 13.
8 *Bulletin of Atomic Scientists*, Vol. X, Nos 8 and 9 (Oct and Nov 1954).
9 *Bulletin of Atomic Scientists*, Vol. XI, No 2 (Feb 1955).
10 *Bulletin of Atomic Scientists*, Vol. XI, No 5 (May 1955).

11 Eventually in October 1958 a three-power conference on suspension of nuclear tests was set up and a moratorium was declared that lasted until September 1961, when first Russia and then the United States resumed testing. See Chapter 10.

12 H C Deb, Vol. 546, No 65, Cols. 2319–22.

13 See *Effects of Atomic Weapons*, (1950), p. 35.

14 Bentley Glass: 'The hazards of atomic radiation to man—British and American Reports', *Bulletin of Atomic Scientists*, Vol. XII, No 8 (Oct 1956).

15 Cmd 9780, June 1956, HMSO.

6 Maralinga—A Permanent Proving Ground

The search for a range

'I am surveying the world, but particularly Australia', wrote Air Marshal Sir Thomas Elmhirst, in July 1953. He had been appointed chairman of Totex (the *Totem* Executive, which was the interdepartmental committee responsible for the general planning of the *Totem* trial). In the Admiralty (which had found the Monte Bello islands for *Hurricane*) Captain Le Fanu was also surveying the world, from the Shetlands and the Hebrides to the Bahamas, from Somaliland and West Africa to islands in the Pacific and Indian Oceans. They were both seeking a 'permanent proving ground' for atomic weapons.

When, after *Hurricane*, Sir William Penney visited South Australia in October 1952 to look at possible sites for *Totem*, he had left with the Australians a summary of the conditions that a permanent range would have to satisfy. Though Emu Field provided an immediate answer for *Totem*, it was never considered as a permanent site—it had too many disadvantages—nor were the Monte Bello Islands, though they were to be used once more in 1956.

In May 1953 the Chiefs of Staff were advised that a permanent inland site was needed. They asked Air Marshal Sir Thomas Elmhirst to look for one, and he wrote to Major-General Stevens, the head of the Australian Atomic Energy Commission (AAEC) and chairman of the *Totem* panel in Melbourne. It was undesirable, he said, to continue with hurriedly prepared and very expensive expeditions to ad hoc sites, well though he thought these improvisations had turned out. He described the ideal site—a 100-mile radius free from human habitation; road and rail communications to a port; an adjacent airstrip; a good water supply; reasonably flat country; a tolerable climate for permanent staff and visiting scientists; not too much rainfall; predictable meteorological conditions, with prevailing winds that would carry fallout away from firing areas. Finally, an island would be excellent for security. The only suitable sites in Australia, Elmhirst thought, were Groote Eylandt, in the Gulf of Carpentaria, and an area somewhere to the north of Emu Field.

Major-General Stevens agreed that hurried preparations like those for *Totem* were 'bad in every way', but the Elmhirst specifications were so exacting that very few, if any, places in the world would meet all of them. A site north of Emu Field would be too near cattle stations or the Aboriginal reserve. Groote Eylandt would not do at all: it was densely wooded and a timber company had sought timber concessions; there were no port facilities; there was a population of seven Europeans and 400–600 Aboriginals. An area in South Australia near Port Augusta seemed best, but a permanent site, he warned, should be selected only after most careful investigation.

In September 1953, Penney was authorized to talk to the Australians about alternative sites that they had suggested after an air reconnaissance. At the same time the Chiefs of Staff asked the Ministry of Supply to make further efforts to find somewhere more suitable than South Australia, but, having again 'scrutinized the world', Captain Lloyd of the Ministry of Supply, like Captain Le Fanu, found no acceptable alternative.

Meanwhile, in October 1953, Penney and two of his staff, with Butement, took time off from Emu Field, between Totem 1 and Totem 2, to visit a remote part of South Australia that had been reconnoitred earlier, first by air and then overland. (A vivid account of the expedition has been published—*Blast the Bush*, by the Australian surveyor, Len Beadell.) It was bush country, but a treeless area of about 100 square miles had been observed, some 50 miles north of the Transcontinental Railway, near a spot marked 'Tietken's Well'. Supplies were dropped here, a camp set up, and a runway constructed in only two days, by four men with Land Rovers pulling a length of railway line. Here Penney and Butement landed and were met by a small Australian party, and together they went exploring for three days.

The region was described in an Aldermaston report:

> The Range is just beyond the Nullarbor ('treeless') Plain lying to the north of the shores of the Great Australian Bight. The Plain has thin soil which carries only a mantle of desert pea and knee-high salt-bush. The Plain which covers about 400 × 450 miles bears traces of the sea which once rolled over it—little cliffs, shells, wave marks hundreds of miles inland. Lost in the salt-bush are the bones of the last diprotodons. Occasional blow-holes, like ancient craters, emit a foetid smell . . . To quote Professor J W Gregory, "These long, low, open plains, with their gentle undulations, suggesting the freedom of the sea with the stability of the land, have to many men an

unequalled fascination . . .".

Beyond the northern limits of the Nullarbor Plain, the country becomes rather more attractive, consisting of low sandhills, thickly covered by mulga and mallee trees. These are up to 20 ft high. As the district has been practically untouched by man . . . many trees of great age still stand. In this country, it is a very simple matter to get lost.

Penney described it as 'gently undulating and covered with low salt-bush and occasional sparse patches of mulga which gave it the appearance of English downland'. To the north lay hundreds of miles of uninhabited wooded country and desert. The Australian geologists were confident of finding water by boring, and their confidence was eventually justified. There seemed no danger of the dust-storms that had been so troublesome at Emu Field. The area, identified as X300 but later named 'Maralinga' by Butement, seemed ideal to Penney. It was very different, however, from the Nevada Test Site, 70 miles from Las Vegas, with its excellent road, rail and air communications with every important military and scientific centre in the United States[1].

Before returning to Emu Field for T2, he had a detailed discussion about the site with Butement[2]. It covered such matters as water supplies, roads, telephones, range layout and the location of the firing sites, the camp and the airfield. Then Penney said, 'You have told me already where the homesteads are and I see no difficulty in getting firing conditions which will give no danger whatever to the homesteads, but I would like to know what is the position about the Aboriginals'.

There used to be a mission at Ooldea, or a little north of there, Butement told him, but it had been abandoned. There had been a track from Ooldea up to the north, but he understood that it was no longer used 'except by one or two elderly blacks and then on rare occasions'. There was no need whatever for Aboriginals to use any part of this country round the proposed site; the main Aboriginal reserve to the north was well away from the area and should not present any sort of problem. This sounded very satisfactory to Penney, but he particularly asked that when the Australians submitted a report on the site they should include a statement about the location of the homesteads and about where the Aboriginals were likely to be. The tests, he said, would be fired in meteorological conditions in which the radioactivity would be in the sector between north and east and would not affect human habitations.

While still in Australia, Penney had talks with the Prime Minister, the Minister for Supply and Major-General Stevens. Menzies, he reported on his return to England, had apparently not realized previously (or had forgotten) that Australia had had no access to the British atomic weapons programme; or indeed that the British had no access to the United States programme. Penney had said that if there were to be further weapon tests in Australia, the British would have to work closely with the Australians, and he would like some integration of effort between the two countries. Since the British would be using Australian facilities and staff, it was only reasonable that some Australians, given security clearance, should receive information about the weapons, and he would welcome Australian scientists into the project in England. Menzies had agreed with these views and Penney believed he would like an invitation on these lines to accompany any request for a permanent range. In his opinion, the offer should be made without waiting for an Australian request.

In further talks, Penney and Stevens had discussed the possibility that Britain might help the Australians to build a reactor, using Australian uranium, to produce plutonium for atomic weapons. Some of the weapons might be returned to Australia. The cost of the scheme would not be great and it would ease Britain's shortage of plutonium. The Australians for their part would assist with the weapon tests. Stevens welcomed some such arrangement, on the grounds that the Australians were nervous about their whole future position, industrial and military, and would be glad to have help from Britain. But Australian views were not unanimous. When Lord Cherwell (the Minister responsible for atomic energy policy in the Churchill government) visited Australia in October 1953, his proposals on very similar lines were rejected by the Australian Cabinet; it doubted whether Australia could afford to maintain any large-scale atomic project for many years to come. It was therefore decided in Whitehall that proposals for a permanent range should simply be linked with an offer for selected Australian scientists to come to England to familiarize themselves with atomic weapons matters.

Meanwhile the United Kingdom High Commissioner in Canberra had passed a list of Penney's requirements to the Australian government. The range must have good road access, an airstrip, and fresh water of high purity. It must be large enough to use for up to three bursts a year. Since the contamination around the firing site would extend to a radius of half-a-mile and would have to be avoided for three to four years after use, some 20 firing sites would be needed. The camp should be 15 to 20 miles from the weapon sites, the orientation of camp and weapon sites depending on detailed analysis of meteorological conditions. Weapon sites and observation sites should be as level as possible.

A detailed Australian report produced early in 1954 by Butement recommended the Maralinga site (see Map 4). It was, he said, reasonably flat, and sufficiently large—some 16 miles from east to west, and at least 12 miles north to south. The south edge of the area was about 32 miles north of the Transcontinental Railway between Ooldea and Watson, and 80 miles north of the coast. The range area would encroach slightly on the northwest corner of an Aboriginal reserve at Ooldea, but the reserve was abandoned. The country was hot and arid, but less so

Map 4   Maralinga and Woomera prohibited areas

than Emu Field, thanks to night breezes from the sea. The rainfall was higher (as the weaponeers were to discover). Water supplies would be easier than at Emu Field.

The camp would be located on a ridge southwest of the trials area, and the airfield would be further south, on the edge of the Nullarbor Plain. Constructing the range—including roads, a railway siding, an airfield, a camp area with semi-permanent buildings for 350 people, laboratories, workshops, offices, stores, and a landline for communications—would cost about £1.9 million. A more westerly area on the Nullarbor Plain, which had also been surveyed, would cost £200 000 more, and was less suitable; alternatively to improve Emu Field to the standard required would cost much more, say £3.6 million. It would be difficult, Butement concluded, to envisage a site superior to Maralinga. The Aldermaston scientists began to study the fallout considerations, assuming that the danger area for contamination could extend out to a radius of 150 miles; as the Transcontinental Railway was well within this distance to the south, firing would not be possible if the wind, at any level, was between 290° and 070° through north.

So far there had been no contact between governments, and the Butement report had not been considered by Australian officials or Ministers. There was still much to be decided and agreed before construction could begin but the British Chiefs of Staff were talking of trials in 1955, or the spring of 1956. They want an airburst to prove the *Blue Danube* (MK1) bomb; the centre section had been exploded at *Totem*, and deliveries to the RAF had already begun, but an operational test was obviously desirable as soon as possible, if only to give at least one aircrew the experience of dropping it. Secondly the Chiefs of Staff wanted a tower test of a smaller bomb (*Red Beard*) for use by smaller aircraft than the V-bombers. Thirdly they wanted a detonation underground or at ground surface—of which neither the British nor the Americans then had any experience—in connection with the War Office's draft requirements for an atomic land mine. Finally they wanted various 'effects' experiments.

Since by now it was likely that the government would soon approve the development of the hydrogen bomb, it was not surprising that Penney was worried that his resources were insufficient for atomic trials in 1955 as well as the thermonuclear research and development. Moreover Maralinga would not be suitable for hydrogen bomb tests, and when the time for them came another site would have to be found.

A decision in sight

The technical case for Maralinga seemed clear; the political arguments now began. If Britain was to continue to develop atomic weapons she would need numerous trials over the next decade. The development of any weapon was a continuous process, requiring trials at intervals—to prove completed weapons; to assist in developing new weapons; and to test new ideas arising in the course of development, or completely new ideas. There were also many secondary objectives. All the Services, and also the Civil Defence authorities, wanted information on the effects of different types of explosions on equipment and stores, on structures, on ships, on aircraft and airfields, and on men with or without various kinds of protection. The need for 'target response' tests would remain, even if more information on weapon effects could now be obtained from the Americans, after the extension of technical cooperation under the *modus vivendi*, early in 1954, to include by experimental simulation 'effects of atomic weapons on human beings and their environment'.

Instead of a permanent site, the alternative—which Duncan Sandys, the Minister of Supply, much preferred—was to carry on *ad hoc*, in the hope of amendments to the McMahon Act which would permit the use of Eniwetok. Politically, it was suggested, *ad hoc* arrangements might also suit the Australians better. But Eniwetok prospects were uncertain; it would cost a great deal, and in dollars; and it was thought that, scientifically, the Americans might prefer independent British tests. A permanent site, it was calculated, would save time, resources and money; it would reduce the length of absence of scientific staff from Britain, and would make possible better living and working conditions. The capital cost of Maralinga—say £2 million— and an estimated expenditure of £750 000 for each test there (excluding the cost of the weapons themselves) looked very attractive if there was to be an extensive trials programme; the cost of *Hurricane* (excluding the weapon and HMS *Plym*) had been some £1.8 million, and the cost of *Totem* (excluding the weapons) £1.325 million.

If the next trials were to be in April/May 1956, the scientists would have to start work at the range in December 1955. Construction would take at least 16 months, and little could be done in January or February (when the shade temperature would average 120°F and metal tools would be too hot to touch). Work must therefore start by July 1954. Time was pressing, but there had still been no formal approval by British Ministers and no approach to the Australian government. A decision seemed unlikely before the Australian General Election on 29 May. There were three questions for the British to ponder meanwhile. Should the Australians be asked to contribute to the cost of the range? If so, what would they want, by way of cooperation, in return? Lastly, how far could they, the British, go in such cooperation without prejudicing their relations with the Americans?

The first question was not only a matter of money, though the British would welcome Australian financial help. The Woomera range was an example of cost-sharing; at first the Australians had been unforthcoming, but after some wrangling their attitude had completely changed, and they became not just 'landlords leasing land' but partners in 'a great scheme of Empire development'. An Australian contribution to the cost of Maralinga would avoid the embarrassment of having a purely United Kingdom establishment on Australian territory. On the other hand, it was argued, if the Australians were asked to contribute, they would then want more information.

On the second question, Penney thought the Australians would want at least as much information as at *Totem*—no papers, but full information on weapons effects, and opportunities to inspect damage to tanks and other equipment. They would also want to send four or five scientists to Aldermaston.

The third question was referred to Washington. As we have seen, atomic collaboration with Commonwealth countries (other than Canada) was restricted by the tripartite Anglo-American-Canadian wartime and postwar agreements, and was inhibited by Britain's fear of damaging her prospects of a renewed Anglo-American partnership. The British Ambassador, Sir Roger Makins, who had unrivalled experience of Anglo-American atomic negotiations in Washington, queried whether it was intended to seek American approval before giving information to the Australians, or simply to offer the Australians what the British themselves considered their agreements with the Americans would permit. He thought the moment inopportune for broaching the subject with the Americans. In his opinion, divulging information on weapons effects would cause no difficulties; but he could imagine no circumstances in which the Americans would agree that information about design and construction of atomic weapons should be given to Australia; apart from its sensitivity, weapons information must be regarded as being of joint origin. The Foreign Office reasonably thought that the complete postwar break in Anglo-American cooperation on atomic weapons after 1945 might by this time justify a different view. However, if the Australians were not going to have a weapons programme, Makins suggested, there was no reason to give them such information, which the Americans themselves were forbidden by law to pass to other countries. If the British did so they would 'certainly lose any chance . . . of getting information about the manufacture and design of United States weapons'.

At last, in June 1954, Ministers agreed to negotiations with the Australian government for the range at Maralinga[3], though Duncan Sandys, the Minister of Supply, doubted that it would be an economy; it might be obsolete before the savings were recouped. He thought too that the Australian government would have difficulty in getting its public opinion to accept a permanent proving ground; Emu Field had been accepted because *Totem* was a 'one-off job'. It was further argued that if Britain was going to concentrate on hydrogen bombs rather than atomic bombs, the site would be wasted; this would also happen if an international agreement to ban atomic weapons, or tests, was reached, although indeed no such agreement was in sight.

The approach to the Australian government was delayed while a proposal linking it to an agreement on uranium supplies was considered, but telegrams were eventually despatched at the end of July. The High Commissioner wrote to Menzies on 2 August about the range and about proposed trials in April/May 1956. He rehearsed the arguments for a permanent proving ground for atomic weapon trials to be carried out during the next ten years. The choice lay between Emu Field and Maralinga, and the British government would be guided by the Australian government who could best assess local factors. The experts believed that Maralinga, in suitable meteorological conditions, would provide a sufficient margin for higher-powered bursts than in previous trials, but there was no question of testing hydrogen weapons. Britain would depend on Australia for much help in works and services, and hoped that facilities could be provided as a joint project; the precise apportionment of costs would be for negotiation. (The rumour of a range in Canada was unfounded, the High Commissioner added; in the uninhabited areas the climatic conditions were unsuitable.)

Within a month, the Australian Cabinet approved the proposal in principle, and Menzies replied in October 1955, agreeing to Maralinga as a permanent range. The power of the weapons to be tested, and meteorological conditions for the tests, would have to be agreed beforehand with the Australian government, and there must be no question of testing hydrogen bombs. Australia would contribute the site and provide such assistance as she could. But she was unlikely to make more than a token contribution towards construction, because of other pressures on her Service and civil resources; labour was very scarce in Australia and the RAAF was fully engaged on a big airfield extension programme in Northern Australia and on construction work in Malaya. Nor would Australia be likely to help financially as the defence budget was already over-stretched. A planning team should be sent from Britain as soon as possible; meanwhile Menzies would talk to Playford, the Premier of South Australia, who was known to have views about the reclamation of the reserve that formed part of the area. The British government thanked Menzies warmly, and deferred questions of finance and defence priorities, perhaps to the Commonwealth Prime Ministers' Conference in the New Year.

A warning came from one British official in the Ministry of Supply:

> I am bound to say that I am left with the feeling (perhaps quite unjustified) that there is a blissful unawareness of the fact that public hostility to A tests has increased many fold since our last efforts . . . I would urge that someone had better be thinking about what . . . to say if they are forced to in response to what may be a torrent of uninformed criticism.

The *Mosaic* repercussions in 1956 proved him right (see Chapter 7).

The Wilson mission

In November 1954 a mission of six officials and scientists, led by J M Wilson, a senior official at the Ministry of Supply, went to Australia for talks in Canberra and Melbourne and a visit to South Australia. Penney commented that it had taken over a year, since his expedition with Butement in 1953, for the British government to ask for Maralinga and the Australian government to agree in principle. (The delays had been mostly in London.) By hindsight, he said, a mission should have gone to Australia in April or May 1954 in anticipation of—but without prejudice to—agreement between the governments.

The Wilson mission returned and reported that the Maralinga site was excellent. The Australians would undertake preparatory work on the site, but labour thereafter would have to be provided either by a United Kingdom Service force of about 700 men, or—more expensively—by a civilian force employed by a contractor and largely imported. Much of the material, including prefabricated buildings and cement, would have to be shipped from the United Kingdom. The range could not possibly be ready by April/May 1956, and the trials should be postponed to September/October 1956; to achieve even these later dates, the main construction force would have to begin work by 1 June 1955, and the Australians would have to complete preliminary work on the site before it arrived. Whatever the difficulties of providing a Service construction force from the United Kingdom, the timetable must be kept, because any delay would hold up important trials programmes in subsequent years.

The Wilson report emphasized that the Australians were much concerned about radioactive contamination, and intended setting up a safety committee of four or five leading scientists to advise the government. It would continue and formalize the arrangements previously made for *Totem* whereby Penney had given information to Martin and Titterton so that they could assess the safety of the tests for themselves.

Finally, the report listed points to be covered in an Anglo-Australian agreement. These included tenure of the site (an initial period of ten years was suggested); compensation for any damage; information to be furnished to the Safety Committee; Australian access to the range; safety responsibilities; joint arrangements for publicity; a joint administrative committee; and weapon effects data for Australia.

Action at last

Aldermaston, while waiting for the two governments, had had to decide how far they could anticipate such an agreement. If all action had been postponed meanwhile, there would have been no hope at all of completing the range by August 1956. Planning had in fact begun immediately after *Totem*, a draft plan had been ready in December 1953, and contract action had been taken on many items, especially those requiring extensive prototype tests (such as weapon towers and recording shelters).

Swift action followed the Wilson mission's report of 6 January 1955. Within a fortnight, the project had been comprehensively examined with Sir Alexander Gibb and Partners as possible consultants, and the Kwinana Construction Group as possible contractors. Treasury approval was sought at the end of February and received on 5 March. All the specifications that Aldermaston had been preparing for the past twelve months, with John Costain Brown Ltd as consultants, were handed over to Sir Alexander Gibb and Partners, who lost no time in subcontracting to the Costain Brown drawing offices. In April representatives of the consulting engineers and contractors visited Australia, where three members of the Aldermaston trials planning staff were already at work, and they were able to exchange ideas very fully on the spot.

On 4 May, Mr Howard Beale, the Australian Minister for Supply, announced to the Australian press that the British and Australian governments were to join in a huge works project in South Australia costing £5 to 6 million. Maralinga would be, he said (inaccurately), 'the Los Alamos of the British Commonwealth'. He explained that the latest types of atomic bombs, developed by Sir William Penney and his brilliant team of scientists, would be tested there, but no hydrogen bombs. The site, selected by Penney and Butement, had been chosen and planned to combine the maximum security with 'the completest respect for life, property and stock', and tests would take place only in meteorological conditions which would carry radioactive clouds harmlessly away into the desert. Each test would require the prior approval of the Minister for Supply, no test would be made until a committee of Australian scientists had satisfied itself that there was no danger, and the Australian Meteorological Bureau would advise the United Kingdom team on safe conditions for firing.

The project was, he concluded, 'a challenge to Australian men to show . . . the pioneering spirit of their forefathers' and 'a striking example of inter-Commonwealth cooperation on a grand scale'. 'England has the bomb and the knowhow; we have the open spaces, much technical skill, and a great willingness to help the Motherland. Between us we shall help to build the defences of the free world . . '.

The Memorandum of Arrangements

The previous understanding between Australia and Britain about trials had been surprisingly informal, based on exchanges of brief personal letters between the Prime Ministers, with no specific agreements on such matters as conditions of occupation, use of the sites, precise allocation of costs, or compensation for damage or injury. The rights and obligations of either side were hardly defined at all. In both countries the organization was *ad hoc*. With a permanent range under discussion, and perhaps 10 years of testing to come, the time for such informality was past. The Australian government, for internal political reasons, had to have a clear understanding of the terms on which the permanent proving ground was to be made available, and in the wake of the Wilson mission Menzies sent a letter outlining an agreement. Its main points were as follows. The period of occupation should be 10 years, which might be extended by mutual agreement. H bomb tests were ruled out. Australian agreement must be obtained before any test was carried out and the Australian authorities must be given enough information to satisfy themselves on safety. The United Kingdom should be responsible for the safety of the area and people entering it, and be liable for damage to persons or property. The Australian authorities should be fully informed and consulted on planning and progress, and should coordinate and control all administrative activities in Australia in connection with the tests. A joint Anglo-Australian committee should be set up in Australia.

Menzies met Eden, the British Prime Minister, and other Ministers to discuss the permanent proving ground during a visit to London in February. They agreed that the main construction work at Maralinga would be undertaken by a United Kingdom civil contractor, but Menzies saw no difficulty in having the firing areas built by Australian Service personnel. The Australian Services would also supply men to assist at the tests, but the question of manning the range between trials was deferred.

A draft memorandum of arrangements was sent from London to Canberra in the following month. One clause in particular was certain to cause problems:

The United Kingdom government undertakes to indemnify the Australian government in respect of valid claims, arising outside the prohibited area, through
(a) death or injury of any person resulting directly from any tests carried out, and
(b) damage to property similarly resulting.

The Australians produced a new draft that was approved by a Cabinet Committee on 4 May and sent to London. They wanted an indemnity 'in respect of *all* valid claims *whatsoever*', for death, injury or damage resulting from the tests, whether inside or outside the prohibited area. They suspected that London perhaps did not realize that the prohibited area extended as far as Woomera and contained 3000–4000 inhabitants, not counting Aboriginals who might pass through. The Australians would not agree to a British proposal to define a smaller prohibited area; they also urged that any claims by Australians present at the tests, under arrangements made for Australia to provide personnel, should be a British responsibility. Opinion in London was divided. 'If we press the Australians too strongly we shall lose the substance for the shadow', wrote one Ministry of Supply official; the Australians, he said, were becoming restive about the amount of their contribution to such projects, they were in many ways apprehensive about the trials, and it would be increasingly difficult to secure their goodwill and cooperation. But against this view, a grudging Treasury view prevailed; the Australian government inexplicably agreed; and in the final version the British government had no liability for claims from Australian nationals present on the range or at the trials in the course of duty.

The most important features of the agreement (Appendix C) are the ten-year term; the use of the range rent-free; the prohibition of hydrogen bomb tests; Australian agreement before tests; the provision by the British of information relevant to safety; Australian responsibility for preventing unauthorized entry into the prohibited area (which was defined in an annex); participation by other British Commonwealth nationals in tests; claims for damage or injury; and the control of the project by a joint committee under Australian Department of Supply chairmanship. The controversial claims question was settled by clause 11, by which the United Kingdom undertook to indemnify the Australian government in respect of all valid claims due to tests carried out on the site (except for claims made by employees or servants of a government other than the United Kingdom government—in most but not all cases the Australian government—who were in the prohibited area specifically in connection with the tests).

A financial memorandum attached to the Memorandum of Arrangements stated that Britain would bear most of the costs, except for:
(a) the cost of any target response or other tests done specifically at Australian request;
(b) the expenses of Australian personnel attending trials at the proving ground, at the Australian government's request; and
(c) the cost of providing Australian Service personnel for specific tasks at the proving ground.

These two memoranda comprised the only formal agreement between Britain and Australia on this big and important project. It was concluded more than 3½ years after *Hurricane*—5 years after *Hurricane* planning began—and there had been three atomic detonations meanwhile and a fourth was imminent. Although the text was finally agreed in March 1956, in September there had still apparently been no exchange of signatures on the two documents. In the close relationship then existing between the two governments, friendly arrangements, rather than legal contracts, were the order of the day.

The Maralinga committee

With the new permanent proving ground, new and permanent organizations were necessary in Australia to replace the *ad hoc* arrangements and special panels created for *Hurricane* and *Totem*. One was a standing committee, with representatives of all the Australian departments concerned[4] and a British representative from UKMOSS(A), the Ministry of Supply's staff in Australia.

This was the committee required under clause 17 of the Memorandum of Arrangements, 'to consider all matters of joint concern in relation to the establishment and maintenance of the proving ground and to the arrangements for any trials thereon as may be approved from time to time and to advise the responsible departments through their respective representatives'. The functions of the committee were to include 'the coordination of all activities within Australia of the United Kingdom and Australian Government Departments and Authorities, and their agents concerned with the project, and such executive action in matters of joint concern in Australia as may be agreed by the representatives of both parties'.

It was set up at the Australian Prime Minister's request in May 1955, by the Minister for Supply, who had been given this departmental responsibility months before the Memorandum of Arrangements was finally agreed. Though named the Atomic Weapons Tests Committee, its first task was to deal with the construction and operation of the range at Maralinga, and it was called the Maralinga Committee until May 1956 when it decided—in view of tests under way on the Monte Bello Islands and being planned in the Pacific[5]—to revert to its proper title of Atomic Weapons Tests Committee (AWTC). It continued work until 1957, when it was replaced by a Maralinga Board of Management with a small executive staff.

During its first year the committee met frequently, to deal with preparing and constructing the range—work that was being done under severe difficulties and great pressure to meet the deadline for trials in September/October 1956. While the AWTC was so heavily engaged in progressing the Maralinga construction programme, it was already involved in *Mosaic* and *Buffalo* planning, as well as longer-term questions of administering the Range.

Maralinga would need a permanent staff, even between trials, and it was agreed that the range commandant should always be an Australian officer. The Australian government rightly attached the utmost importance to retaining administrative control of the range, as a duty to the Australian people and a necessary indication that Australian sovereignty was being safeguarded. The British concurred, not only because it was right and reasonable, but also because it involved Australia in responsibility for the project and in sharing any criticism. But inevitably the commandant (an Australian Army colonel) had divided responsibilities—to the United Kingdom staff (or the trials director when present) for the technical operation of the range; to the Department of Supply for the general administration of the range; and to the Service authorities in South Australia for the discipline and administration of Australian forces. The Australian government provided a Service contingent of nearly 200 men during construction at Maralinga and some 370 for the 1956 trials period, and promised between 40 and 50 for care and maintenance between trials. After *Buffalo*, Maralinga arrangements were to be reviewed and considerably altered, as we shall see later.

The Atomic Weapons Tests Safety committee

With the prospect of atomic trials at regular intervals—and especially in the context of worldwide concern about fallout—the Australian government was anxious about radioactive contamination. When the Wilson mission had raised the question of *Kittens* tests, the Australians had asked for full details, and in February 1955 Aldermaston provided a comprehensive report, *The Scope and Radiological Hazards of* Kittens *1955*. It was referred to the Australian Department of Defence for Professor Martin's comments. He saw no objection, but suggested some formal arrangement for checking the safety aspects of these and subsequent tests; a safety committee of four or five leading scientists might be considered and an independent study by a small committee would enable the government to reassure the Australian people that they were not being endangered[6].

The Department of Defence agreed and proposed five names (though it later favoured a committee of three). Of the five, Martin, Titterton and Butement had already been involved in *Hurricane* and *Totem*. The new names were Dr C E Eddy, the Director of the Commonwealth X-ray and Radium Laboratory, and Professor J P Baxter, member (and later Chairman) of the Australian Atomic Energy Commission. Menzies accepted the five names; he believed the committee must include members 'sufficiently well known to command general confidence as guardians of the public interest' who were not 'in any way to be identified as having an interest in the success of defence atomic experiments'[7]. He doubted if a committee of less than five could meet these requirements, particularly if the Defence Scientific Adviser and the Chief Scientist of the Department of Supply (Martin and Butement) were members.

The list included, in Dr Eddy, one scientist with special expertise in radiological protection; he was responsible nationally for precautions against the radiation hazards of X-ray and radium equipment. Somewhat surprisingly the list had no meteorologist, but L J Dwyer, the Director of the Australian Bureau of Meteorology, was later coopted. As we saw in Chapter 2, Professor Oliphant, Australia's most distinguished nuclear scientist, was not included.

The list of members was sent to London before the AWTSC was formally constituted. All the members, as we saw in Chapter 2, were well known in British circles. The committee was established in July 1955, and was enjoined, at some length:

(a) to examine the information and other data supplied by the United Kingdom government relating to atomic weapons tests from time to time proposed to be carried out in Australia for the purpose of determining whether the safety measures proposed to be taken in relation to such tests are adequate for the prevention of injury to persons or damage to livestock and other property as a result of such tests and

(b) to advise the Prime Minister, through the Minister for Supply, of the conclusions arrived at by the Committee as a result of such examination, and in particular as to whether and if so what additional, alternative or more extensive safety measures are considered necessary or desirable.

The committee was to have the power to coopt other persons subject to the prior approval of the Minister for Supply and the United Kingdom government[8]. Like the AWTC, it was reorganized in 1957, after *Buffalo*.

Safety regulations

The health physicists at Aldermaston prepared comprehensive radiological safety regulations for everyone concerned with the trials, whether at Maralinga itself, Emu Field, Salisbury, the RAAF airfield at Edinburgh Field which was the main airbase for trials, or anywhere else in Australia. These regulations, which were agreed with the AWTSC, placed responsibility for radiological safety during trials on a health physics adviser to the trials superintendent, appointed by the Director of Aldermaston. In periods between trials, an Australian health physics representative at the range (the AHPR), appointed by the Australian authorities, would take over.

The MPLs for external gamma radiation laid down in *Radiological Safety Regulations, Maralinga* were based on the current (1955) ICRP recommendations, and were:

(a) A normal working rate of not more than 0.3 r a week of gamma radiation

(b) A lower integrated dose of up to 3 r of gamma radiation

(c) A higher integrated dose of up to 10 r of gamma radiation

(d) A special higher integrated dose of not more than 25 r of gamma radiation.

The regulations also set limits for beta and neutron radiation, and for internal radiation, and they emphasized that every endeavour must be made to keep the average exposure as low as possible. The lower integrated dose (b) required the express permission of the health control officer, and would be given only when necessary for the smooth running of the operation. The higher integrated dose (c) applied only in cases of necessity, in order to recover records and information that might otherwise be lost; it required the personal permission of the trials superintendent, after consultation with the health physics adviser and medical adviser. Anyone receiving either the lower or the higher integrated dose—(b) or (c)—would not be further exposed to radiation until his average weekly exposure, from the start of the operation, was below the normal working rate. The special higher integrated dose, (d), was new since *Hurricane* and *Totem*. It applied only in cases of extreme necessity, and only to personnel not normally exposed to radiation. It required the personal permission of the trials director, with health physics and medical advice as before, and of the AWTSC in the case of Australian personnel. (There is no record that this last provision was ever required.) Anyone receiving a 25 r dose would not be further exposed to radiation for three years.

The regulations also defined non-active and active areas, and classified active areas—BLUE (no special clothing needed), RED (protective clothing to be worn as instructed) and YELLOW (fully protective clothing essential). There were rules about entry to different areas, about film badges and personal monitoring, about laundering and waste disposal, about storage and movement of radioactive materials. They emphasized that officers in charge of any task must ensure that their staff understood the hazards, and must see that the regulations were rigorously observed; Service officers in command of Service units or personnel must see that the regulations, and any other safety instructions, were brought to the notice of their men and were enforced.

Construction of the range

By December 1954 an Australian survey party from the weapons research establishment at Salisbury, near Adelaide, had moved in, first to Maralinga and then to Giles, 600 miles away and 450 miles southwest of Alice Springs. At Giles a new meteorological station[9] was later to be set up to improve weather forecasting for trials; it was of great importance to the trials (as well as to Woomera), and Butement was later reported as saying that without it the Safety Committee would not permit any trial at Maralinga.

The South Australian Department of Mines began boring for water, at first with disappointing results. The Department of Works cleared a site to be used for *Kittens*, built a camp, laboratory and stores, and made roads and tracks, in time for the *Kittens* series in May 1955—all this in spite of the overpowering summer heat between January and March. Land lines were laid from Port Augusta to Maralinga and communications equipment installed. Emu Field was opened up again as an active station, to assist in fallout measurements. The Australian 'token contribution' was proving extraordinarily generous and effective.

The contractors began work at Maralinga in June 1955. There were formidable problems in accommodating some 700 workmen in bush and desert country '500 miles from anywhere'; the medical authorities warned that the construction camp was too crowded; all the water used still had to be transported by rail; supplies were delayed by shipping strikes. Unfortunately, site management was inefficient, and progress reports were so discouraging that the prospects of completion in time for *Buffalo* looked poor. In London, the Minister of Supply and his senior officials held frequent and anxious meetings with the consulting engineers and contractors.

By April 1956 there had been a reorganization, and a complete change of atmosphere on the site was reported. Captain Lloyd, of the Ministry of Supply, visited Maralinga in May and June, and was much impressed by the friendliness and whole-hearted cooperation he found there, the excellent work done by the resident engineer who had 'given his utmost', and the new and very efficient range commandant who was about to take over. Despite continuing water problems, and the recent derailment of more than 20 trucks of urgently needed freight, there was a feeling of confidence that the range would be ready in time for *Buffalo* though at greater cost than estimated.

Meanwhile another major trial was in progress in the Monte Bello Islands. *Mosaic* is the subject of the next chapter.

Notes and references

1 See Menaul: *Countdown*, p. 61.
2 A verbatim record is reproduced in Symonds: *A History of British Atomic Tests in Australia*, Appendix 11.2.
3 At the same time they asked the Lord President to examine the possibility of the South Polar regions for atomic tests; a thermonuclear explosion from an aeroplane near the South Pole was being considered.
4 The Department of Supply (which provided the chairman and executive secretary), the Department of Defence, the Service departments, the Treasury, the Department of Works, the Australian Atomic Energy Commission (AAEC) and the Australian Security Intelligence Organisation (ASIO).
5 i.e., the first *Grapple* series in 1957 in which the Australians were to play some part.
6 See Symonds: *A History of British Tests in Australia*, pp. 290–91.
7 See Symonds: *Ibid.*, p. 294.
8 See Symonds: *Ibid.*, pp. 295–96.
9 The British government met the capital cost and Australia paid for operation and maintenance.

7 Mosaic—1956

The first step to the H bomb

After the Government's hydrogen bomb decision in the summer of 1954, the scientists had expected their first test to be in 1958, but by early 1955 they hoped to be ready by 1957. However they lacked essential scientific data on thermonuclear reactions in light elements that they could only obtain by experiment. They needed a third series of tests in order to judge the likely success of the megaton weapon as they then conceived it. But Maralinga would not be ready until September or October 1956, and was already booked for a fourth test series, *Buffalo*. Emu Field was unsuitable. A return to the Monte Bello Islands was the only possibility.

Captain Cooper had already made a post-*Hurricane* appreciation of the Islands as a possible site for further atomic tests. Whether trials could be held there again, he said depended mainly on whether there was enough room. Contamination would make operations inconvenient, and the areas remaining for use were considerably restricted in size and shape; however if there was not enough space on land, some equipment might be installed on rafts or barges in the lagoon. Weather and sea conditions were crucial; although the climate was pleasant from April to October, boatwork was difficult, and more boats would have to be provided, as well as helicopters. For *Hurricane* the resources deployed had been dangerously small and planning had been very rushed; planning for the next trials could not begin too early.

A British scientific party led by W N Saxby of AWRE visited the Islands in November 1953, and found them still very contaminated and unlikely to change for ten years or more. They surveyed the Islands and re-defined the 'slight risk' and 'no risk' areas.

Aldermaston and the Service ministries discussed the matter, especially the best method of approach to the Australian government. The difficulty was, how to explain the use of light elements in the proposed trial: as an important step towards testing a megaton weapon? or as the next step in the development of fission bombs, with added light elements which might give a small, even insignificant, fusion yield but still with a total yield measured only in kilotons?

The Minister of Defence, Selwyn Lloyd, wrote to the Prime Minister, Anthony Eden, that experiments were needed in April 1956, involving atomic devices that would incorporate unspecified 'light materials'. The experts' advice was that the Australian government should be asked for the use of the Monte Bello Islands, without which the whole weapons programme might be delayed. However the Australian Minister for Supply, with British agreement, had categorically stated that no thermonuclear tests would be carried out in Australia, and though these experiments would not be tests of thermonuclear weapons, there might be difficulties. It was a problem of presentation.

The Prime Minister cabled Menzies on 16 May, and was frank about the purpose of the trial if vague about its nature.

> You know well the importance we attach to speediest development of efficient nuclear weapons and the great part they can play in interests of Commonwealth strategy. Our research and development work is going so well that we hope to carry out certain experiments early in 1956 and to have a full-scale test of thermonuclear weapons in 1957 . . . I should like to ask for your help in making arrangements for experiments in early 1956. As you know, Maralinga cannot be ready until September/October of that year, when we are already planning to carry out certain weapon trials. If we can carry out experiments in April 1956 we shall not only save 6 months valuable time in our weapon development programme, but we shall get greater value from Maralinga tests in September/October.
>
> Our people here . . . suggested that your agreement should be sought to a programme of two firings in the Monte Bello Islands in April 1956. The experiments would consist of atomic explosions with the inclusion of light elements as a boost. It would of course be made clear in any public announcement that the explosions were atomic and not thermonuclear . . ..
> The smaller of the two shots [would] be fired first and if this was completely successful the second and slightly larger shot would not then be fired. Neither would give a yield more than 2½ times greater than that in the *Hurricane* operation[1].
>
> The explosions would be on towers to reduce contamination and fallout would be less than one-fifth that of *Hurricane* bomb.
>
> We should of course ensure that shots would not be exploded unless conditions were such as to involve absolutely no danger to health of people or animals on mainland, and should give your people the same facilities[2] for checking safety measures as they had at previous trials and as they will have at Maralinga.
>
> We should be prepared to bear cost of operation but should be grateful for all such logistic support as Australia could provide . . ..

Menzies quickly agreed in principle. His reply was very friendly and cooperative, but firm. Australia, he said, would continue to assist within the limits of her resources, but he was in the dark about the logistic support involved. Manpower was short and he was anxious about the cumulative effect on Australia's resources of so many commitments, including her contribution to the strategic reserve for Malaya and the operations at Woomera and Maralinga. He was also concerned about safety:

> I notice from your description of the nature of the shots to be fired that each would give a yield considerably greater than in the case of the bomb fired in the *Hurricane* operation. In view of this I ask that the most meticulous care be exercised in the scientific checking of safety measures to ensure the safety of people and animals on the mainland.

Eden assured him that safety measures would be meticulous, that as before the British would welcome discussions on safety checks with the Australian scientists, and also that senior Australian Service officers would be welcome as observers at the test. Resources required for the test would only be about 10 per cent of those used at *Hurricane*. A British party would, as suggested, visit Australia shortly for discussions.

The agreement between Prime Ministers cleared the way for planning. The Monte Bello Islands were familiar territory, and the Aldermaston scientists by this time had experience of three tests. But *Mosaic* was unlike previous tests, partly because of its novel purpose, partly because it was the first to take place under the new dispensation. In Britain, as we saw in Chapter 1, the Atomic Energy Authority had been created in 1954 and had taken over Aldermaston, and responsibility for weapon trials had been divided between it and the Ministry of Supply's Controllerate of Atomic Weapons, headed by General Morgan. In Australia the Atomic Weapons Tests Safety Committee had been set up in 1955; the Memorandum of Arrangements had been agreed by Australia and Britain, and although it referred specifically to Maralinga it was tacitly assumed to apply to all weapon trials in Australia. Anglo–Australian relations in respect of trials had thus been put on a more formal basis, with clearly defined rights and obligations, and though the Australians had certainly not struck a hard bargain their position had been strengthened.

Planning the operation

Captain Cooper had said of *Hurricane* that it was a rush job and that more time should be allowed for planning later trials. Then the second test—*Totem* in October 1953—was proposed and approved in December 1952, and because there was insufficient time to mount another naval operation the new site at Emu Field was quickly prepared. One argument for the permanent inland range was that it would speed up the programme, since any naval expedition to Australia would need two years' notice. But *Mosaic*, once again, was a Royal Navy operation, and mounted with little time to spare; it was fifteen months, not two years, from its conception in February 1955 (as Operation *Giraffe*) to the planned firing dates in 1956. By June 1955, when intergovernmental agreement was reached, only ten months were left; there was much work to do and a long voyage lay ahead. An appreciation in March 1955 by the Aldermaston trials staff had been 'over-optimistic and unrealistic in terms of time and manpower', the Operational Commander said later, and after *Mosaic* he commented that a further three or four months of planning and preparation would have made the task easier and more certain of success. There had been no margin; this theme recurs again and again.

At a preliminary meeting of the Service departments and Aldermaston, on 3 May, it was tentatively decided to place the weapons on towers, one on Trimouille Island, and one on Alpha Island, and to control the firing from the base ship, anchored 15 miles away in the lagoon. The scientific party, it was estimated, would number 35 to 40—it proved an underestimate—and an engineering force of about 30 would be needed. A timetable was agreed. The ships would have to be refitted and ready for sea-trials by mid November; they would have to sail from the United Kingdom by 5 January 1956 and reach the Islands by 7 March; the sites would then have to be prepared by 18 April; the full rehearsal should be not later than 30 April; and the two shots should be fired on 1 and 10 May, weather permitting. Compared with *Hurricane*, there were two time-saving factors; the ships would go through the Suez Canal and not round the Cape, and the scientific party and the main Royal Engineer Force would go to Australia by air instead of by sea—a *Hurricane* lesson well learnt.

In London the Atomic Weapons Trials Executive, under the chairmanship of General Morgan of the Ministry of Supply, was already planning Operation *Buffalo*; its terms of reference were extended to include *Mosaic*, and it became the executive authority in London dealing with all aspects of the operation, sitting as 'Mosex' or Buffalex', according to the agenda. The Royal Navy appointed Captain (later

Commodore) Hugh C Martell RN as Operational Commander in June 1955; C A Adams, who had been deputy to Dr Tyte at *Hurricane* and to Sir William Penney at *Totem*, was appointed scientific director, to be assisted overseas by I Maddock as scientific superintendent. Group Captain S W B Menaul was to command the RAF *Mosaic* Air Task Group.

Captain Martell decided at once that joint planning should be done at Aldermaston—another *Hurricane* lesson well learnt—which resulted in a successful integration of operational and scientific plans and an admirable understanding between the Service and scientific elements throughout the operation. The Operational Commander, besides being in command of all HM ships, was responsible—under the Atomic Weapons Trials Executive—for overall control, planning and execution of the operation, including safety and security. Army, RAF and scientific personnel were to be commanded by senior Army and RAF officers and the scientific superintendent respectively—Lieut-Colonel R N B Holmes RE, Group Captain Menaul and I Maddock. At Aldermaston, AWRE planning of the trial was the responsibility of J T Tomblin, head of Trials Planning Branch, which was part of the Trials Division under R Pilgrim. The latter was one of the British scientists who had been at Los Alamos during the war and at *Cross Roads* in 1946, and he had been invited to visit the Nevada Test Site in 1955.

Planning in Australia

On 22 July 1955, as promised in Eden's message to Menzies, a small mission led by Martell and including Adams and Menaul went to Australia to discuss all aspects of *Mosaic* with the Department of Supply, the Maralinga Committee, the Services, the Bureau of Meteorology and the Australian security staff. Adams gave Butement, as a member of the AWTSC, a broad description of the scope of the operation and the probable yields. He suggested to him that safety precautions and firing conditions should be governed by the principles in Report A32 (which the Australians already had) and showed him fallout contours for the *Totem* shots—'nominalized' to 20 kilotons, i.e., re-drawn as they would have been if the yields had been 20 kilotons—demonstrating the effects of windshear and absence of windshear. They decided to correspond further about safety questions and to meet again early in 1956, and it was agreed that at least two members of the AWTSC would be on board the headquarters ship, HMS *Narvik*, when decisions to fire were taken.

Meteorological plans were discussed with Dwyer, the head of the Bureau of Meteorology. One or two Australian meteorologists, it was agreed, would be attached to the Operational Commander's staff as consultants. A RAN frigate might be stationed to act as a weather reporting ship, and a second weather ship would be necessary to give warning of hurricanes—not infrequent in the area—and willy-willies coming from the Timor Sea.

As a counterpart to Mosex, in August the Australians set up the Monte Bello Working Party, under a naval chairman; paradoxically but sensibly, it operated as a sub-committee of the Maralinga Committee. Plans went forward rapidly in Britain and Australia. A revised time-table was agreed, with HMS *Narvik* reaching Fremantle by 11 February instead of 28, since Martell and Adams were both worried about Monte Bello weather conditions in April/May and wanted more margin for possible delays in firing. They had every reason to be apprehensive about limited opportunities; the prevailing winds in the area in April and May were westerlies, and the Australian meteorologist, H R Philpot, had concluded that in these months the chances were low of winds between 30 000 ft and 50 000 ft blowing into the appropriate sector (i.e., from 270° to 045° through north). Moreover, favourable winds nearly always meant rough weather, which would hamper boatwork. A further constraint on firing opportunities was the political ban on Sunday firings.

Menzies asks questions

Eden sent a message to Menzies at the end of August to say that a public announcement of the test could not be delayed, as preparations would soon be too visible to be kept secret:

> I understand that the planning of the Monte Bello test is going ahead and that your government is proposing to send naval vessels to the Islands early next month to begin the laying of the moorings. This raises the question of publicity, to which we have been giving some thought. It seems desirable to issue in the near future a general statement about our plans for tests in 1956 both at Monte Bello and Maralinga. We have therefore prepared a short draft . . . .

On receiving Eden's original request in May, Menzies had evinced no concern about the nature of the trial or the light elements mentioned. Now he became anxious and wanted a fuller explanation. Some of his officials had gained the impression from Australian scientists that

Mosaic might be described as a hydrogen bomb test; if it was by any definition an H test, he and his Government would want background material to enable them to deal with questions after the public announcement that the trial was to take place.

A prompt reply to Canberra said 'Australians can be reassured. An H bomb in normal parlance is a weapon of large yield, that is, in the megaton range, which employs the fusion reaction of light elements on a large scale. The proposed tests are not of this character but are the fission weapons used as vehicles for certain diagnostic and experimental tests'. As for the explanation Menzies wanted, the answer given was:

> The smaller yield weapon is a fission weapon which in order to get scientific data contains small quantities of the light elements used in thermonuclear bombs. The light elements are expected to react but the quantities are so small that the effect on the yield is small. The larger yield weapon is a fission weapon containing somewhat larger quantities of the light elements, but containing no uranium[3] with which the light elements can react. The behaviour of the light elements will be diagnosed with the help of traces of various materials.
>
> An H bomb is essentially a bomb in which the major explosion is due to a reaction of considerable amounts of light elements, and the yield is large—in the megaton range. The two rounds at *Mosaic* are of low yield—a few tens of kilotons—and the small amounts of light elements incorporated are solely to investigate the nature of the reaction.

These doubts apparently dispelled, a carefully agreed statement about the forthcoming operation was released simultaneously in the United Kingdom and Australia, on 12 September 1955. It explained that rapid progress in the atomic weapons programme made further trials necessary before the range at Maralinga would be ready in late 1956. The Australian government had therefore agreed to the use of the Monte Bello Islands for trials in April/May 1956. Fallout on the Islands and the nearby sea would be less than that from the *Hurricane* explosion in 1952; there would be no danger to people or stock on the mainland, and detonation would only take place when the meteorological conditions were fully satisfactory. After this third series at Monte Bello, a fourth would take place at Maralinga later in 1956. None of the tests would exceed a few tens of kilotons in yield, and some would be smaller. The Australian meteorological service would provide meteorological information for both series. As in earlier tests, the decision to fire would only be made after eminent Australian scientists, nominated by the Australian government, had made their own independent assessments. (This last sentence does not accurately describe the arrangements at *Hurricane* and *Totem*, where there had officially been no such procedure; however at least three eminent Australian scientists had been present at both of these trials and had been consulted by Penney when the decisions to fire were being taken.)

The Services complete their plans

At Chatham, refitting of HMS *Narvik* began early in July, and she was commissioned on 25 November—thanks, said the Operational Commander, to feverish activity by all dockyard departments working day and night. An already tight time-table was made more difficult by changes of plan and inaccurate briefing due to security restrictions, and most of the officers and crew joined the ship late, but the sailing date was met. One useful change of plan was the decision to use *Narvik* only for operational control and not for scientific activities; in particular, the firing control was to be on Hermite Island, where a camp for eight scientists would be set up. This made more space available on board; even so it was barely adequate and the meteorologists, for example, worked in very cramped conditions. Electronic instrumentation was simplified as a result of the change and scientific sea trials became unnecessary, with a valuable saving of time; arrangements for movement of personnel before firing were also made easier.

The ships of Task Force 308 were in four groups. The first was HMS *Narvik* and HMS *Alert* (loaned by the Commander-in-Chief, Far East). The second group consisted of RAN vessels, HMAS *Fremantle*, HMAS *Junee* and HMAS *Karangi*, and two lighters. In the third group were five Royal Navy destroyers, from the Far East and East Indies stations, employed on weather reporting duties. Lastly, HMS *Diana*, a destroyer on special detachment from the Mediterranean Fleet, was to carry out Admiralty-sponsored experiments on fallout.

By the end of December, HMS *Narvik* had completed her refit and trials, had loaded all stores, and was ready to sail. A small party of Royal Engineers was on board; the other RE, together with two Aldermaston staff, were to fly to Australia to join HMS *Narvik* at the end of February 1956. The main scientific party would leave London by air on 1 April. Stores were to be carried by HMS *Narvik* and by commercial shipping, but a considerable tonnage had to be sent by air freight.

The RAF air task group, originally formed with the Maralinga trials in mind, was responsible for air communications and transport, safety patrols, long range meteorological reconnaissance flights over the

Timor Sea, the collection of cloud samples, cloud tracking, radiological surveys of the Islands and the coastal area, and aerial photography. Twenty-five aircraft were engaged, including three RAAF Neptunes used for safety patrols, and 107 officers and 407 NCOs and men, most of them volunteers. Most were based at airfields at Pearce and Onslow, but four RAF Shackletons flew daily weather flights from Darwin. Seven specially equipped RAF Canberra bombers were to collect and deliver cloud samples, and to track the radioactive clouds until they were clear of the Australian continent. Five RAF Varsity aircraft were to assist in cloud tracking at lower levels and to carry out low-level radiological surveys. Two Whirlwind helicopters were to provide a ferry service (and air-sea rescue service if needed) and to help the Varsities in low-level surveys. Special air transport between the United Kingdom and Australia and between bases in Australia was provided by four Hastings aircraft.

The air task group had some early difficulties with too little time for planning, late delivery of equipment, aircraft needing modifications, and hitches over movement of personnel, but the advance party of 84 officers and men duly moved to RAAF Pearce in January 1956. The main party followed in the second half of March; the travel arrangements were chaotic, but once at Monte Bello all went well. Liaison with the scientific staff, and cooperation between the RAF and RAAF, were both excellent.

The Army contribution, though less obvious, was outstandingly good. Royal Engineers under Lt Colonel Holmes worked in intense heat, ten hours a day and seven days a week—reportedly 'cheerfully'—on construction and civil engineering work. This included the erection of aluminium towers for the two weapons; there were difficulties due to bad drilling by the manufacturers, and none of the men were trained erectors—one was a plumber whose hobby was mountaineering—but they did their job admirably.

Meteorology and theoretical predictions

By the end of October the AWTSC had specified a need for two ship-borne weather reporting stations—one 600 miles west and one 600 miles northwest of Monte Bello. As two or even three ships were required to keep one ship on station, the Admiralty suggested that one should be replaced by a wind-finding radar station on Christmas Island (that is, Christmas Island in the Indian Ocean, 190 miles south of Java, *not* the Christmas Island in the Pacific, used for the *Grapple* trials in 1957 and 1958). The AWTSC agreed and the Royal Naval Weather Service set up a station there. On HMS *Narvik* there was to be a meteorological office with two Australian meteorologists, a Royal Navy meteorological officer and six naval ratings. This group would work closely with the scientists in the theoretical predictions group, whose task, before firing, was to correlate the theoretical fallout patterns with the forecasts provided by the meteorologists, and to advise whether the forecast conditions were suitable for firing. After firing, they and the meteorologists had to determine the probable position of the cloud, so that the tracking and sampling aircraft could be told where to look for it; it would soon become invisible and would have to be found by means of radiation-sensitive instruments.

The procedures leading up to a decision to fire were carefully defined in the Joint Operational Plan:

> The scientific conduct of the trial will be under the control of a scientific superintendent who will notify the operational commander and the scientific director when the groups have completed their preparations. When Service units have similarly notified the operational commander that they are ready, a standby state will be declared and the decision to fire will be taken when the meteorological forecast is suitable.
>
> During the standby period the operational commander and scientific director will be kept informed of forecasts by the staff meteorological officer. The representatives of the Australian Safety Committee, who will be similarly kept informed by the senior Australian meteorologist, will jointly with the scientific director decide when the forecast shows that firing is permissible in relation to radiological safety. This decision will be given by the scientific director to the operational commander who will authorise final preparations and firing if he is satisfied that all other operational requirements are met.

It is clear from these procedures that the AWTSC representatives had an effective veto on firing.

Health and safety planning

In the Maralinga Safety Regulations, which it had been decided should apply to *Mosaic*, the standards laid down for trials personnel were almost the same as those for *Hurricane* and *Totem*. The difference was that, above the higher integrated dose of 10 r, a 'special higher integrated dose' of 25 r was permissible in cases of extreme necessity.

As for population exposure limits, it should be remembered that firing was to take place only when the predicted winds would blow the bulk of the fallout away from the mainland and across the ocean, so that no significant radioactive contamination would be expected to reach the Australian population. During September 1955, Aldermaston sent two papers to the AWTSC. The first, entitled 'Safety levels for contamination from fallout from atomic weapons tests', defined two levels for guidance on contamination, A and B, to replace those previously defined in A32 as 'zero risk' and 'slight risk'; these descriptions were dropped because 'slight risk' might be thought to imply an exaggerated possibility of injury. Level A was 'that level which will not cause any observable effect on the body'. Level B was 'that level which could cause a small observable effect, such as slight temporary sickness, in a few people if they had a low threshold sensitivity to radiation'; these hypersensitive people were considered likely to be only a fraction of one per cent of a population[4].

At their Nevada Test Site the Americans applied a derived limit approximating to level B, but the Aldermaston scientists did not wish to seek Australian agreement to such high level, and they suggested a level between A and B—at ½B instead of B. This, they believed, would give only a slight chance (if any) of any physiological effect which, if it occurred, would be temporary and hardly observable. They hoped by accurate fallout forecasts to keep exposures well below this level, but, as a marginal possibility, the half-level seemed reasonable. The AWTSC took some time to consider this suggestion, but then decided that level A should apply to Aboriginals, because they would be less sheltered from radiation exposure by housing, clothes and footwear, and less likely to remove contamination by washing. Half level B could apply to the rest of the Australian population.

The second paper Aldermaston sent to the AWTSC gave upper limits for the yield of the *Mosaic* weapons as 'one and four nominal' (i.e., 20 kilotons and 80 kilotons), and presented the evidence of *Totem* contamination as a guide to estimating probable contamination from *Mosaic* under various meteorological conditions. A third paper was being prepared on the probable frequency of favourable weather, and the meteorological conditions to be laid down for firing, matters which the AWTSC was studying independently. For both Aldermaston and the AWTSC, Adams emphasized, safety must be the paramount consideration and an appropriate safety margin must be allowed, but if an unnecessarily large margin of safety was required they might wait in vain for an opportunity to fire.

Scientific planning

The operation being planned was stripped to its scientific essentials, with no ancilliary experiments except the Admiralty exercise to be carried out by HMS *Diana*. Even so, the tasks detailed in the Joint Operational Plan seemed a formidable load for fifty scientists. They were organized in nine groups under Adams, the scientific director, and Maddock, the scientific superintendent, with a small headquarters staff of four. The largest groups were the Radiochemical Group with ten men at RAAF Pearce; the Radiological Health Group with six at Monte Bello and four at RAAF Pearce; and the Electronic Operations Group, with nine at Monte Bello. The other groups were very small; four for weapon assembly, three for weapon functioning, two for theoretical predictions, two for blast measurements and two for photographic measurements (all at Monte Bello), with two decontamination specialists at RAAF Pearce.

Everyone, British and Australian—dockyard workers, Servicemen of all ranks, and scientists—worked desperately hard to meet the *Mosaic* deadlines. But the whole operation might have been aborted by one item. The fusion reaction which it was the purpose of the trial to investigate depended on the presence of a small quantity of a lithium hydride. The Atomic Energy Authority's Production Group had no experience of making it—few people in the world had—and was having the utmost difficulty in getting a production process to work. William Cook, Penney's deputy at Aldermaston who had special responsibility for hydrogen bomb research and development, saw that the whole trials programme might have to be rephased. 'If the *Mosaic* trial at Monte Bello is delayed until September', he wrote, 'we shall be unable to hold the naval support there without jeopardizing the 1957 trial [i.e. *Grapple*, in the Pacific]. If the trial is delayed this far we propose firing the Monte Bello rounds at Maralinga in the autumn. In view of the large yield of one weapon this can only be done if we fire it on a high tower, much higher than the towers we have provided for *Buffalo*'. In October 1958, he sought, and obtained, approval to order a 300 ft tower, which, he said, would not be wasted if the lithium hydride was ready after all. It was ready just in time and *Mosaic* went ahead as planned.

Arrival in Australia

Mosaic passed from the planning to the operational phase. The RAF advance party arrived at Pearce on 10 January; HMS *Narvik* had sailed on 29 December and reached Fremantle on 23 February, where the Royal Engineers came aboard. The Australian ships of the task force assembled at Fremantle and soon all were ready to sail to the Monte Bello Islands. But first Commodore Martell met the Monte Bello Working Party (MBWP) to review the situation and discuss outstanding questions. The target dates for the two tests were amended to 16 May and 11 June and the terminal date was agreed as mid-July to avoid overlapping of *Mosaic* with the preparations for Operation *Buffalo* at Maralinga.

Meanwhile the Australian Minister for Supply, Howard Beale, had made a public statement about the test, explaining the arrangements made to ensure that firings only took place in satisfactory weather conditions. He described the 'vast network of hundreds of reporting stations' throughout Australia, New Zealand, Indonesia and islands in the Indian Ocean, the Royal Navy's weather ship and weather station at Christmas Island, and the special meteorological flights from Darwin. On the basis of reports from all these sources, and analyses by the Australian Bureau of Meteorology in Perth and Melbourne, forecasts would be jointly compiled on HMS *Narvik* by the British meteorology officer and a senior Australian meteorologist. They would keep both the scientific director and the AWSTC fully informed. Then, after Commodore Martell declared standby, the AWSTC and the scientific director together would decide when the weather pattern showed that firing was permissible. They would tell Commodore Martell of their decision, and he would authorize final preparations and firing if he was satisfied that everything was in order. The problem for the forecasters was to predict the approach of suitable conditions early enough to enable all preparations to be completed, and then to satisfy the AWTSC and the scientific director that the conditions would persist long enough after the firing for the atomic cloud to drift out over the sea and diffuse harmlessly into the atmosphere.

Daily meteorological flights from Darwin began on 2 March. Three days later, delayed by a hurricane, HMS *Narvik* sailed for the Islands, and arrived on 8 March. Reconnaissance and construction work began at once, and a camp on Hermite was ready by the end of March; meanwhile at Onslow the Royal Australian Navy was building a mainland base camp. The main scientific party reached the Islands on 7 April and Adams arrived on 22 April. He missed two very distinguished visitors; on 15 April the First Sea Lord, Earl Mountbatten, and Lady Mountbatten called in at the Monte Bello Islands to see the *Mosaic* expedition.

Operation *Mosaic*—G1

A tremendous amount had been done before the scientists came, but they had much work to do before the first round (referred to as G1) could be fired. Scientific rehearsals were held on 27 April and 2 May, followed by a full rehearsal on 5 May. Preparations for G1 were complete, except for the fissile material. It was delivered by a special RAF Hastings flight to Onslow. HMS *Alert* collected it on 11 May and assembly of the weapon began next day. On 14 May, the members of the AWTSC reached Monte Bello, and standby began. A small party of VIPs—six Australian Service chiefs—and press representatives arrived to observe the explosion from HMAS *Junee* and *Fremantle*. D−1 was declared on 15 May, the favourable weather conditions held, and on the morning of 16 May G1 was successfully detonated.

Twenty minutes after the explosion the sampling Canberras entered the cloud, and four hours afterward cloud tracking began. By sunset the seagulls were back, circling the ships. The Radiological Health Group, in a specially fitted motor cutter, surveyed the lagoon, and next day re-entry operations began. On 18 May, HMS *Diana*, after carrying out the Admiralty's fallout experiment, sailed for Singapore.

The AWTSC, after getting results of the mainland surveys, left the Islands—they were to return for G2—and the chairman, Professor Martin, sent a brief report on G1 to the Prime Minister:

> The requests of the Safety Committee for meteorological predictions of safe firing conditions and for examining the subsequent radioactive fallout by air and sea operations were fully met.
>
> The control of movements of shipping and aircraft worked smoothly. The air search of restricted areas showed with certainty that there was no shipping, other than that associated with the experiment, in the prescribed danger area.
>
> The meteorological predictions were complete and accurate and the operation was carried out without there being any hazard whatsoever to life on the mainland, ships at sea, or to aircraft.

The whole operation proceeded with precision and was a complete success.

Nevertheless it had not been entirely plain sailing. The Australians had thought they were going to do the forecasting, and the methods used by the British and Australian forecasters were greatly at variance. Then, at busy periods, the volume of incoming meteorological information tended to saturate *Narvik's* communication system. Prediction of a possible D day, Maddock said, was undoubtedly the problem needing most attention since he came to the Islands. He had been dismayed by the uncertainties in the wind forecasting; during the rehearsal, wind conditions at the instant of mock firing were significantly worse than had been predicted at midnight or even in the early morning forecast. Large uncertainties were also likely in forecasting wind forces, and a predicted windspeed of 10 knots might turn out at anything from 5 to 15 knots. For the real firing, fortunately, predictions proved much more reliable, but there seemed to be no solution to the problem of a 16-hour gap between the latest meteorological information used as a basis for the decision to fire, and the actual time of firing.

Adams, Maddock and the British meteorologist, Matthewman, met Dwyer and Philpot in Melbourne a few days later to try to resolve the difficulties; the atmosphere was friendly but the Australians could not accept the British point of view. The British thought the Australian method of prediction unsatisfactory and unrealistic; since the meteorological conditions they were seeking were very elusive, excessive constraints could make them unattainable. Dwyer made it clear that, for his part, this consideration was secondary to maintaining absolute safety, and he added that public opinion in Australia was strongly opposed to the trials. Adams and Maddock went on to meet the Monte Bello Working Party and the AWTSC. The MBWP was whole-heartedly cooperative; the AWTSC they found extremely reasonable, but acutely conscious of the political atmosphere and possible press and public reactions to any untoward incident.

Martell sent Penney a full, personal, handwritten account promptly after the first detonation.

G1 was fired yesterday after a very successful set of met. forecasts—far more successful than the average practice ones we have had. The only point on which I have regrets . . . is in the concessions I made to ensure the cooperation of the Safety Committee. The question of their seeing anything of the assembly luckily didn't arise, as we went straight into D−1 on the morning after their night arrival. However they asked for a meeting with me in the morning 1½ hours before the decision had to be taken. From their attitude, not only at this meeting but in conversation the previous night, it was clear that they are very perturbed about the Australian political situation, and about the organization and knowledge behind the opposition to atomic tests. Both Martin and Titterton show this apprehension most markedly . . . . Martin took the attitude that they could not function as a Safety Committee unless they were given more information about the nature of the tests. I therefore said I would repeat and confirm what had already been stated to Mr Menzies and, after an assurance that the information would be treated as [Top Secret] said:

(a) Although the major part of the yield of the explosions would come from fission we had for scientific purposes included a small amount of material to give information on thermonuclear processes.

(b) An increment of yield would result from this inclusion which would be proportionally small.

(c) We would give them predicted fallout patterns for both the probable yield and the maximum figure for safety purposes, and that both these figures would include an allowance for the presence of the thermonuclear material.

. . . I ought, I think, to have stone-walled on the lines that such information as UK was prepared to give had already been given to Mr Menzies and that they should get their information from him . . . . However my reaction at the time, with the knowledge of a particularly favourable met. situation coming up, was that it was expedient to repeat to the Prime Minister's committee information that had been given to him . . . . The risk of a deadlock seemed large at the time . . . . They particularly wanted to know how they stood in relation to public assurance that this is not a hydrogen bomb and wanted more than a repetition about the range of yields.

There is a background to this, of which you have probably seen the Press reports—trouble with the Seamen's Union over a ship, *Kytra*, which might be within 500 miles of Monte Bello, and protest marches through Perth with placards about Australians becoming guinea pigs. The Safety Committee is on our side, but a bit jittery . . . .

The results—G1

What did Penney and Cook and the staff at Aldermaston think about G1? It neither elated nor depressed them. Excellent records had been obtained, and the experiment had been technically successful (moreover without American help in measuring the multiplication rate, which Penney had sought in vain). The results agreed pretty well with their calculations and the yield was in the 15–20 kilotons range as expected. But G1 also showed that their more optimistic hopes about the effects of the thermonuclear reaction had not been realized; the effect of the small quantity of lithium hydride had been slight. In this respect, G1 did not give all the information required and there was no question that G2 would be needed, despite the Prime Minister's expectation. Nevertheless, it did give confidence in the improved performance of the implosion system.

The G1 results immediately affected plans for the larger G2 detonation. It had been intended in G2 to use lead, instead of natural uranium which would undergo fission by fast neutrons and might result in a higher yield than that agreed with the AWTSC (i.e. a planned upper limit of 80 kilotons, with 100 kilotons as a conservative basis for safety calculations). However the results of G1 meant that natural uranium could safely be used in G2.

The first *Mosaic* shot had been satisfactory. All had gone smoothly, and there had been no delay due to unfavourable weather. But after the disagreements over meteorology, and the Australian anxieties reported by Martell, the prelude to the bigger G2 shot was full of suspense.

An observer's view

How did G1 look to a keen observer, an American journalist in the press party on board HMAS *Fremantle*? (No journalists were to witness G2, and the fact that there would be a second shot at all was not disclosed to them.)

> Go-it-alone Britain [he reported in telegraphese] produced its own open-shot atomic test off W Australia coast today with typical casual indifference in contrast to tub-thumping ballyhoo of Las Vegas tests.
>
> Today's test could have been RN gunnery practice for all anyone seemed to care and left this lone American observer wondering what hell all excitement had been about yesteryear at Las Vegas.
>
> Missing were tail-chasing governmenters who upsnarled Press arrangements Las Vegas. Two men—one Perth, one Port Embarkation Onslow—handled Press here. Battalions of uniformed securiters who guarded American secrets from Nevada newsmen be ashamed to hear British assigned lone securiter protect its secrets from Press and cost to British taxpayers from M B test would be microscopic compared with bill footed by Americans for practically same result.
>
> Way British conducting tests here you impressioned they old hands at game been doing it for years and downplaying bare facts today's blast will determine whether Britain going to be able to compete world atomic race and whether her months painstaking groping research been down blind alley or crowned success.
>
> From time of announcement Atomicers—in contrast American publicists—repeatedly emphasized there be little news value and quote nothing spectacular unquote in blast. Casualness with which tests treated is deceptive and hides months preparations behind today's blast and discounts thoroughness in way entire show . . . being handled.

In contrast fleets American planes which crowded Nevada fields with transports fighters drones jet VIP craft there only few bomber transports handling chores here and brasshats riding in minesweepers sleeping in cots and living same as junior officers in contrast to chauffeured transport swank accommodation accorded Las Vegas VIPs.

You get impression here that austerity dominates British atomic budget and every shilling being scrutinized before spent and Britain has neither time nor money to squander on open shot à la American.

Did the Treasury officials in Whitehall, I wonder, read these comments while they worried over the cost of *Mosaic* and the rising estimates for Maralinga?

Operation *Mosaic*—G2

Scientific rehearsals for G2 were held on 28 and 31 May and a full rehearsal took place on 4 June. On 6 June the fissile core was delivered by air to Onslow and was again collected by HMS *Alert*, and assembly of the G2 weapon began. Standby was declared on 10 June.

Then came the most trying time of the whole operation. The chances of favourable weather were not good; ever since HMS *Narvik* arrived in early March there had not been a single day suitable for firing a weapon like G2. There were now only 30 possible days until 15 July, set as the terminal date for the operation, since—apart from the approaching *Buffalo* trials—*Narvik* had to be home in time to refit for the 1957 *Grapple* trials in the Pacific. No sooner did the weather look promising than it suddenly changed, but everything was kept in a constant state of readiness so that any opportunity could be taken without delay. This meant continually preparing, moving to action stations—the ships had to be at least twice as far away from ground zero as for G1—and then cancelling when the predicted conditions worsened.

Weather was not the only problem. 'Adams is in considerable difficulty with the Australian Safety Committee over the firing of G2', Cook wrote to the Admiralty, 'and he had to be very restrictive about weather conditions to meet the Safety Committee and so to obtain agreement to fire'. Adams was very worried that before 15 July there might be no weather that would satisfy the AWTSC, and he urged that everything should be done by both British and Australian governments to make an extension possible, if it should prove necessary. The AWTSC must have been the more uneasy because after G1, the decontamination group had found that aircraft based at Onslow had measurable radioactive material in their engines and on their under-carriages, though radiological surveys by the Varsities had found the mainland clear of radioactive contamination from the shot. The explanation seemed to be local winds, blowing onshore in the evening.

The situation was all the more sensitive as Howard Beale, the Minister for Supply, had mistakenly said in a radio programme that G2 was going to be smaller than G1.

Why he said this is a mystery. Butement, in Beale's Department, certainly knew the figures. Yields for G1 and G2 had been given to the AWTSC when Adams visited Australia in mid-July and he had discussed the whole business informally with Martin, Butement and Titterton. If it had not been for Beale's broadcast, a longer danger area than that for G1 would have been declared for G2, but to avoid embarrassing the Minister this was not done, and no public correction of his mistake was made.

The AWTSC was also pressing Adams for further information about the G2 weapon. Penney was always more inclined than Whitehall to be candid, and he appreciated that Adams was in an awkward situation. Nevertheless he strongly advised against showing the committee any significant weapon details, though he did not object to their seeing the outside of the cabled ball in the centre section. They could be told that the fissile material was at the centre of a large ball of high explosive and that elaborate electronics were necessary 'to get symmetrical squash', but no details of the explosive's configuration or the inner components might be disclosed.

The weather continued unfavourable until 18 June. Then conditions suddenly changed, the wind moderated to 25 knots and wind directions up to 60 000 ft were suitable for firing. D − 1 was declared, all was made ready, and ships moved to their stations. At 10.10 am on 19 June Maddock began the countdown. (After having spoken the countdown on three occasions he was known as the 'Count of Monte Bello'—see Photograph 11).

At 10.14 am (local time), G2 was detonated. The explosion was spectacular; G1, by comparison, was like a penny squib competing with a Brock's thunderflash, said Martell. Two newspaper photographers who were watching from the mainland wrote, 'We saw the bomb explode. First was the glow of the fireball, then a brilliant orange light suffused the horizon and waned, and immediately the atomic genie rose gracefully into the upper atmosphere. It was a magnificent sight'. The mushroom cloud was seen at Port Hedland, 265 miles away, and the 'rumbling blast' of the explosion was felt 280 miles away at Marble Bar.

Tracking of the cloud began at once, but next day, 20 June, the RAF Canberras from Darwin could no longer locate it. It was clear that the cloud had not passed over the mainland at any point—though some radioactive material did—and the Safety Committee decided that further tracking was unnecessary. But that was not to be the last of the G2 cloud.

'Task Force 308 deactivated'

Re-entry sorties began on 20 June, the day after G2, and packing up and re-embarkation began on 22 June. The scientific director and the main scientific party left the Islands in HMS *Alert* on 23 June and on the 26th, the rest left with the Royal Engineers in HMAS *Karangi*. From Fremantle they flew back to Britain. Next day HMS *Narvik* sailed for Singapore; well before the terminal date of 15 July, after all the suspense about weather and the possible need for an extension. On Martell's suggestion he and Adams went on a goodwill tour to Onslow, Pearce, Fremantle, Adelaide and Melbourne, to meet as many as possible of the people who had helped, and to thank them.

Prefabricated posts shipped to the Islands were placed to cover all the possible entrances to contaminated areas, and warning notices were erected in English, Greek, Malay, Chinese and Japanese. *Mosaic* was over, and technically and logistically it had gone very smoothly in spite of the rushed planning. The troubles of the 1952 Monte Bello expedition were entirely avoided—thanks to good personal relations between Martell and Adams, to joint planning from the outset, to the sensible decision to fly the scientists to Australia to join the expedition, and to the care taken over mutual understanding (for example, a booklet about 'Life on Narvik' was given to every civilian on the ship).

Clouds of confusion

Before considering the achievement of the operation and its safety, we must follow the vagaries of the G2 cloud. On the evening of 20 June— the day after the detonation—'something of a panic' arose when it was mistakenly reported that a dangerous atomic cloud had drifted inland.

Beale was entertaining some newspaper editors to dinner at Woomera and while he was making a speech, one of them received a message and immediately left the room; as the message was passed on, others quickly followed. The story had started when a miner in Western Australia got a reading on his geiger counter that he considered high; deciding that it was due to the nuclear test he told a local journalist, who at once telephoned his newspaper, which in turn alerted its editor at Woomera.

While the newspapermen were pressing Beale for a statement, in Canberra the Cabinet and the Deputy Prime Minister, Sir Arthur Fadden—Menzies was abroad—had heard the story and were frantically trying to find out what was going on. Beale, as the Minister responsible, was expected to know; they asked him what the hell he was doing and if he wanted to ruin the government. But the only people who could give him the facts were the AWTSC and the scientists on HMS Narvik and, as luck would have it, the radiotelephone was out of order. Meanwhile, someone in Beale's department in Melbourne told him that the Bureau of Meteorology had sent a message to Narvik which suggested that the radioactive cloud had crossed the coast. This was not the case, but some material was carried inland by low-altitude winds and there was some low-level radioactivity dispersed over the mainland—less than level A.

Beale felt obliged to issue a Press statement that night, though he had not been able to obtain authoritative information, and though its terms had not been agreed with the British as they should have been. He told the press that at altitudes of 5000 to 10000 ft all significant particles of fallout had gone into the sea, but at 18000 to 20000 ft some cloud containing minute particles had drifted inland, although it was now tending to drift back towards the coast. When communications with Narvik were restored late that night, Martin informed him that the main cloud was safely over the Arafura Sea, 100 miles away, and that there had never been any danger to the mainland. In the morning Beale therefore gave a further statement to the press, but it was still inaccurate; it was based on what Martin had said, but it implied that the cloud had been overland but had moved out safely to sea again.

That same morning, 21 June, Sir Arthur Fadden told the House of Representatives that the AWTSC had stated that there had been no risk to life or property on land or elsewhere. The Opposition led by Dr Evatt pressed for, and were promised, more information. The AWTSC then had the task of trying to reconcile the conflicting statements. It said that the bulk of the radioactive fallout had been deposited in the sea and the remaining activity had moved as a cloud at a very high altitude over the sea. There had been *no* cloud between 5000 and 10 000 ft, and activity between 15 000 and 20 000 ft had been very small. On these facts there was no present or future risk to property or life. Ministers were still not entirely satisfied, and Beale sent a further enquiry to the AWTSC asking specifically whether the cloud had drifted over land at any time. The AWTSC reaffirmed that the cloud did not pass over the coast but added that nevertheless there was a little activity over land, as was normally to be expected. If atmospheric temperature inversions trap some of the rising radioactive material at altitudes where the wind is in a different direction from that determining the path of the main cloud, the trapped material may be blown in other directions. It was not at any time dangerous.

Four days later Sir Arthur Fadden issued a long statement. After describing the behaviour of the light and heavy particles in fallout, he explained that conditions for the G2 test were chosen so that radioactive particles would remain over the sea until the harmful concentrations had fallen out. It was inevitable that small quantities of fine particles would fall in other directions, including some on the Australian mainland; measurements confirmed that there was some deposition but that it was completely harmless. He was satisfied that the whole operation had been carried out without risk and assured the Australian people that, for both governments, safety was the highest consideration. But the Deputy Leader of the Labour Party declared that the next Federal Labour Government would vote no money for nuclear tests or for the development of the means of waging nuclear war.

The Australian newspapers gave front page and sometimes sensational treatment to G2 but editorial comment was generally restrained. The fact was not mentioned—though it was picked up later—that G2 had been much bigger than G1 whereas the Minister had said that it would be smaller. There was less tendency to blame Britain than might have been expected, though some press reports did point the finger at her. The Sydney *Morning Herald* considered that pressure to discontinue the tests would be little short of calamitous since it was in Australia's interest for the British Commonwealth to have atomic weapons. The Melbourne *Herald* suggested that the way to reassure the public was for the Safety Committee to publish regular reports about the amount of fallout—as indeed the AWTSC was to do. The Melbourne *Age* wrote of a terrible responsibility resting on the authorities concerned, 'to make sure "charged" clouds to not stray'. *Truth* warned that if one Australian were maimed through any miscalculation in these tests 'the Australian people will hurl you and all your guilty colleagues into oblivion'. Some Australians remained imperturbable; when a Sydney *Daily Telegraph* reporter telephoned a small northwestern town to ask about local reactions, he was told, 'Oh, they're a fairly complacent crowd here. It takes something fairly important or severe to make them take notice'.

The G2 cloud story is instructive. Adams commented later that it was always known that the explosions would cause a small increase in radioactivity; if this had been publicly explained beforehand the outcry could have been avoided. The information had been available in Australia, and in Britain, in an unclassified document, which made clear that some radioactivity overland was inevitable. But it had been classified by the Australian authorities—presumably to avoid unnecessary public alarm. This, Adams conceded, was perhaps politically understandable, but by hindsight it was exactly the wrong decision. In all public statements politicians and officials had tried to avoid any mention of contamination; the Australians had asked for the word to be deleted from a pre-*Mosaic* press release drafted by London. This was a classic example of the familiar dilemma of nuclear public relations: candour requires difficult explanations and may mean trouble; lack of candour may mean even more trouble and require even more difficult explanations later.

Martell complained of a lack of imagination in Whitehall. He himself was well aware that the trials were of the utmost interest to the Australians but he doubted if London appreciated the tremendous impact they would have on the Australian public. 'If it can be imagined that a Commonwealth nation were planning to explode a bomb in the Scilly Isles—the British public would be howling for information . . . .. Some adverse criticism after G2 would have been avoided if more facts had been given to the press'.

Proposals that the press should attend *Mosaic* had not been favoured by the British. From a purely practical point of view, Adams thought that the journalists might get very bored and frustrated, cooped up on a small ship waiting for the weather, and with little of interest to see. But British Ministers had disliked the idea on principle and had only concurred because the Australians were insistent. The elaborate arrangements made for agreeing and coordinating public statements[5] might have been adequate for press releases issued at leisure in advance of operations; though even as early as March the British Minister of Supply, Reginald Maudling, complained that 'Mr Beale has already made two announcements on his own initiative and without following agreed procedure with us'. There were British breaches of the procedure too. But the G2 affair showed that the arrangements could not cater for the unforeseen, or for emergencies in which events moved fast and radiotelephones broke down. The story of the G2 cloud is much more about politics, public relations and communications, than about safety.

Whitehall's lack of imagination appears not only at *Mosaic*, where Martell observed it, but generally—in a failure to appreciate either the true extent of Britain's indebtedness or the generosity of Australia's contribution. The Australian Government took political risks in accepting the trials on Australian territory, but was astonishingly unexacting. Whitehall for its part was mean at times, showed little awareness of Australian public opinion, and was often insensitive to Australian feelings—for instance about the control of the Maralinga Range, or the preferential position of Canadian scientists at the trials. However Anglo-Australian relationships at the working level were generally very good, and a strong sense of camaraderie developed.

What did *Mosaic* achieve?

G1 and G2 together made essential contributions to Aldermaston's knowledge of the fusion reaction, of the high energy neutrons it releases, and of the very complex effect of the fission they cause in natural uranium. The Aldermaston scientists also gained improved techniques for measuring the multiplication rate in nuclear explosions and were led to a salutary re-examination of basic questions about yield—its meaning, and its measurement by a variety of methods (radiochemical analysis of debris, ultra high speed photography, and gamma flash and blast measurements). The purpose of *Mosaic*, Penney had said, was 'to confirm that we have not made a fundamental mistake'; it did so and was crucial to the plans for *Grapple*, the megaton bomb tests to be mounted in 1957 in the Pacific.

HMS *Diana*

Unlike the other trials in Australia, *Mosaic* was not accompanied by ancillary investigations of weapons effects and target response. The only ancillary experiments were those carried out for the Admiralty by HMS *Diana*. *Mosaic* was the only trial that would afford an opportunity for these experiments (code-named *Hotshot Foxtrot*) which might very loosely be regarded as a RN counterpart of the RAF's Operation *Hot Box* in 1953 (see Chapter 4). The objectives were to obtain scientific data on fallout, and to study the protection of ships in fallout conditions during nuclear combat.

The destroyer's movements had to be planned so that after the detonations she would be in the right place, at the right distance from ground zero (65 miles for G1 and 130 miles for G2), to receive the required amount of fallout without breaching the safety standards laid down for *Mosaic*; exactly the same radiation rules applied to the crew of HMS *Diana* as to all other participants in the trial. This meant close liaison with the theoretical predictions staff and meteorologists. If the direction or intensity of the fallout was wrongly predicted, HMS *Diana* might either miss the fallout, or she might receive more than intended. If the predictions were right, and if she was correctly stationed, and if the protective measures ('pre-wetting', and washing down) worked as expected, the radiation exposure to a man on deck would be 1.25 r—but no one would be on deck—and the dose below deck would be 0.3 r, the normal weekly working limit. At the worst—supposing fallout was 20 times greater than estimated, protective measures were ineffective, and a man was actually on deck—his exposure might be up to 25 r (equivalent to the special higher integrated dose).

In the event, *Diana's* movements were flexibly controlled and she intercepted the fallout, though not without some problems of tracking; the prediction aspects of the experiment were judged to be satisfactory. The intended degree of fallout on the upper deck was achieved, and decontamination procedures were rapid and thorough. No member of the ship's company received a measurable exposure to gamma radiation. The only misfortune was the loss of an unmanned whaler fitted with scientific equipment. *Diana*, on her way to station after G2, was to drop this boat in an area not far from ground zero where fallout was expected to be intense. However the whaler was lost in bad weather, during one of the many ship movements which occurred between G1 and G2, and it could not be recovered.

A mystery on Delta Island

The Navy made one strange discovery during the *Mosaic* operation. A petty officer one day found a skeleton buried, in a sitting position, in the sand on Delta Island. The discovery was reported to the Australian authorities and bones were sent to the mainland for analysis. The skeleton was believed to be of an Asian fisherman, about 20 years old.

How safe was *Mosaic*?

Safety of *Mosaic* personnel

For the *Mosaic* trials personnel, both Servicemen and scientists, the general levels of radiation exposure were low (see Appendix H). About 5 per cent of them received a total of 0.05 r or more—one sixth of the normal *weekly* working rate of 0.3 r. The exposures of the cloud-sampling crews were lower than expected, and those of the HMS *Diana* crew were below 0.02 r, which was the threshold of measurement. Only eight men received over 5 r. The two highest exposures during the whole operation were incurred by two of the senior scientists present, who volunteered to collect early samples from near to ground zero. They knew that such sorties would mean high exposures—but less than the special higher integrated dose—and they undertook them, with the scientific director's permission, after carefully weighing the value of the scientific information to be gained.

Safety of the Australian population

If *Mosaic* was acceptably safe for the participants, how safe was it for the Australian population? By far the greater part of the fallout was carried out to the open sea but, as we saw, low levels of radioactivity reached the mainland. Adams reported to the *Mosaic* Executive that the highest level detected was a third of Level A, which gave a safety margin of 3 for Aboriginals and 12 for others.

As at previous trials, there were radiological surveys by low-flying aircraft to detect ground surface activity (to be supplemented if necessary by ground-survey teams), but for the first time there was also a static monitoring system. The Memorandum of Arrangements (Appendix C) had specified that 'in collaboration with the United Kingdom government the Australian government [would] set up a chain of fixed monitoring stations at agreed sites in Australia' (clause 9). At these stations fallout was collected on air filter papers and on strips of gummed film. By the time of *Mosaic*, 29 stations were in action, along the northwest coast and at strategic points throughout the continent. Sampling began before G1 and continued daily until the end of July, and then every four days for some time. In addition, water and mud samples from fourteen reservoirs all over Australia and Tasmania were taken from March to August. There was also, as we shall see later (Chapter 9), an extensive study of uptake of radioactivity in the thyroids of sheep and cattle.

Altogether, there was a wealth of information about fallout from *Mosaic*. The samples from reservoirs showed no radioactivity above normal background levels, and the fixed monitoring stations showed no airborne radioactivity in any of the large population centres—Adelaide, Brisbane, Melbourne, Perth and Sydney. From the fallout readings at the 29 stations it was possible to derive an upper limit for the integrated (total) dose of gamma radiation that people at each place would receive. However from these same fallout readings different ranges of dose might be derived, according to the assumptions made. Three sets of calculations have been done. The first, by the AWTSC shortly after *Mosaic*[6], is extremely conservative and based on pessimistic assumptions, which do not suggest that the Committee was indulgent to the trials or complacent about safety.

At Port Hedland, where the highest activity was found, the AWTSC calculated the individual radiation exposure, from G1 and G2 together, as 58 millirems (580 microsieverts) over 50 years. This dose however depended on four unlikely assumptions: that the recipient remained at Port Hedland for fifty years; that he was out of doors all the time; that he wore no clothing; and that the contamination was reduced only by radioactive decay, with no weathering. As a suggestion had been made that the gummed film might be only 62 per cent efficient[7], the figure of 58 millirems might have to be multiplied by 1.6, giving 93 millirems. (This was one-third of the normal weekly working limit of 0.3 rem for test personnel or for radiation workers). Of the radiation doses which the AWTSC calculated on these assumptions, only six were over 25 millirems and twenty were 6 millirems or below.

In 1983 the Australian Ionising Radiation Advisory Council (AIRAC) reviewed the AWTSC figures[8], using the original data from the 29 monitoring stations. It was unrealistically conservative, AIRAC thought, to assume that weathering would not reduce contamination, or that people would remain in one place for 50 years, with no clothing or shelter. As most of the calculated 50-year exposure would be received in the first six months, AIRAC integrated the dose over six months only, and ignored weathering, as little would occur in such a short time. It then produced revised figures based on alternative assumptions: (i) that people were out of doors all the time, and (ii) that they spent a normal amount of time indoors; the shelter factor used in the calculations was taken from the 1977 Report of UNSCEAR. The second set of figures would provide, it said, a reasonable upper limit of the possible radiation dose for most of the population.

Table 7–1 shows the comparative figures for the six places in Australia with the highest fallout readings after *Mosaic* (AIRAC gives the figures in microsieverts but they are shown here in millirem for easier comparison).

Table 7–1

	AWTSC	AWTSC (with 1.6 factor)	AIRAC (i)	AIRAC (ii)
Broome	42	67	12.5	5
Fitzroy Crossing	25	40	7.7	3.1
Liveringa	25	40	9	3.7
Noonkanbah	38	61	8.9	3.5
Onslow	34	56	8.2	3.3
Port Hedland	58	93	21	8.5

By any existing standards the largest lifetime dose of gamma radiation due to *Mosaic*—even based on the more pessimistic AWTSC figures—was insignificant. The highest dose, at Port Hedland, was less than the amount of radiation the average Australian receives annually from natural sources. All the figures calculated for Port Hedland are only a small fraction of the annual limits, obtaining in 1956 or today, for radiation workers and for members of the public, as the Table 7–2 shows.

Table 7–2

Doses	Millirems
1 Integrated dose at Port Hedland: calculated from fallout measurement by	
(a) AWTSC	58
(b) AWTSC (increased by factor of 1.6 to compensate for suggested inefficiency of monitoring 'sticky film')	93
(c) AIRAC	
(i) without shelter factor	21
(ii) with shelter factor	8.5
2 Annual exposure of average Briton or Australian to background radiations (including radon, thoron and their daughter products)	200 approx
3 Exposure of average Briton or Australian to background radiations over 70 years	14 000 approx

Limits	
4 ICRP-based annual limit for radiation workers (1956)	15 000 milliroentgens
5 ICRP-based annual limit for radiation workers (1959–77)	12 000 millirems in one year and 5000 per year on average since age of 18—dose equivalent
6 ICRP annual limit for radiation workers (post–1977) for 50 years of occupational exposure	5000 millirems effective dose equivalent
7 ICRP limit in any one year for individual members of the public (post-1958)	500 millirems—dose equivalent
8 Lifetime limit for radiation workers proposed by Medical Research Council (1956)	200 000 millirems dose equivalent
9 ICRP lifetime (70 years) limit for individual members of the public (1985)	7 000 millirems effective dose equivalent

(These figures (except item 4) are given in millirems for easy comparison. It will be noted that the figures for 1, 3, 8 and 9 are integrated doses, whereas those for 2 and 4 to 7 are annual.)

In 1985 Wise and Moroney[9]—whose reassessments of *Hurricane* and *Totem* have already been referred to—also reassessed the public health impact of the three later series of trials, in 1956 and 1957[11]. For these, especially for *Buffalo* and *Antler*, they had much better data, from the static monitoring stations. They used these fallout records—correcting for proven inefficiencies of the monitoring techniques used—and other contemporary data, including radiological surveys and records of cloud trajectories, and they brought to bear on them the most up to date knowledge on radiation pathways.

Their calculations, covering all twelve nuclear explosions from 1952 to 1957, yield a population dose about 30 times higher overall than that of AIRAC[10], largely because the contribution of ingested radioactivity was dominant in their analysis. However they warn that their population-weighted averaged doses may be too low by a factor of 2, or too high by a factor of 10. No comparison of their *Mosaic* figures with those of AWTSC and AIRAC is made here, as they are not on a directly comparable basis. The conclusions that they draw from them, and from their studies of all other tests, about the public health impact on the Australian population are discussed in Chapter 12.

Notes and references

1 The *Hurricane* yield was approximately 25 kilotons and the expected *Mosaic* yields would therefore be about (or less than) 60 kilotons. In the event the second shot (*Mosaic* G2) had a yield of approximately 60 kilotons, that is about 2½ times that of the *Hurricane* device, and about four times larger than that (approximately 15 kilotons) of G1, the first *Mosaic* shot. See Appendix E2.
2 There had been no formal facilities at previous trials. With the Memorandum of Arrangements and the establishment of the AWTSC the Australians would have to be given much greater facilities.
3 This was not so in the event, as uranium was used.
4 It has been suggested that the scientists should have known whether the proportion of such hypersensitive people was more common in some races than others; in particular, whether the Aboriginals might be more sensitive to radiation. There is no available knowledge on this subject. Knowledge of the effects of radiation on human beings was and is mainly derived from studies of either Japanese bomb survivors, or of radiotherapy patients (in countries where medical radiation is extensively used).

5 The arrangements for clearing public announcements were as follows:
   (a) All public announcements or publicity arrangements in Australia to be submitted to the Australian authorities for approval.
   (b) All press releases in Australia to be made by appropriate Ministers.
   (c) All press releases to be agreed between UK and Australia before release—also time and date.
   (d) Some discretion allowed if UK requests that announcement be made in Australia other than by a Minister.
6 Butement, W A S, Dwyer, L J, Eddy, C E, Martin, L H and Titterton, E W: *Radioactive fallout in Australia from Operation Mosaic (Australian Journal of Science*, V **20**, No 5, 21 Dec 1957).
7 By the American scientists, Eisenbud and Harley. *See* D W Keam *et al.*: *Experiments on the 'sticky paper' method of radioactive fallout sampling (Australian Journal of Science*, V **21**, No 4, Nov 1958).
8 AIRAC No 9: *British Nuclear Tests in Australia—A Review of Operational Safety Measures and of Possible After-effects.*
9 Keith N Wise and John R Moroney: *Public Health Impact of Fallout from British Nuclear Weapons Tests in Australia, 1952–1957* (July 1958).
10 Wise and Moroney calculate the collective dose equivalent commitments for *Mosaic* as 10 man-Sv (1000 man-rems) for G1 and 52 man-Sv (5200 man-rems) for G2.

8   Buffalo—1956

The first Maralinga trial

Operation *Buffalo*, in September/October 1956, broke new ground; the first major trial at Maralinga, its planning was from the outset bound up with the planning and preparation of the new permanent range, and the Australians were more closely involved, especially through the Maralinga committee and the AWTSC (see Chapter 6). *Buffalo*, with four shots, was more extensive than the three previous trials and it included the first airdrop from a bomber aircraft with an operational weapon. Associated with the weapon tests was a substantial programme of biological studies and target response experiments. A novel feature was the so-called 'indoctrination' exercise, designed to give some 200–300 Service officers a practical understanding of atomic weapons and their effects and of the nature of atomic warfare. Altogether it was a big and complex operation.

Buffalo was part of the main A bomb development programme and more time was allowed to the planners than had been the case for *Totem*. However everybody, especially the weaponeers, was being affected by the speed at which new ideas appeared. The orderly sequence of development was interrupted by a special job, the *Mosaic* trial. *Mosaic* was designed to provide thermonuclear information and required small quantities of thermonuclear materials to be inserted into fission bombs. A contingency plan was made in case these materials were not ready in time: it envisaged a shot in the *Buffalo* series containing a small amount of thermonuclear material; details were not worked out but action was taken to procure and build a 300 ft tower. But this contingency plan was cancelled when it became clear that *Mosaic* would · proceed.

Besides the scientific and technical preparation for *Buffalo*, the British and their Australian colleagues had four serious concerns. How could the Australian public be informed and reassured? What should be the radiological safety standards for the Australian population? How could meteorological forecasting and the prediction of safe firing conditions be improved? Most immediately, would the range be ready in time?

Preparing the range

The original *Buffalo* plan set 1 August 1956 as the arrival date of the main scientific party at the range, and 29 August as the first possible firing date for Round 1, but by the beginning of 1956 the prospect of completing the Maralinga range in time for a major trial in September/October looked uncertain. Progress made on the site by the Kwinana Construction Group was unsatisfactory, but in the forward area, for security reasons, work was to be done by Servicemen, not the civilian labour force. The Australian task force—including an augmented Army field engineer troop and RAN and RAAF personnel—was due to arrive soon.

The task force moved into 43 Mile Camp (see Map 5) in February as planned. Their morale, it was reported, was high, despite a shortage of water for washing, and temperatures up to 105° in the shade and a ferocious 132° on the ground.

Clearly, to meet the deadlines, a lower standard of construction would have to be accepted and even some of the major work, as well as minor jobs, would have to be deferred until after *Buffalo*. Serious delays were caused by an Australian dock-strike and the continuing shortage of water; however by late June it appeared that the basic essentials would be ready by 31 July. The advance scientific party arrived on 20 June but the Village was not yet habitable; buildings were unfinished, the power station was not yet functioning, water was scarce and hygiene was appalling. The scientists had to join the task force at 43 Mile Camp for two or three weeks. The water supply, from four bore holes, was still disturbingly inadequate. Then, ironically, the range was deluged with continuous heavy rain for three weeks, which further delayed progress, especially on road and runway construction.

The main body of the scientific staff reached Adelaide during July. Then, instead of coming by special train to Watson as originally planned, they were flown to Maralinga by the RAF in parties of 50; the last—which included Roy Pilgrim, the deputy director of the trial—arrived on 17 August.

Very soon, between 19 and 23 August, the Indoctrinee Force (IF) of some 250 men would be arriving also. The Australian Army had set up

Map 5 The Maralinga range

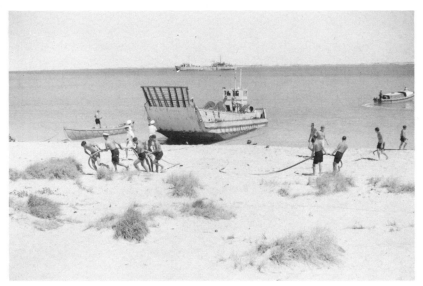

Photograph 1   Cable laying in the Monte Bellos. For *Hurricane* some 150 miles of cable had to be laid between the islands (p. 22).

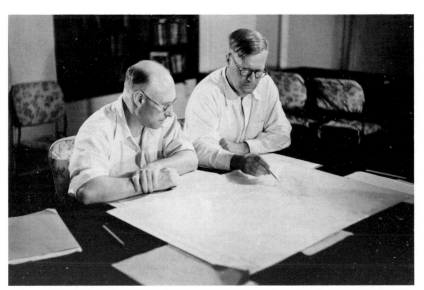

Photograph 2   Before *Hurricane*—Dr W G Penney confers with the Scientific Superintendent, Dr L C Tyte (Chapter 3).

Photograph 3 On board HMS *Campania* at Monte Bello. Right to left: L C Tyte, W A S Butement (Chief Scientist, Commonwealth Department of Supply and Development), Captain A B Cole RN, Rear Admiral A D Torlesse, W G Penney, L H Martin (Melbourne University) O M Solandt (Chairman, Canadian Defence Research Board) (Chapter 3).

Photograph 4 A re-entry party at *Hurricane*, wearing protective clothing (p. 47). Light-coloured clothing was used for later trials to minimize heat stress.

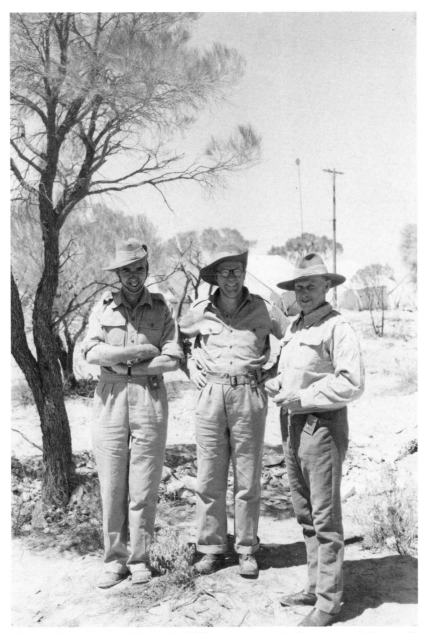

Photograph 5 At Emu Field—Sir William Penney with C A Adams (left) and E Titterton (right) (Chapter 4).

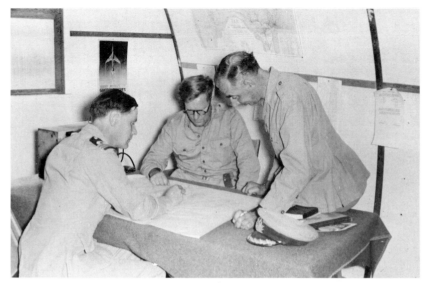

Photograph 6   At *Totem*, Sir William Penney and C A Adams discuss meteorology with Lieutenant Commander Fotheringham (Chapter 4).

Photograph 7   The terrain at Emu Field (p. 58).

Photograph 8 Operation *Hotbox*—the aircrew and their Canberra at *Totem* (pp. 67 to 69). Right to left: Group Captain D A Wilson (observer), Wing Commander G Dhenin (pilot) and Wing Commander E W Anderson (navigator).

Photograph 9 Radiological protection—a fixed monitor in the Health Control Centre at Emu Field (Chapter 4).

Photograph 10 *Mosaic*—a portable radiation monitor in use on the beach.

Photograph 11 Firing Control—Ieuan Maddock at *Mosaic* (p. 127).

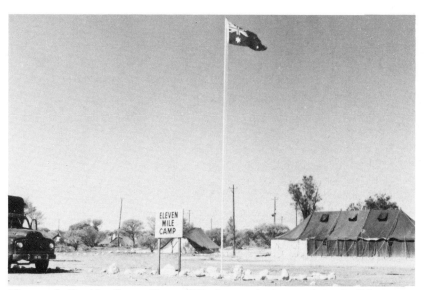

Photograph 12 Maralinga—Eleven Mile Camp, the home of the *Buffalo* Indoctrinee Force (p. 153).

Photograph 13 For grazing experiments at *Buffalo*, boxes planted with grass had to be placed where close-in fallout would be deposited on them (p. 156).

Photograph 14 Dummies were used to study the effects of atomic explosion on Servicemen and to determine the best methods of protection. The dummies used at *Buffalo* were well made and very life-like (p. 155).

a separate camp for them, eleven miles from the railhead at Watson and twelve miles from Maralinga Village; officially named Gundulph, it was usually called Eleven Mile Camp, or Seaview Holiday Camp.

Weeks before, on 1 August, Reginald Maudling, the British Minister of Supply, had written to Beale, his opposite number in Australia, to express satisfaction at the completion of the Range and gratitude for Australian cooperation. At the same time he wrote to the consulting engineers, Sir Alexander Gibb and Partners, to thank them and in particular to commend the indefatigable resident engineer. But considering the immensely difficult conditions and the impossibility of working during the hottest weeks of the summer, there had been too little time, and much work was still unfinished when the Kwinana Construction Group handed over. However, after all the delays and difficulties—including the last-minute derailment of a train carrying essential stores—Maralinga was sufficiently ready for *Buffalo* to proceed very much as planned. How ready for *Buffalo* was the Australian public?

The publicity campaign

In the United Kingdom, a senior official commented, there was not much cause to be anxious politically. 'Atomic tests' he wrote, 'tend to be treated here as fairly routine events . . . . As regards Australian opinion, reports indicate that there may be some opposition'. The scientists were certainly alive to the need for more public information in Australia about the trials, to allay anxiety in so far as it was due to ignorance and misunderstanding. Public opinion had been alarmed by the United States' 15 megaton test at Eniwetok in 1954 (*Castle Bravo*) but no British test in Australia was more than 1/200 of the size of that shot, and most were less than 1/1000.

Public information about *Hurricane* and *Totem* had been too little and too late, and *Mosaic* had been a public relations fiasco. The difficulties were partly due to secrecy (and some Australians regarded excessive secrecy as a typically British fault), but even more to the fact that, because the trials were on Australian soil, the Australian authorities had to be clearly seen to be in control. All public statements had to be made by Australian Ministers, not by British spokesmen, although the British also had a legitimate interest in how it was released and presented.

There had therefore to be procedures for consultation and agreement before statements were made, and these procedures sometimes broke down on one side or the other.

British High Commission staff took the view that, if the necessary facts were in the hands of the Australian authorities, notably the AWTSC, it was 'entirely up to them to educate their own people having regard to their own political problems'. However the Australians expected some assistance and, after *Mosaic*, made it clear that they would positively welcome British technical advice on publicity. Beale appointed a press secretary and it was arranged that the Aldermaston scientists should provide him with information through the head of the United Kingdom Ministry of Supply Staff (UKMOSS(A)) in Melbourne.

By mid-1956 there were substantial reasons for concern about public relations. Up to this time, there had been little opposition in Australia to the trials but worldwide hostility to all nuclear tests was growing (see Chapter 5) and in Australia it naturally focused on the British tests. *Hurricane* and *Totem* had been tolerated as 'one-off' operations, but the establishment of Maralinga as a permanent range implied a continuing programme of tests. By June 1956, 60 per cent of the Australian public was against the tests, according to an opinion poll, and the Opposition party in Parliament had taken up the issue.

Moreover since Maralinga was in the centre of the continent, assurances could not be given, as at Monte Bello, that the fallout would be blown out to sea. The British scientists therefore had to be able to convince the Australian scientists, and through them the politicians and public, that the tests would not deposit harmful radioactive fallout on the mainland (at least, beyond the test area). It was always obvious that at Maralinga radioactive clouds must traverse much of the continent before reaching the coast. But after the G2 scare at Monte Bello, Beale had decided that the best line to take was to emphasize, as a guarantee of safety, that the cloud had gone out to sea. This, as we saw, had not been a success and, as Adams ruefully pointed out, by focusing attention on whether or not the cloud had crossed the coast, Beale's statements had fostered two erroneous beliefs, both prejudicial to Maralinga. The first fallacy that had to be belatedly explained away after *Mosaic*, was that as long as the cloud did not cross the coast there would be no radioactive fallout on the mainland. The second fallacy was that no place under the trajectory of a radioactive cloud was safe. But the truth was that the deposition of fallout, not the cloud trajectory, was the crucial factor, and the trajectory was only important for prediction and cloud-tracking purposes. The real facts would have to be effectively presented to the Australian public before *Buffalo* if panic headlines were to be avoided. A publicity campaign, strongly advocated by Penney, was launched in the summer of 1956. British Ministers had wanted to keep publicity about *Mosaic* to a minimum (because it was mainly of a scientific character and was in aid of *Grapple*), but they agreed that *Buffalo* was quite another matter. Facilities should be offered to the press, and 15 Australian and British press representatives should be invited to witness the first shot.

The publicity plan included feature articles on Maralinga prepared by the Ministry of the Interior, articles by Howard Beale, and papers on scientific aspects of the trials written by British experts for use by the Australian authorities. A long article by Beale, dealing with the trials comprehensively, appeared in all the main daily newspapers on 6 August 1956. Australia, he wrote, had both the wide empty spaces and the facilities needed for atomic weapon tests that, he argued, were essential to the defence of the Commonwealth and also provided invaluable information on civil defence, crucial to the protection of the population in the case of an atomic war. He went on to describe the nature of fallout, and to outline the findings of the recently published Himsworth and Bronk reports. Australia, he said, was firmly in control of the tests and, through the AWTSC, of the safety standards applied. As for the demand that tests should be stopped, he would strongly support an end to testing by all the nuclear powers—as proposed by the British Prime Minister—but not by Britain unilaterally.

On 14 August, the day after Penney's arrival in Australia, Beale and Penney held a joint press conference in Sydney. Penney, Beale wrote, was masterly. He was also invited to make a guest of honour broadcast, and gave some effective press conferences and radio and television interviews.

The most telling contribution—though not arranged as part of the campaign—was probably the visit by Australian Parliamentarians to Maralinga during *Buffalo*. In April 1956, after a Parliamentary Question in the House of Representatives, Menzies had asked the British Government if a party of a dozen Parliamentarians could be invited to watch one of the *Buffalo* shots. British Ministers took some time to decide but at the beginning of June agreed that they should attend Round 1, with the press party; only two plane loads could be managed and facilities were such that it would be impossible to give anyone VIP treatment.

It has been suggested that the publicity campaign was a brainwashing operation intended to ensure the continuation of the tests. It could also be considered simply as a way of providing the Australian public with sufficient information to understand the tests being carried out in their country, to give them the facts and to dispel some erroneous notions. Beale's articles, for example, were certainly informative, as well as enthusiastic and persuasive in tone.

Safety of the population

Once again, the safety of the Australian population depended on its exclusion from the danger area, on the setting of adequate safety standards and safe firing criteria, on accurate meteorological forecasting and fallout prediction, and on post-firing checks—by cloud-tracking aircraft, aerial and ground radiological surveys and monitoring. The network of fixed monitoring stations had been extended from 29 to over 80.

Exclusion from the danger area

In the area that would be affected by short-range fallout (see Appendix I) there were no stations, homesteads or missions, and the only danger would be to intruders, or to Aboriginal nomads who might be moving across the Range. As we saw, Butement had assured Penney—who had no reason to doubt the assurance—that no Aborigines lived on the Range, few ever traversed it and none needed to. Butement clearly regarded the area as a vast, empty, arid and uninhabitable space.

The rocket range established in 1949 had already created a large prohibited area stretching across the continent from Woomera, and a native patrol officer, W B MacDougall, had been appointed to cover the South Australia section; later his responsibilities were extended to Western Australia. There was at that time no coordinated Australian Commonwealth approach to Aboriginal welfare and to such major issues as reserves, segregation, protection of nomadic life-styles, or assimilation, and the policies of the Western Australia and South Australia governments were different. MacDougall thought that the reserves should be gradually eliminated, and that the Aboriginals should be assimilated and given opportunities in Australian society—'we have taken away their beliefs and customs and trespassed on their lands, and we have a moral obligation to give them something in return'[1]—but meanwhile their interests must be protected. One of his responsibilities was to identify ceremonial grounds or sacred localities and to advise the authorities on how to avoid giving unnecessary offence to the Aboriginals.

At first he had no staff and few resources for patrolling his enormous parish, in which he estimated that about 1000 Aboriginals were living, though he had not been able to carry out the thorough population surveys he wished to do. In 1955 a young assistant native patrol officer, R A Macaulay, was appointed to work at Giles, where the new meteorological station was being built, in an area where Aboriginals had been living in virtual isolation from white men. MacDougall and Macaulay were responsible for assessing the Aboriginal situation at the time of tests at Maralinga, getting information from their own patrol activities, from local homesteads and missions, and from police and security officers. On the basis of this information—and of air surveys (the value of which has been much debated) before each trial—the scientific director was advised, before he took a decision to fire, that there were no people in the danger area on the Range.

Shortly before *Buffalo* an Aboriginal gathering (or corroboree) took place near Mount Penrhyn and MacDougall was concerned that after the trial some of them might cross the fallout area on their way home again. Arrangements were made for security and police officers, and the twenty members of the Australian Radiation Detection Unit (ARDU) engaged in fallout surveys, to keep watch for any parties, to tell them which way was safe and to move them out of danger if necessary.

Safety outside the danger area

Safety outside the danger area was, as before, a problem of intermediate range fallout. The primary requirement for safe firing was that such fallout should not cause anyone to receive a dose of radiation above the acceptable dose for members of the public; however, at the time of *Buffalo*, ICRP was still concerned with the protection of people occupationally exposed to radiation, and had made no recommendations about limits for exposures of the public.

The secondary standard, derived from the radiation dose limit, was the level of radioactive material on the ground that it was calculated would give rise to that dose. It was defined in microcuries per square metre. It may be noted that the microcuries per square metre could not be measured directly but had to be derived from readings given by monitoring instruments which measured radiation dose rates either in counts per second or per minute (cps or cpm) or in millirads per hour.

The main business of the theoretical predictions staff was to plot the theoretical fallout contours, showing—for a weapon of a given yield and in various specific conditions—how far from ground zero the unacceptable levels of fallout would extend. It was the responsibility of the meteorological staff to provide forecasts so that the fallout contours could be predicted and advice given when it would be safe to fire.

For *Buffalo*, the safety document (report 041/55) relating to fallout levels was one that Aldermaston scientists had produced in 1955 in succession to A32. It replaced the 'zero risk' level with level A, and the 'slight risk' level with level B (corresponding to 3r and 25r respectively). For *Mosaic* and *Buffalo*, levels of surface activity were calculated that—taking into account all kinds of radiation and all modes of exposure (external and internal)—would result in theoretical exposures at level A (3r) or half of level B (12.5r). These values were used for plotting fallout contours before a decision to fire was taken.

It had been during *Mosaic* that Adams had suggested to the AWTSC that, as an additional safety factor, half of level B should be adopted instead of B. The AWTSC had been concerned that the limits calculated by Aldermaston applied to people wearing clothes and living in houses, and had therefore asked the Aldermaston scientists to think about special limits to safeguard Aboriginals living in a tribal state, unprotected by buildings or clothing or footwear. The result was an appendix to report 0.41/55, produced in April 1956, which defined reduced levels A and B (later designated A^1 and B^1); these levels were lower by a factor of 5, a reduction that would entail a considerable extension of the fallout contours beyond the original A and B lines and would therefore impose more restrictive firing conditions.

The AWTSC also decided that more information was needed about the number and distribution of Aboriginals in the areas outside the prohibited area which might nevertheless be affected by early, or intermediate, fallout. It is surprising that such an enquiry, which Mac-Dougall had wanted, was not put in hand before the original decision to conduct trials at Maralinga was made, but it was at least made before major trials began there. A survey by MacDougall and Macaulay estimated the population in question at about 1600, and the limit of their migrations at about 150 miles from the trials area.

A report by the AWTSC to the Prime Minister, via the Minister for Supply, set out the position and gave examples of fallout patterns from a nominal (i.e., 20 kiloton) detonation at Maralinga, using the most recent data from the two *Totem* shots, which had been fired in such contrasting meteorological conditions—T1 with practically no windshear and T2 with a high degree of windshear. In their report the committee recommended that level A should be used as the criterion for trials at Maralinga. It was lower than the level thought acceptable for a white population; at 3r, it was only a quarter of half level B (used for *Mosaic*) and one eighth of level B which was understood to be the American standard for the Nevada Test Site. The whole matter was submitted to the Australian Cabinet which in September 1956 approved the adoption of level A. But—as Maralinga, unlike Monte Bello and Emu Field, was to be a permanent range—they made it a condition that fallout contours should not overlap so as to expose the same areas repeatedly.

It would be confusing to attempt to compare the various levels of surface activity, in terms of radioactivity per unit area, tabulated in the various scientific reports. What is important is the radiation exposure to which the levels correspond; the relationship between them is not a simple arithmetical one. The radiation dose limit for *Buffalo* was fixed with particular regard to the vulnerability of any Aboriginals who might be in a fallout region. Between *Hurricane* and *Buffalo* the dose limit, for external gamma radiation, had come down from 25r ('slight risk' or level B) to 12.5r (half level B, for *Mosaic*) to 3r (level A). It should be remembered that these were the radiation standards used for planning; they were not actual radiation exposures.

It may well be argued that the authorities, British and Australian, had been slow to take account of Aboriginals in their fallout calculations. It may also be thought that the various arrangements made to keep Aboriginals away from danger were insufficient. However the AWTSC, once set up, took the safety of the Aboriginals seriously, and the British scientists—with limited knowledge of the problem, and necessarily relying on Australian information, advice and action—had always been concerned about it. The wider question of Aboriginal interests, the restrictions on their movements and the denial of access to territory is a separate one (see Chapter 12).

Planning the operation

The original *Buffalo* plan envisaged four bursts. Two, which would be part of the weapon development programme, would be on towers. One would be an airburst, partly an operational airdrop by the RAF and partly an acceptance trial of the Mark I bomb. The fourth would be a groundburst, for investigating effects, including ground shock.

It was always apparent that *Buffalo* would not be an easy operation. Maddock, in a prescient note in 1954, said that this first trial 'with a fair number of bangs', given the 'somewhat depressing meteorological probabilities', would mean a long time at the site unless plans were made to minimize delays in every way. The whole duration of one operation, and the sequence of preparation, should be limited, he said, to about 6 hours so that opportunities could be quickly seized. The trials staff were very likely, he thought, to strike a similar period to that before *Totem* 1, with consistently unfavourable meteorological conditions; staff morale was vital in such a situation. The airdrop would present novel problems; though the weapon was intended to fire high above the ground, the worst must be assumed—that is, that the radar fuzes would fail to function. If the weapon detonated on impact with the ground, contamination would be severe and the ground shock considerable. Before the live drop, both the RAF and the telemetry group would therefore need practice drops, including drops with small H E bombs.

The interdepartmental executive committee that functioned as Mosex or Buffalex, according to the matter in hand, held its first meeting on 11 November 1954. Penney was appointed as scientific director of *Buffalo*, and Pilgrim was his deputy and chief planning officer. Later Air Commodore C T Weir RAF was appointed as Task Force Commander. Planning, and visits to and from Australia, proceeded throughout 1955 and early 1956, and the problems of Maralinga and *Buffalo* were inextricably intertwined. The main preoccupations of Buffalex were the readiness of the Range, the target response programme, the biological experiments, and the Indoctrinee Force (see below).

By March 1956 an outline timetable was drawn up, and a summary plan was ready in June. This plan set out the organization of the trials staff. The scientific groups came under the headings of HQ, Safety, Weapon, Measurement and Target Response; those concerned with safety were the meteorology, theoretical predictions, health physics and decontamination groups. Australians were to staff the seismological, meteorological and radio-flash measurement groups, and were to make a big contribution to the health physics and target response work. Twenty-five Canadians were to take part as a radiation detection unit (RDU).

As before, there were to be considerable RAF and RAAF contingents, responsible for air patrols, surveys, cloud sampling and tracking and so on, but on this occasion the RAF was to have the new and demanding task of assembling and dropping the test bomb. A provisional timetable gave 1 August 1956 as the date of arrival of the main scientific party, 22 August for the scientific rehearsal of Round 1, 26 August for the operational rehearsal and 28 August as the beginning of standby. The order of firing was expected to be tower burst, ground burst, second tower burst, air burst. Practice flights for the live airdrop were planned to begin on 12 September.

Except for the airdrop, firing was expected to be early in the morning, at 0700 hrs (local time). The timetable required that on each day of standby, meteorological forecasts were to be made at 0700 hrs, 1400 hrs and 1900 hrs. If the last was favourable D−1 would be declared and the firing phase would begin; forecasts would follow at midnight, 0200 hrs and 0600 hrs, with wind balloon ascents at 0500 hrs and 0615 hrs; at 0655 hrs, the scientific director would give instructions to start the master clock, and firing would take place. After firing, movement control would be established at Roadside and a mobile health unit (the health physics 'circus' of caravans) would be set up.

The plan envisaged a total of 1350 men at Maralinga. There would be 200 scientists from Aldermaston and Harwell, 70 from other departments, 30 Australians and 50 Canadians. The indoctrinee force was expected to be about 250. There would be 500 RAF and RAAF personnel, and about 250 Australian Servicemen responsible for keeping the Range and the camps running. There would besides be various short-term visits—the Australian Parliamentarians, six high-ranking United States observers, and journalists. The numbers were much larger than had been envisaged when Maralinga was planned, and the Village and the camps would certainly be overcrowded at times.

Guinea-pigs in battle dress—the IF

A story about troops being used as human guinea-pigs in the *Buffalo* operation appeared in the London *Daily Mail* on 2 February 1956 and was picked up by the Australian press the next day. About 200 troops, it said, all volunteers, were to be disposed in danger areas in a new type of dugout, which scientists would share with them. The troops would be told that there was 'some margin of danger'. Pressed strongly by the Australian newspapers for comment, Beale told them that Servicemen would be present as observers but certainly not as guinea-pigs.

The proposal that Servicemen should attend the trials was first made, and agreed by the British Chiefs of Staff, early in 1955. Few Service personnel had witnessed an atomic explosion or had any realization of its effects, and *Buffalo*, it was thought, would be an opportunity 'to spread the confidence which comes from personal experience and dispel fear of the unknown'. The Americans had already made use of atomic tests to indoctrinate whole formations of troops, on a scale that the British could not begin to emulate.

The Australian government agreed in principle in June 1955. At first 400 'indoctrinees' were envisaged, but this number was too ambitious and plans were worked out for 250. Places were allocated to the British and Australian forces, predominantly the two armies. The RAF's *Buffalo* commitments were already so heavy that the Air Ministry did not want any places on the Indoctrinee Force (IF). The Chiefs of Staff approved plans in December 1955, and nominations were called for— all officers, most of them captains, majors or lieutenant-colonels. After many changes, due largely to the Suez crisis which began to loom in July 1956, there were eventually 178 British officers and civilians, about 70 Australian officers and five from New Zealand.

The stated purpose was to enable these selected officers:

(a) to experience the effects of a nuclear explosion;
(b) to examine the effects of such explosion on the ground and on weapons and equipment;
(c) to pass on their experience to other members of the Armed Forces at the conclusion of the trial.

The programme for the IF was to consist of lectures and general instruction very much on Staff College lines, including syndicate work and the writing of original appreciations of military aspects of the new weapon. Before round 1, there would be a tour of the Range, particularly to see the target response material; the nuclear explosion would be observed from a stand at a distance of about 4½ miles; and there would be a post-firing conducted tour to see the effects of the explosion. The timetable of instruction for the first week was intensive, with highly expert lecturers, including Penney, and lecture topics ranging over 'blast, genetics, nuclear physics, nutrition, meteorology, heat effects, ionisation and decontamination'. The Army officers were to be much impressed by the importance of meteorology, and by their 'abysmal ignorance' of it.

The IF, due to arrive at Maralinga at the end of August, was expected to stay 10–14 days; it turned out to be 41 days, and longer for some men. The Australian Army prepared a camp with great efficiency, twelve miles from Maralinga Village and eleven miles from the railhead at Watson. Conditions at Eleven Mile Camp were spartan (see Photograph 12), and high winds, rain and the all-pervading red dust made the tents uncomfortable, although the food was reported to be excellent. The first party arrived at Maralinga on 20 August and most of the United Kingdom group was there by 29 August. This was the date for which the first shot had been planned, but as we shall see it had to be repeatedly postponed. The IF was kept busy meanwhile, and not only with academic work. Even before the first group arrived, working parties were organized for various tasks on the Range, where preparation was behindhand because of bad weather, and the indoctrinees were set to work building a biological laboratory, erecting aerials, digging weapon pits, laying cables, and preparing target response materials. The brigadier commanding the IF found it 'a pleasure to watch highly responsible senior officers manipulating power drills, filling sandbags and cleaning up 25-pounders with complete abandon and a certain lack of skill', and they all took their turn at washing up and other camp tasks.

During the long wait, the GOC, Central Command, Australian Army, lived at Eleven Mile Camp with the IF and remained until after round 1. The delay and the working party schemes benefited the indoctrinees, who—even though they were not living in the Village—were able to get to know the scientists and to learn a great deal more about atomic weapons and atomic tests. The formal training programme too was extended, thought it was somewhat erratic at times because of repeated standbys and 1.30 am reveillés in order to arrive in good time at the spectator stand.

Round 1 was eventually fired on 27 September, and on D+1 and D+2 all the indoctrinees, wearing protective clothing and respirators, entered the target response area in small parties, each led by a conducting officer and with one IF member briefed to monitor radioactivity. They were taken on 2-hour tours to inspect the area and the target response items, and afterwards each man passed first through an experimental Army decontamination centre, designed for use by a unit in the field, before going through the civilian Health Control. After showering, no one was found to be contaminated, and no one received as high a dose as the permissible 3 r.

Most of the IF left on 30 September, but at Penney's suggestion the military authorities agreed that 65 officers should remain for round 2. Their time was fully occupied between rounds, with more training, discussing tactical problems relating to the low-yield weapon, and digging shelters with overhead cover. Twenty-four of the indoctrinees were in these shelters to experience the ground shock produced by the round 2 explosion, and four others were in a Centurion tank in the same area.

Contaminated clothing trials were also carried out by 24 volunteers, wearing three different types of clothing. The officers moved in groups through a fallout area three days after the detonation; some were in a vehicle, some marched along a track, and some crawled 30 yards 'in the accepted military manner' and then marched through the bush. Health escorts accompanied each group. The object was thoroughly practical—to discover what types of clothing would give soldiers the best protection against radioactive contamination in conditions of warfare. Exposures were satisfactorily low (see p. 166).

The indoctrinees were 'shaken by the devastating effects on weapons and equipment' of this very small bomb; they realized 'the devastating effect on the morale of troops not expecting one, and/or not knowing what to expect'. One hardy soul, however, would have liked to be 'much closer, in a properly constructed infantry position'. The lectures had been well worthwhile, but films, demonstrations and lectures were no substitute for the real thing. Discussion of the effects with brother officers and with scientists had been very valuable. The experience would be a stimulus to further study. They would be able to lecture and carry out their training duties with greater conviction and authority. As field commanders they would have more confidence. As their comments showed, most of them found the whole experience professionally rewarding.

In spite of delays and discomfort, the atmosphere of Eleven Mile Camp was cheerful. In their spare time, which must have been scanty, there were cricket, chess, darts and volley ball, as well as botanical walks, fossil hunting and conversation. One officer wrote later, 'All British indoctrinees will always remember the friendliness of the Australian and New Zealand officers . . . and the sharing of good times and bad, hardship and alcohol'. 'Throughout the whole of the six weeks', wrote another—it sounds almost too good to be true—'in conditions that were sometimes frustrating, I never heard of one cross word being spoken, nor was there even a jarring note'.

Another guinea-pig story that gained currency in 1984 was that soldiers were placed close to ground zero to demonstrate the effects of an atomic explosion on human beings. This story arose from a Chiefs of Staff paper, by that time in the Public Record Office, that outlined plans for atomic weapon trials and for associated investigations of 'the detailed effects of various types of explosion on equipment, stores and men with and without various types of protection'. A reader assumed wrongly that this meant using troops for the purpose. What the plans really involved was the placing of dummies in various positions and at various distances from ground zero, as described below. The dummies used at *Buffalo* were well-made, and were dressed in Army uniform; photographs show them to be extremely lifelike (see Photograph 14).

The target response and biology programme

Maralinga afforded greater opportunities than Monte Bello or Emu Field for target response experiments, and this advantage had been one of the arguments for the permanent Range. Nevertheless, in its unfinished state and with scanty water supplies, the Range could only accommodate limited extra numbers at *Buffalo*, and proposed experiments had to be rigorously scrutinized. At an early stage in planning, the *Buffalo* Executive (Buffalex) asked government departments to submit bids, and it set up a target response sub-committee to coordinate them. With its assistance, J T Tomblin, Pilgrim's deputy, and later the target response coordinator, E R Drake Seager, produced order out of the chaos of proposals.

The Services put forward an extensive programme, to which the Australian Services also contributed. It included the exposure of six Swift aircraft; three Centurion tanks; guns of various types; ammunition and explosives; structures (including bridges, runways and sheds); equipment (Service clothing, respirators, radio sets, telephones and instruments of various kinds); medical supplies; and materials (plastics, paints, packaging, etc).

The Services also had a strong interest in some of the work of the

Biological Group, which had an extensive and—by British standards—ambitious programme. When Buffalex invited bids, the Medical and Agricultural Research Councils (MRC and ARC) replied promptly that they wanted to take the opportunity both of validating certain laboratory conclusions in the field, and of carrying out some biological experiments that were only possible with an actual weapon detonation.

They proposed two different ingestion studies, and some blast-effect experiments. For the first, they wanted to pasture some grazing animals on an acre of grassland sown and maintained in the fallout area within a few miles of the explosion. These animals would be slaughtered at the site after a few days, and autopsied to investigate the uptake of radioactive fallout. For the second, they wanted to determine the effect of fallout on sheep downwind of the test area; samples of tissues and organs would be required for analysis, and in this biological monitoring programme they needed the cooperation of the Australian agricultural scientists. For both types of investigation, the MRC recommended joint Anglo-Australian teams, especially as these studies were of particular interest to the Australian authorities. The blast experiments were expected to use mice and a few large animals, say ten sheep, in shelters. Penney commented on the proposals:

> I have to admit that the suggestion rather frightens me, because I know from experience what tremendous complications arise at trials when animals are included, especially large animals like cows and sheep. The building of shelters and the introduction of test animals is another matter of great complexity . . . very difficult to get useful results.

Plans for the experiments were discussed in May 1955 by the Research Councils and Aldermaston, and then by a biology subcommittee of Buffalex chaired by Dr J F Loutit of the MRC. It was agreed that the ingestion experiments could not be simulated by sprinkling radioactive material on grass, and that the grass must be exposed to real contamination downwind of the explosion. As the direction of the fallout could not be determined until a few hours before firing, it would not be practicable to sow a sufficiently large sector of pastureland; about 100 trays of grasses, 18 inches square and 9 inches deep, would have to be strategically placed shortly before firing (see Photograph 13). This would limit the number of sheep that could be grazed, but six would be the minimum. They would not be taken into the area of the explosion or exposed to an injurious level of external radiation.

The blast experiments were to be done for Dr (now Lord) Zuckerman who was investigating for the War Office the effect of hydrostatic pressure in a blast wave on living creatures. Much of his programme was carried out in the laboratory, using small animals and a simulated blast wave in a shock tube; to extrapolate with confidence from small animals to man, he needed experiments with intermediate-sized animals, such as goats. The experiments would be concerned only with the blast wave, and not with radiation or heat or with secondary effects of blast, and the caged animals were to be placed in hollow pits or shelters to reduce secondary or thermal injuries. The numbers proposed were 200 mice, 140 rabbits and 20 goats. All this would mean a few extra trials staff and some additional facilities.

These plans were approved in August 1955 for submission to British Ministers; the use of live animals was clearly a politically sensitive topic in Britain. On 29 August Eden sought Australian agreement. In a message to Menzies he said:

> We are naturally anxious to make the fullest use of the opportunity afforded by these trials to carry out experiments to cover not only matters of purely military interest but also those affecting the assessment of the effects of atomic warfare on both public health and agriculture . . . . The authorities responsible for research into medical and agricultural aspects of atomic explosions are pressing for the inclusion in the trials of a number of experiments which involve the use of live animals. This is always a contentious subject and we have therefore . . . reduced the programme to what we regard as a minimum . . . . It covers experiments for which an actual weapon explosion alone can give the necessary conditions . . . . I should be grateful for your sympathetic consideration . . . .
>
> There is another associated matter. We are anxious to study the effects of distant fallout from atomic explosions on the bone tissue of animals. A conventional way of doing this would be to arrange for the collection of bone samples from sheep or rabbits from a number of widely separated places in Australia. This could, I believe, readily be done by your agricultural services and I should be grateful for your agreement in principle so that our experts may make an approach to yours.

With this message went a description of the proposed experiments. Menzies agreed but, as the use of live animals could arouse considerable public interest, he wanted Australian scientists to be given full information about the experiments so that the Australian government could deal effectively with any critical comments. Eden thanked Menzies warmly. Indeed, without the active participation of Australian scientists at Maralinga and in the universities of Sydney and Adelaide, the experiments would have been quite impracticable. The following month Dr Scott Russell, of the ARC and the Department of Agriculture, Oxford University, went to Australia to see Professor J Wood, of

Adelaide University, who was to be the Australian adviser on the programme, and his team of animal and plant experts.

Besides the animal experiments on blast effects, and the two ingestion studies, there were several other biological studies. One involved the weekly collection of sheep thyroids from three sheep stations 150–200 miles from Maralinga, to be assayed for radioactive iodine. Another was a survey of local flora and fauna after rounds 1 and 2. A third was the exposure to radiation of cereals ripe for harvest. Other activities included the collection of fission product samples and contaminated soil to be flown back to the United Kingdom for experimental use by the MRC and ARC.

The Biology Group planned two other sets of investigations not involving animals, which were important both for civil defence and the protection of troops. The first, conducted by Dr W J H (now Sir John) Butterfield, of the MRC, was into the hazards of broken glass, since it was known that flying glass from broken windows had been a serious source of injury in Japan. In one of these experiments, glass samples were place in steel fragmentation boxes at various distances up to 10 miles from ground zero. In another, glass fitted in steel window frames was mounted in four 8 ft wooden packing cases. In both experiments telephone directories fixed inside the box or packing case were used to catch the glass projectiles, and to enable calculations to be made of the depth of penetration.

The second set of investigations was to be carried out with the human dummies already mentioned. Thirty dummies, each representing a man six feet tall and weighing 12½ stone, dressed in Army uniform, were to be positioned at various distances from ground zero, some standing, some crouching and some prone (see Photograph 14). Some had accelerometers in the chest. Forty-eight other dummies were to be placed in tanks, scout cars, and various other vehicles; in groups with field guns or anti-aircraft guns; in large steel shelters; and in medium machine-gun pits. The experiment was concerned with blast rather than radiation or thermal effects; the object was to see how soldiers could best be protected, or could protect themselves, from injury by blast from an atomic weapon.

In the *Buffalo* Summary Plan of April 1956 one section was devoted to the Biology Group, which numbered 16 in all. The group leader was Dr Scott Russell, and his deputy was Dr Butterfield. There were six Australian members (from the Commonwealth Scientific and Industrial Research Organisation—CSIRO), and one Canadian scientist. The group was to be assisted by Professor H R Marston of Adelaide University, chief of the CSIRO Division of Biochemical and General Nutrition, and three of his staff. Professor P L Krohn and Dr J McGregor, of Birmingham University, were also members, and there were others from the MRC, the RAMC and Harwell.

The four shots are fired

One Tree—Round 1

The first round, One Tree, was to be a tower-mounted test of the new plutonium warhead, *Red Beard*. Though its expected yield was about 16 kilotons, it was much smaller in dimensions than the Mk I bomb, *Blue Danube* (which was already in production), and was intended for use by light bombers. Round 1 was also the main target response round, and the one to which the Australian Parliamentarians and the press were invited.

Standby was declared on 11 September, with Martin, Titterton, Butement and Dwyer, of the Australian Weapon Tests Safety Committee, all present. The party of Australian Parliamentarians, led by Beale, had left Canberra by air for Maralinga on 10 September, and it was hoped that round 1 would be fired soon after they arrived. Meteorological conditions had been favourable for two or three days before standby, but then the weather changed; firing was cancelled on 12 September, and the Parliamentarians had to return disappointed.

Conditions continued unfavourable from 13 to 18 September. A revised schedule of forecasts was then introduced, allowing for either morning or evening firing (at 0700 or 1700 hrs), and the timetable was compressed into 12 hours or less, instead of 24. Maddock had been right two years earlier! On the statistical evidence available, not more than one satisfactory occasion in a month was likely to occur; however, experience at the site showed that other opportunities occurred but remained favourable only for a few hours. The change of plan imposed a heavy load on the meteorological group, and Penney cabled home urgently for an additional meteorologist from the United Kingdom to reinforce the team; he arrived on 1 October. A Canadian scientist and another Australian were also added.

Firing on 20 September was again cancelled, but preparations for firing on 21st continued through the night. The Parliamentarians from

Canberra arrived once more, but were again disappointed. 'We have had a tough night', Penney signalled Aldermaston:

Met forecasts, originally rosy, got progressively worse, until we ended with forecast and observed winds over wide area showing less than degree variation ground to 35 000 ft pointing precisely at Oodnadatta. [See Map 3, p. 56]. With several homesteads nearer could not prejudice future of Range, and therefore cancelled without last-minute fight with Safety Committee undoubtedly ending with their veto. Showed Press and Parliamentarians non-secret apparatus, and hope we made deep impression on care which we exercise and quality of our work. Three of most important Labour leaders appeared to become friendly and sympathetic. Press had discovered reason for postponement so saw them and told them what they knew already. I believe that this abortive night may have valuable long-term effects . . . . I have done my best to win confidence of Australians and keep long-term use Maralinga . . . . Everyone here behaved magnificently and took the disappointment like men. Parliamentarians will not return for first shot, but some may come to second shot, which is much easier . . . .

Another alert was declared for 23 September but by the evening of 22nd rapid changes in low level winds caused yet another cancellation. The weather remained unsuitable until 25th, when forecasts for the morning of 26th were promising. Penney signalled:

Tried again last night and cancelled in last few minutes. Winds at cloud height were rapidly turning towards south. Firing opportunity was real but lasted six hours and we missed. Main worry Safety Committee thunderstorms Adelaide to Melbourne. This was political and not safety. Last minute telephone consultation Martin to Beale resulted in advice to postpone. I should probably have delayed one hour at last minute because of danger to Maralinga and small settlements on railway and would then have postponed.

Speaking for people at site we are going to try to catch every firing opportunity that is safe. Am asking Safety Committee to get Beale and Menzies approached to accept political disturbance due to counts in rainwater magnified by the trouble makers.

Real culprit is completely exceptional weather. Conditions vary widely every few hours and Australian meteorological grid cannot cope with fine structure.

Am studying arrangements firings but not easy. Have Olympic Games dates in mind but still believe weather will not continue bad. [The Olympic Games were to be held in Melbourne in November 1956]

Grateful advise if my No. 1 priority not to prejudice future of Maralinga is correct. Difficult for me here because I cannot fully assess strength of trouble makers raising scares by rainwater counts. We can never guarantee that activity will not be found in rain 500 or more miles away.

Penney was assured that his policy was correct; he must take note of political objections that were represented to him by official sources and which were real to the Australian government. Although fear of scaremongers should not inhibit him from pressing for agreement to fire when conditions were safe, the first priority was to reassure the Australian people and to retain the government's confidence.

Apparently the Australian journalists were sharply critical of the cancellation, alleging that Beale had prevented the firing on political grounds. What happened was that the Safety Committee had informed him that the winds would carry the clouds over Adelaide and perhaps Melbourne; possible thunderstorms there would result in high Geiger counter readings. Though not necessarily dangerous, they would cause anxiety. Beale confirmed their advice not to fire, but as we saw Penney decided against firing without waiting for the AWTSC to say no. Press signals also suggested that Maralinga was an unsuitable site for atomic weapon trials and that there was dissension among the scientists there. There must certainly have been much frustration, but it had been known from the beginning that favourable opportunities would be elusive.

Then at last, at 0600 hrs on 27 September, the forecast was good and, thanks to the new compressed timetable, round 1 was successfully detonated in the evening at 1700 hrs, in conditions that were considered completely satisfactory but short-lived, during a minor interruption in the prevailing westerly airstream. Penney described the test in a cable to Cook at Aldermaston:

> Cloud top 38 compared calculated 29 . . .. Think yield was as expected and cloud height theory is in error and unreliable. Cloud top went right into tropopause[2]. High level cloud moved just north of east at 70 knots and should pass coast line north Brisbane during morning. Low level secondary cloud 15(?) moved ENE. Aircraft tracked both clouds during the night. Magnificent work. Congratulate Air Ministry. Panic here all night because winds began to stack at all local stations. Ground surveys at nearest inhabited places show nothing more than total dose infinity one tenth roentgen or one-fifth level A. All safety worries gone. Think we have excellent complete records. Will [send] second report late tonight. Everyone cheerful.

After the explosion the main cloud, and a secondary cloud that formed between 16 500 and 23 000 ft, moved almost due east. Its height was some 12 000 ft in excess of the estimation, and this failure in their calculations worried the theoretical predictions group. The upper-level winds were from 254°, with little angular windshear, but changes in the lower-level winds caused the slow-settling fine material in the atmosphere to diffuse to the north and west. The nearest inhabited area in the fallout path was at Coober Pedy, 197 miles from ground zero. The main cloud crossed the east coast about 18 hours after firing, and the secondary cloud some 12 to 18 hours later. No rain was observed in the area over which the main cloud moved, but on the afternoon of 29 September rain brought down some radioactive material in the Brisbane–Lismore area. Fallout from Round 1 is discussed on pp. 161–169, together with that from the other *Buffalo* shots.

When the scientists had had a few days to assess round 1, Penney sent a further report to Aldermaston:

> Lovely blast records. Blast yield 17 kilotons . . .. Complicated fallout pattern but most complete survey we have ever had . . .. Target response and medical side had high percentage excellent results . . .. Still puzzled by height of cloud . . . Hope to shoot ground burst this Thursday but rain threatens. We shall be ready . . . .

The story of the first round at *Buffalo* exemplifies the problems the scientists had to face. The problems for the biology group of having repeatedly to deploy and then remove their animals, grass trays and so on, were especially trying, both to scientists and animals. It also shows how determined Penney and the AWTSC were to wait for the right conditions, even if the Australian Parliamentarians had to make two abortive flights to Maralinga. From their point of view, the repeated cancellations must have been reassuring even if frustrating.

Marcoo—Round 2

Round 2 was a *Blue Danube* bomb, with a low yield Mark I uranium core[3]. It was to be fired on the ground to give information about cratering and ground-shock effects, on which the British scientists had no information. Nor had the Americans, and it was hoped that sharing the results with them might encourage fuller cooperation. The low yield of the test weapon meant a predicted low cloud height, and therefore if lower level winds were suitable it would be safe to fire even when a strong westerly airstream persisted at altitudes above 10 000 ft.

The Australian Parliamentarians returned once again to Maralinga, and this time there was no long wait. Round 2 was fired on the afternoon of 4 October, at 1630 hrs (local time). Of the AWTSC, Titterton, Dwyer and Stevens were present. Penney reported:

> Second shot appears to be exactly as predicted. Worried at last minute by approaching rain. Fallout 100–200 miles very slight. Shear exceeded right angle. Main cloud very dispersed. Expect very low level counts if there is rain at E coast. Best estimate yield just under 2 kilotons. Have had solid rain

for last 8 hours. Parliamentary party delighted with their visit—and very friendly.

There were good fallout data up to 30 miles, and no contamination could be found further away, though the cloud was somewhat higher than predicted, and just penetrated the region of the westerly airstream. Moving almost due east the cloud crossed the coast 25 to 30 hours after firing; a secondary cloud at about 5500 ft drifted away very slowly over the desert to the north west and was soon too diffused to be tracked by aircraft. The lower-level winds were from the south, and the high-level winds were westerly, with a large angular windshear. Fallout was thinly spread over a wide sector; deposition in inhabited areas was negligible, and the ARDU ground survey reported zero readings.

The bomb made a crater 160 ft across, perhaps 40 ft deep, with steep sides and surrounded by a lip 4 ft to 10 ft high.

After Round 2 came heavy continuous rain 'More gales', Penney signalled, 'thunder and heavy rain, see Ecclesiastes chapter 1 verse 6'. His message, decoded with the help of a Bible, read: 'The wind goeth toward the south and turneth about unto the north; it whirleth about continually and the wind returneth again according to his circuits'.

Kite—Round 3

Penney decided to change the original order of the shots, making the airdrop Round 3 instead of Round 4. It was to be a Service operational test of a *Blue Danube* bomb, and originally the expected yield had been some 40 kilotons, which would have produced little fallout from firing at an altitude of about 1200 ft. But there was a remote possibility that the fuzing system might fail and that the bomb would hit the ground before exploding. A groundburst of 40 kilotons would be quite unacceptable, and various safety devices were considered that would prevent detonation on impact. But in the end, after correspondence with the AWTSC in the person of Professor Martin, it had been decided—because of the risk, however slight, of a groundburst—not to use a standard production *Blue Danube* bomb. A low-yield version was used instead, to be dropped from a Valiant bomber and fuzed to detonate at 500 ft. The expected yield was 3 kilotons.

Titterton and Dwyer, of the AWTSC, were present for the shot. It was successfully carried out on 11 October, at 1530 hrs. Later, Penney reported back to Aldermaston:

RAF did a lovely job. Brilliant flash and fireball. Some trees set on fire and many scorched. Terrific dust cloud and stem. Impressive scar on desert, surface torn and rocks scattered in central area. Atmosphere very dry and stable with big inversion at 14 000 ft where cloud stopped as predicted. Blast and heat indicate 3 to 4 kilotons, nearer 3 . . .. We shall be ready for the last shot early afternoon Thursday . . ..

There was a small amount of low-level fallout on Maralinga Village some hours later—not dangerous but a slight nuisance because it affected instruments there. Otherwise fallout from Round 3 was minimal.

Breakaway—Round 4

Martin, Butement and Dwyer were present at the site for Round 4. The device was essentially a variant of the *Red Beard* warhead with a small quantity of the light elements inserted to supplement data obtained from *Mosaic*. The device was to be exploded on a 100 ft tower. A somewhat larger yield that from Round 1 was thought to be possible, so this shot, Penney said, would need excellent weather. If the weaponeers were unlucky, there might be a wait of two weeks, but he thought this most unlikely. Two favourable firing occasions were just missed on 18 October, because rain had flooded the instrumentation sites. Standby was then declared, but on 19 October the meteorologists predicted a light northerly component in low-level winds; this might cause contamination of Maralinga Village. Conditions were good on 21st but it was a Sunday, and Sunday firing was not permissible. Shortly after midnight—on 22nd—the round was successfully fired, with an estimated yield of rather less than 16 kilotons. 'Beautiful clear night with full moon until 10 minutes before shot, then suddenly thick cloud 2000 (ft) above ground', Penney cabled. 'Rather spoilt night vision test and ruined cloud photography . . .. Safety aspects extremely satisfactory . . .'.

The cloud rose some 35 000 ft and reached the coast just south of Darwin within 24 hours; no rain fell in the areas over which the cloud passed. There was no secondary cloud. Because of extensive windshear, the radioactive material became widely diffused and was deposited very thinly over an arc from Darwin to Newcastle. The highest reading by the ARDU ground survey was obtained at Ingomar, 190 miles from ground zero.

Reporting on *Buffalo*

Operation *Buffalo* was completed in an overall time of 26 days in spite of persistently bad weather. The long period of planning had paid dividends, and so had experience gained in previous trials. The AWTSC reported to the Australian Prime Minister that stringent safety conditions had been imposed for all firings; detonation had only occurred when Safety Committee members present and their British colleagues had arrived at the considered opinion that no dangerous effects would arise. Subsequent analysis of the data, they said, showed that the safety measures were completely successful; there had been no risk to any human beings, livestock or property at any time during the series.

The British scientists drew some important general lessons from *Buffalo*, especially about meteorology and about public relations.

Meteorology

Meteorology, as always, was a major preoccupation. For this first Maralinga trial, past meteorological data that would have made it possible to estimate the frequency of good firing conditions were almost nonexistent. The desired conditions that had been originally defined were found to occur only once a month or less; there were only two such periods during the whole operation—once just before Round 1 and once just before Round 4—and neither could be used. The wind structure at Maralinga turned out to be so complex, and so difficult to forecast in detail, that little confidence could be placed in the predicted fallout pattern. The most important consideration was that the fallout should be along a safe line; provided the fallout direction was acceptable, the contamination would remain within permissible distances in most wind conditions. The extra meteorological facilities in use for *Buffalo*—including the new station at Giles (the mobile station between Maralinga and Broome) and improved communications with the Central Weather Bureau in Melbourne—had been invaluable, but still better meteorological provision was required; meteorologists never had enough information, Penney thought. At Maralinga, firings had to be carried out in essentially transient conditions markedly different from those expected, and, to catch these fleeting opportunities, procedures at future trials would have to be so streamlined that all groups would require only 9 to 12 hours' notice and could maintain a state of readiness for a further 12 to 18 hours. Experience at *Buffalo* showed the need for still more detailed meteorological information, especially better upper air observations, for predicting suitable weather conditions and rain and for tracking radioactive clouds. Penney commented:

> By a combination of good judgment and good luck, the offsite fallout from Buffalo was minute. Every university, and numerous cranks, were waiting with Geiger counters to detect radioactivity. They got either zero results or such minute traces that many of them were convinced that the margin of safety was even greater than we claimed. Sooner or later, however, there is going to be rainfall with 20000 cpm and then the political scare will start again. This amount of radioactivity is quite safe but a carefully reasoned case will have to be presented.

Public relations

The attention paid to public relations between *Mosaic* and *Buffalo*, and the campaign of public information already described, undoubtedly had the desired effect. The existence of the AWSTC, the publication of its reports, the increased Australian participation and the network of monitoring stations all promoted confidence. Above all, nothing had gone wrong. *Buffalo* had been an ambitious and complex operation, and all parts had been carried out successfully.

Safety

Safety of test personnel

Of the 1250 test personnel for whom there are radiation exposure data, 24 received more than 3r (19 of them in the Services, none of them Australians). In three cases, 5r was exceeded, but there were none over 10r for the whole operation.

Fallout

Aerial and ground surveys were, as previously, carried out after each round. From the two tower bursts—Rounds 1 and 4—fallout was detectable at about 200 miles downwind; after the ground burst (Round 2), at about 60 miles. (Fallout from a groundburst is unlike that from a tower burst because a large proportion of the radioactivity is left behind when the cloud rises.) From the airdrop (over *Kite*—Round 3) the fallout was purely local and very small in quantity.

Adelaide University, which ran a regular monitoring programme to measure the radon and thoron content of air due to emanations from rocks and soil, found a marked increase in radioactivity for 12–14 October. It fell away rapidly and would not have been shown by rainwater monitoring as these were rainless days. H R Marston, the head of the University laboratory concerned, concluded that after the *Kite* shot the plume had passed close to Adelaide and had contaminated the city and surrounding countryside. (See Chapter 9 for a further account of Marston's report.)

The AWTSC report makes clear that the plume did not pass within 160 miles of Adelaide. The primary cloud moved east and crossed the coast in the Newcastle area. However a slight temperature inversion just below 6000 ft trapped a small quantity of radioactive material, and the veering of light low-level winds after the explosion caused a southerly diffusion of slowly settling material of low activity, which was detected in South Australia, Victoria and New South Wales between 12 and 16 October.

As in the case of *Mosaic*, fallout was measured at fixed monitoring stations all over Australia, which were in operation from 27 September to 5 November. Water and sludge samples were also taken from sixteen reservoirs and rainwater was collected at thirteen meteorological stations. Detectable rises in radioactivity were found in samples from these reservoirs, but were too small to have any health significance for human beings or livestock. Of the rainwater samples, most of the activities measured were very small; the highest were at Oodnadatta and Brisbane. Even if the water had been collected as run-off water from roofs and used for drinking, the AWTSC calculated that the maximum dose to the whole body would have been 0.2 r, which would have been of no consequence, but in a normal household water-tank a large dilution factor would have reduced the dose correspondingly[4].

As after *Mosaic*, readings from the monitoring stations were again used by the AWTSC to calculate the maximum integrated gamma doses. From Round 1, eleven out of 86 stations gave results of 1 millirem or above. Only four were 3 millirems or above; the highest was 22 millirems, at Lismore where rain had occurred shortly after the shot. From Rounds 2 and 3, there were no doses above 1 millirem; most were zero. Round 4 gave many zero results, but 8 were 5 millirems or over; the highest was at Birdsville, Queensland (11 millirems).

The combined *Buffalo* results showed that radiation doses in six of the main population centres—Canberra, Adelaide, Melbourne, Perth,

Darwin and Sydney—were 1 millirem or less; the figure for Brisbane was 2 millirems. Elsewhere the highest figures were 24 millirems at Lismore, 15 at Marree and 12 at Birdsville. The places which had received most fallout from *Mosaic*, such as Port Hedland, were untouched by *Buffalo*.

The AWTSC doses for *Buffalo*, as for *Mosaic* (see p. 136), were recalculated by the Australian Ionising Radiations Advisory Council (AIRAC)[5] and comparative figures are shown in Table 8.1 for the three highest instances.

Table 8.1

Location	AWTSC (millirems)	AIRAC (millirems)
Lismore	24	3.5
Marree	15	2.7
Birdsville	12	1.5

The AWTSC figures are for doses integrated over 50 years, with no allowance for weathering or shelter. The AIRAC figures (as explained on p. 135) are integrated over 6 months; they do allow for weathering and shelter, and to calculate the corresponding dose for a person without clothing or shelter, the figures have to be multiplied by 2.5.

The figures may be compared with ICRP limits, and with the figures for annual exposure given at the end of Chapter 7. *Buffalo* exposures are far below the A level—or 'zero risk' level of 3r (3000 millirems) recommended by the AWTSC and approved by the Australian government.

The network of monitoring stations was planned to provide an extensive coverage of the Australian mainland, but it would be assumed that some higher doses might have occurred elsewhere or as a result of 'hot spots'. Wise and Moroney[6], in their 1985 study already mentioned, estimated higher external radiation doses from *Buffalo* for two other places, Coober Pedy and Ingomar, where fallout contours for Rounds 1 and 4 overlapped (as they were not supposed to do), as shown in Table 8.2. Their figures for total population doses are much higher than the highest AIRAC and AWTSC figures, largely because of a much greater contribution calculated for internal radiation. It should be remembered that Wise and Moroney state that their figures may be 10 times too high, or too low by a factor of 2. Their assessment of the total dose to

Table 8.2

| | Effective dose equivalent (millirems) | |
	External dose	Total
Round 1		
Coober Pedy	20–68	120–400
Ingomar	17–30	100–180
Round 4		
Coober Pedy	4.5	2.6
Ingomar	12	72

the whole Australian population (over all time) from fallout from the four *Buffalo* shots is 250 man-sieverts (25 000 man-rems), or about one-third of that from all twelve nuclear explosions from 1952 to 1957. The possible public health impact is discussed in Chapter 12.

Bombs on a shoe-string

Previous trials had been planned with little time for preparation and with barely adequate resources. *Buffalo*, the biggest and most elaborate, had the advantage of a longer planning period—though none too long for the work involved—and had the largest scientific staff. It was still a rush, because of the delays at the Range and the uncertainties about its completion (or rather its partial completion, as a good deal of work was still left to be done after *Buffalo*). Resources, both of men and material, were barely sufficient. The most serious handicap, one senior member of the trials staff wrote later, was lack of adequate transport and mechanical handling plant. The planners had had to cut requirements below the essential minimum to keep down high transport costs; and insufficient allowance was made for servicing or contingencies, or for additions to the scientific programme.

The Australians had made an invaluable contribution, besides providing the Range. The Range Commandant and the Services task force had done 'a magnificent job'—Penney's words—'in the forward area and in providing domestic support'. In all, well over 400 Australians, about 100 of them civilians, took part in *Buffalo*—in the task force, in the indoctrinee force, in the target response programme, as meteorologists, as security officers, as members of the health physics and biological teams, in the Australian radiation detection unit (ARDU), and as observers in a seismic survey designed to investigate the ground shock effects of atomic explosions.

Rumours that Maralinga was unsuitable as a permanent testing ground for atomic weapons were dismissed; nothing better, it was said, could be found anywhere in the British Commonwealth. In all the circumstances this was no doubt true, but from a meteorological point of view Maralinga—like Monte Bello—had been far from ideal, and had never looked very promising.

Notes and references

1 Native Patrol Officer Report, August 1956, in J L Symonds: *A History of British Atomic Tests in Australia* (p. 393).
2 Tropopause—the plane of discontinuity between the troposphere (the lowest layer of the atmosphere) and the stratosphere. The thickness of the troposphere varies from 20 000 ft at the Poles to 60 000 ft at the Equator.
3 The yield of a test warhead or device bore no necessary relation to that of a production bomb, since the yield of a given weapon could be varied at will.
4 *Australian Journal of Science*, October 1958 (Butement, Dwyer, Martin, Stevens and Titterton).
5 AIRAC 9.
6 Keith N Wise and John R Moroney: *Public health impact of fallout from British nuclear tests in Australia 1952-1957* (July 1985).

9 *Antler*—1957

Two busy years

The years 1956 and 1957 were climacteric in the British nuclear weapons programme. The technology of nuclear explosives by 1956 was being rapidly developed against a political backdrop that nuclear weapons tests might soon be banned by international agreement. Aldermaston, encouraged by Ministers, the Foreign Office and the military, sought to consolidate into established technology the maximum amount of knowledge and hardware. In the situation, the quickest and cheapest was not necessarily what would have been the best if the development time had been longer.

The test programme had to be flexible. From month to month, the priority of terms in the programme changed. In total, many more shots were considered and partially planned than could possibly be managed. The results of one shot often caused an immediate modification or even the cancellation of a shot that was in the course of preparation.

Mosaic and *Buffalo* took place in 1956 but plans were already going forward in early 1956 for a series of high-yield tests, to be held at various times in 1957 and collectively called *Grapple*. A completely new test-range with different characteristics was to be established on two remote islands in the Pacific, Christmas Island and Malden Island. In spite of all this activity, Aldermaston scientists decided it might be possible also to manage another series of tests in 1957 at Maralinga. The precise make-up of this series was changed several times and several code names were used, but in the event the series was held in September/October 1957 with the code name *Antler*.

The pressure of work on Aldermaston's staff was severe. In January 1956 there were only about 225 scientists (some 700 scientific and technical staff altogether) of whom 100 or more were abroad at any one time for long periods, and many others were engaged at Aldermaston in trial planning, preparation of trial weapons and devices, and support for the teams overseas. (There had been about 150 scientists—and fewer than 400 scientific and technical staff—soon after *Totem* in 1953.) Moreover, trials were only part of Aldermaston's work; other tasks ranged from theoretical research to production of parts of the Service weapons for the defence stockpile. It is commendable that the trials staff managed to write up the trials data as comprehensively and in such detail as they did; it is hardly surprising that there appear to be some gaps in the reports literature.

Shifting plans

The code name *Sapphire* was given in early 1956 to a second series of tests that the Aldermaston scientists contemplated holding at Maralinga in 1957, if possible. It was clearly understood that the details of the shots could not be defined at that time, but provisions had to be made in forward plans.

By July 1956, Cook had drawn up a list of objectives to be covered by atomic tests. Some would have to wait and it would be some time before it was clear what shots would be ready by September 1957. Soon afterwards, he and Penney discussed the two main *Sapphire* objectives. The first, said Penney, was to investigate lightweight weapons of low yield using plutonium; the second, to study new weapon principles opening the way to cheaper, lightweight high-yield warheads for a ballistic missile. At this time the world's first long-range rocket able to deliver a nuclear warhead had not yet been made, but it was known that the USSR had been engaged since 1953 in a major effort to develop such a rocket; their first test ICBM—intercontinental ballistic missile—was launched in August 1957. The Americans had six crash programmes during the fifties, and their first test ICBM was launched in December 1958[1].

The urgency of the *Sapphire* tests was less to meet production dates for weapons than to beat the ban on tests, which might be stopped internationally—or in Australia for local reasons—before the weapon scientists had gathered essential information. If major trials were to be mounted at Maralinga in the latter part of 1957, the Australian government would have to be approached soon, even though it was too early to put forward firm proposals. In September 1956 advance information about the trials for which agreement might later be sought was despatched to the Australian government. This information had to cover all the possibilities. There might be up to five tower tests; the scientific party would be smaller than for *Buffalo*; there would be no target response programme. The AWTSC must in due course be satisfied on the safety aspects. The Range staff required would be a basic 228, increasing to 354 during the preparatory phase, and 400 during the operational phase; if it was difficult for the Australian government to provide the whole force, the British government would have to consider supplementing whatever numbers Australia could provide.

A further matter needing attention was the work left unfinished by the Kwinana Construction Group when the labour force vacated the Range to allow Operation *Buffalo* to proceed. This work was readily taken on by the Australian Department of Works.

In January 1957, Tomblin produced an outline plan for *Sapphire*— renamed *Volcano* by someone with no public relations sense; it was later changed at the request of an Australian official and became *Antler*. The plan included up to five shots; two were to be on 300 ft towers and three suspended from balloons. The balloon project, begun in late October 1956, was novel, though it was known that the Americans had used balloons at the Nevada Test Site. The advantage was that the test weapon could be suspended very high in the air, so that the explosion would not suck up contaminated material from the ground (including tons of metal from the tower itself) and the amount of fallout would be greatly reduced; at such altitudes the fine radioactive particles would return to earth very slowly, allowing more time for dispersal and radioactive decay. Britain had considerable experience of balloon operations, though not of course for this use, but if the technique could not be developed successfully, all the detonations would have to be on towers and the programme would have to be recast.

The plan was to lift two of the test weapons by a double or triple balloon system using 110 000 cubic ft balloons, and the third by a double or triple system using smaller balloons (70 000 cubic ft). By the end of the 1956 contracts had already been placed for the development and production of balloons and handling gear and for hydrogen sufficient for three shots. A final decision on the use of balloons would have to be made by the end of January 1957.

The estimated total of scientific staff was 200, with the addition, it was hoped, of some Canadian scientists to help with radiological surveys and health physics. The Services would again be asked to help, especially with health physics and control. The air support required would be similar to that for *Buffalo*, but with the balloon operating personnel and without the airdrop. Meteorology would be an Australian responsibility, as at *Buffalo*, but four or five United Kingdom staff might be needed as reinforcements. No target response programme was envisaged but the plan was changed later to provide for a modest programme; no Indoctrinee Force was included. The preparatory phase of the operation would be from 1 March to mid-August, and the operational phase from mid-August to 28 days after the last firing. Once again the timetable would be very tight. It would require all stores to be packed and shipped at the beginning of April; all stores to be delivered and all site engineering work to be finished by 1 August; all scientific staff to be on the Range by the end of August. The first possible firing day would be at the end of September and the operation should be completed by mid-November.

The Defence and Service Ministers strongly agreed that *Antler* was essential and urgent, and the Foreign Secretary concurred. The primary aims, the Prime Minister was told, were to develop nuclear warheads, small in physical size and yield, for defensive use in surface-to-air guided weapons; to develop more efficient (Service) versions of the tactical aircraft bomb, *Red Beard*; and to increase scientific knowledge in order to produce smaller fission bombs as triggers for megaton weapons. An approach to the Australian government, with detailed proposals, was becoming urgent, if the trials were to be in 1957. Recent United States disarmament proposals made it particularly important to go ahead with essential nuclear testing without delay. The Foreign Secretary added that, apart from these proposals, growing public opposition to tests might make it more difficult to carry out tests in 1958; so too might future reports of the recently set up United Nations Scientific Committee on Effects of Atomic Radiation (UNSCEAR). However *Buffalo* had not aroused much foreign comment in 1956, and tests at Maralinga in 1957 might attract little attention, especially as they would be overshadowed by the *Grapple* tests in the Pacific. The Prime Minister agreed that plans should proceed as rapidly and quietly as possible, even though they might be affected by whatever emerged from the current discussions on disarmament.

The proposed plan was forwarded to the Australian government on 12 February 1957. They accepted it but soon their decision seemed likely to be reconsidered. Penney wrote giving further details to Martin, as chairman of the AWTSC, but the AWTSC felt unable to recommend final approval by the Australian government without further investigation. The Committee's doubts, Martin wrote to Penney, arose from the magnitude of some of the proposed yields and from lack of knowledge about the use of balloons. He, Martin, had advised the

Minister for Supply that Titterton, shortly to become chairman of a reconstituted AWTSC, should visit the United Kingdom immediately to discuss *Antler* plans. If possible he should return via Nevada to get the general feel of United States balloon experiments. Butement would be visiting England at the same time.

Penney, previously informed of this suggestion, had already approached Admiral Strauss, chairman of the United States Atomic Energy Commission, to explain the position and to ask if Titterton might visit the Nevada Test Site. Two of the Aldermaston staff, Tomblin and Saxby, with an RAF balloon unit officer and an RAE official, had already been invited there to see the NTS balloon work which differed considerably from the techniques the British were developing. Penney wrote to Strauss[2]:

> There is, of course, an agreement between the Australian and British governments about tests at Maralinga. The Prime Minister of Australia has a Safety Committee and . . . one member is Professor Titterton who you will recall made distinguished contributions at Los Alamos in the early days. The Australian government have asked me if I would be willing to request that Professor Titterton be allowed to visit Los Alamos and possibly Nevada to see how the fallout problems at the Nevada site are handled. He would be particularly interested in the fallout computer . . . and also any work you have done on balloons. There is understandable anxiety in Australia about the dangers of fallout from atomic tests but the successful operation of Operation *Buffalo* last year did a great deal to allay fears. However the continuous agitation against tests will undoubtedly regenerate some public nervousness about fallout in Australia. The Australian government wishes to prepare accurate and convincing publicity to counteract this nervousness, and it would be a valuable point for them if they could claim that a member of the Prime Minister's Safety Committee had visited Nevada. Your excellent publicity showing how you have run so many tests in Nevada without mishap or hazards has had a great effect in Australia.

This useful visit duly took place.

Antler

In mid-April 1957 Penney put forward a programme for *Antler* that was however liable to be modified by the results of the first *Grapple* series of three rounds in May/June. This *Antler* programme, forwarded to Canberra on 18 April, consisted of a maximum of six rounds—a 20-kiloton round and a 3-kiloton round on 100ft towers; a 30-kiloton round on a

300 ft tower; and one round of 30 kilotons and two of 80 kilotons as free air bursts, each suspended from a balloon assembly. Safety and fallout precautions, he said, would be based on the maximum expected yields, and the fallout on the Range and at distances up to 200–300 miles would in no case exceed the *Buffalo* tower shots. The balloon shots would give very high clouds and the debris would be in very fine particles. The main meteorological conditions required would be fast upper winds, with no expectation of rain below the cloud tracks; the cloud would then quickly clear the mainland, and the fallout on Eastern Australia would be similar to that of *Buffalo*. Trials with balloons had been very successful. All the safety precautions would be discussed with the AWTSC.

The *Antler* plan

By mid-June, the detailed *Antler* plan had been compiled by the Aldermaston Trials Planning Branch. It provided for five rounds, two free-air bursts on balloon systems, two on 100 ft towers and one on a 300 ft tower. There would be a small target response programme after all; Penney was sceptical about target response but the Service departments in particular had insisted that no opportunity should be missed and that these expensive experiments must be utilized to the full.

The Trial Director was to be the very experienced C A Adams, with Dr J A T Dawson GM as his deputy and J T Tomblin as Trial Superintendent. The Services Commander was Air Commodore W P Sutcliffe, and the RAF task group was commanded by Group Captain H A S Disney. There would be 22 scientific groups, totalling 170 men, and a target response team of 25. There would also be 28 Australians forming the Australian Radiation Detection Unit (ARDU), 11 Australians in the meteorological unit, and 17 Canadians. The whole scientific and technical staff would be about 320. The Australian Range Commandant's staff of 450 would support the entire operation.

The biggest single contribution, as at *Buffalo*, was to be made by the RAF. The RAF air task force, with 31 aircraft and about 700 men, would cover all the flying activities that are now familiar—transport services, meteorological flights, photography, safety and security searches, cloud sampling, cloud tracking, and so on—as well as aircraft decontamination, and would also provide the 70-strong balloon unit. Twenty-five RAF Regiment personnel would be attached to various groups, in particular to the health physics group. The task force's main base was to be at RAAF Edinburgh Field, 15 miles from Adelaide, whereas most of the operational flying would be from Maralinga. The Shackletons were to be based 1400 miles west, at RAAF Pearce, near Perth. This situation, Group Captain Disney commented, was like having a headquarters in London, a forward airfield near Berlin, and meteorological aircraft east of Leningrad. The distances involved—the great distances within Australia as well as the distance from the United Kingdom—are easily forgotten.

A new timescale for the standby and firing phases, even more streamlined than that developed for *Buffalo*, was to be used, in order to take immediate opportunity of transient weather conditions. All the activities that had to be carried out immediately before firing were to be completed in six (for tower rounds) or eight (for balloon rounds) hours. Members of each group had to know precisely how their activities must be timed to fit into the overall pattern so that Control could make appropriate arrangements for moving and accounting for each man present in the Maralinga area.

An idealized programme was drawn up, with the scientific teams arriving on site on 15 August. The earliest possible firing dates for the five rounds would then be 12, 19 and 26 September, 3 and 10 October. The plan for weekly firing was based on the 7-day weather cycle which had been observed during *Buffalo*. Between these firing dates, scientific and operational rehearsals had to be fitted in, but all was, of course, dependent on weather conditions. Meanwhile minor trials would be going on in another part of the Range (see Chapter 10).

The estimated yields of the five proposed rounds were now in the range 5 to 30 kilotons for the tower explosions, but the two balloon rounds were to be 25–30 kilotons and 50 kilotons.

The special advantages of the balloons were not confined to reducing fallout. Their use had three operational advantages. It did away with the civil engineering effort required for erecting towers; weapons of larger yield could be detonated without infringing the safety criteria; and the absence of contamination at ground zero meant that, instead of using a new firing site for each round as hitherto, a permanent firing site could be set up, with a permanent cable system for instrumentation. The disadvantage was that the weapon could not be positioned so precisely. There were other problems, as will be seen later.

The balloons to be used were developed from the designs of those used during World War II to discourage low-level air attacks, and were procured in cooperation with industry and the RAE establishment at

Cardington, former home of the great airships of the twenties and thirties. If successful the technique was likely to be used in future trials, as indeed it was for the first and fourth shots in the *Grapple* Z series at Christmas Island in August/September 1958.

The *Antler* programme was again modified in July 1957 as a result of information obtained from *Grapple*, and the Australian government was informed that it would be possible to reduce the number of rounds and the maximum yield. Instead of five or six shots, there would only be three shots, two on 100 ft towers and one on a balloon assembly; the maximum yield of the last would be 25–30 kilotons and of the tower rounds less. Penney would send full particulars to the Safety Committee.

This reduction must have been a great relief to the Australian authorities. For the British it meant welcome economies in a programme whose costs were anxiously counted—by the leading scientists as well as by the Treasury—and a simplification of the timetable; six shots, with all the rehearsals between, might have proved difficult or impossible to squeeze into the time available if weather conditions turned out as unfavourable as they had been in 1956.

As a result of the tests before *Antler*, the British scientists had acquired the knowledge to produce three types of weapon:

(1) a fairly efficient tactical bomb of nominal yield, which could be carried in a Canberra as well as a V-bomber;
(2) an extremely expensive high-yield warhead for a ballistic missile; and
(3) a medium-to-large-yield free-falling bomb, or a warhead for a propelled bomb, which was heavy and which could only be carried in a V-bomber.

They did not as yet have the knowledge necessary to produce small kiloton warheads for defensive missiles or small tactical weapons, to make (comparatively) inexpensive megaton weapons, and to maximize a weapons stockpile from a given cost in nuclear materials.

Antler would lead to significant progress. It would become possible to produce a much cheaper and operationally safer tactical bomb; preliminary ideas on the design of small tactical and defensive weapons would have been tested; and the way to major design changes in thermonuclear bombs might be opened. But if no more tests were possible after 1957, the British would still be unable to make efficient use of nuclear materials, in comparison with either the Russians or the Americans, who could produce larger stockpiles of weapons from similar quantities of nuclear materials. There was a pressing need to continue kiloton and megaton tests after 1957 for the reasons just explained. Moreover the Services, following the lessons of military history, began to enquire if nuclear weapons could be made more resistant to attack in combat situations, thereby raising a new range of problems in component development and design.

Safety arrangements

Reorganization in Australia

Rules for the safety of test personnel were, as before, governed by the Maralinga Radiological Safety Regulations (see p. 105). For the Australian population, radiation safety standards were to be the responsibility of a new body, the National Radiation Advisory Committee (NRAC), set up as the result of an Australian reorganization after *Buffalo*.

Martin had proposed in December 1956 that the AWTSC should be reconstituted as a three-man committee—Titterton as chairman, L J Dwyer, head of the Commonwealth Meteorological Bureau, and D J Stevens, head of the Commonwealth X-ray and Radium Laboratory (CXRL)—to be responsible for all public safety aspects of the atomic weapon tests. He suggested that another committee should be set up with more general functions, as the national authority on all radiological hazards. It should advise the Government, through the Prime Minister, and it should include medical scientists, nuclear physicists and experts in human, animal and plant biology. Its scope would be similar to that of the Medical Research Council's Committee on Hazards to Man of Nuclear and Allied Radiations—the Himsworth Committee—in the United Kingdom (see p. 80), but unlike the latter it was to be a permanent body.

Martin's recommendations, with suggested names, were submitted to the Ministers for Supply and Defence, and the formation of NRAC was agreed in May 1957, under the chairmanship of Sir Macfarlane Burnet, a medical scientist of the greatest eminence. This was a wise, indeed overdue change; the NRAC not only met wider needs outside the scope of the AWTSC but it was also more fully representative in having biological scientists in its membership.

The new AWTSC forwarded a report to the NRAC on 30 July 1957 on safety levels for radioactivity in fallout from atomic weapon trials, and it was considered at an NRAC meeting on 26 August. In this report, the AWTSC explained the basis of the standards it had approved for the general population. The external gamma dose recommended by ICRP was 0.3 r a week for a working life-time, and for beta radiation 1.5 rep a week. ICRP considered a level permissible if 10 times the weekly dose was not exceeded in a period of 10 weeks; thus for a single trial period—approximately 13 weeks—the external dose should not exceed 3 r (gamma) and 15 rep (beta). Though ICRP recommendations already embodied large safety factors, the AWTSC had decided to recommend a further safety factor, setting the external radiation limit for the public at 0.5 r (gamma) and 2.5 rep (beta). For internal radiation, the AWTSC recommended as a limit an integrated dose of 0.5 rep from all sources. AWTSC concluded by noting that the highest integrated dose so far recorded in any inhabited area was a factor of 10 below these limits, and the doses generally recorded were many orders of magnitude lower[3].

Safety limits for *Antler*

For Round 1 of *Antler*, firing criteria were based not on 0.5 r but on the requirement that predicted fallout contours were such that half level A (equivalent to an exposure of 1.5 r gamma and 7.5 rep beta) would not be exceeded in any populated spot. Level A, it may be remembered, was defined in the Aldermaston report 0–41/55 as that level of surface radioactivity that would not give rise to any observable effect on people living under 'civilized' conditions—i.e., wearing footwear and some clothing (see p. 148).

For Rounds 2 and 3 the criteria were changed, following the NRAC's acceptance of the AWTSC report. The predicted fallout contours should have been based on a surface radioactivity equivalent to an external gamma exposure of 500 milliroentgens (0.5 r) and 2.5 rep of beta. This would have been a more restrictive limit than that for Round 1. However by some failure of communication, the limit actually applied was simply 0.5 r (gamma). This was a reduction compared with 1.5 r, but because of the varying beta component, exposure of surface tissues could be up to 40 times that from the gamma; as the 0.5 r limit, with no corresponding beta limit, was actually a slight relaxation, though not one intended by the AWTSC.

These changing limits are complicated and are difficult to compare, as they are defined in so many ways—in terms of radiation dose; as units of activity per square metre; as levels A, B, zero risk, slight risk, and so on. The important point is the limit on the radiation exposure of members of the public that is implied. This had been reduced from 12.5 r (gamma) and 25 rep (beta) at *Mosaic*, to 3 r and 15 rep at *Buffalo*, and then to 1.5 r and 7.5 rep for *Antler* (Round 1). These are limits and do not imply anything about actual activity levels or actual exposures.

The efforts made to ensure that no Aboriginals strayed into potential hazard areas before or during *Antler* appear to have been more thorough and systematic than for previous trials. The air task group reported as follows:

> The Aboriginal tribes have complete freedom in South Australia but tend to stay within their own reserves where there are mission posts from which they obtain medical services etc. The Native Affairs Officers exert a great influence over the tribes by whom they appear to be highly regarded, so there is no great difficulty in preventing a large-scale influx into the Range area. Nevertheless there is always the possibility that individuals or isolated groups of Aboriginals or other people might enter the area by accident or with malicious intent. Searches of the Range area were therefore flown by day and night [by Varsity aircraft] during the last 48 hours before each shot. Detailed briefing for all searches was prepared in collaboration with the Range security staff, a member of which normally flew on each search.

The Varsity crews flew low searching for Aboriginal camp fires but none were found and there were no incidents.

Meteorology

The meteorological provisions made for *Buffalo* were enhanced for *Antler*. Besides the meteorological stations at Maralinga itself and at Giles, a mobile unit operated from Giles. The Maralinga meteorological office received surface three-hourly synoptic charts from the Commonwealth Bureau at Melbourne, as well as daily prognostic and upper air charts and extended period forecasts. Perth provided daily prognostic statements, giving valuable information about weather approaching from the west. Precipitation forecasts came in from all over Australia. The Southern Ocean analysis was received every 24 hours. Daily wind observations, by radiosonde or radar, were sent in from 18 stations; a new radar station was set up at Woomera and two new radar sets were installed by the British authorities at Albany and Carnavon. Additional upper wind soundings were requested from at least 7 other stations after each firing, to assist with cloud tracking. RAF Shackletons based at RAAF Pearce made routine meteorological flights over the ocean south of Australia, and special sorties were flown by RAF Canberra and Varsity aircraft.

The Maralinga Village meteorological office was well equipped—though it wanted rather more space, some fluorescent strip lighting, and a wire screen so that the door could be left open in hot weather. With excellent communications—telephone, telex and Mufax—it had a wealth of information pouring in. The importance of meteorology in the trials was very fully appreciated. L J Dwyer, Director of the Commonwealth Bureau of Meteorology, was a member of the AWTSC, was present at the weapon trials and was involved in the firing decisions. There were some meteorological deficiencies at the early trials, but by the time of *Antler* everything that could possibly be done to ensure safe firing conditions was done.

Public relations and privileged observers

By May, the United Kingdom High Commissioner in Canberra, Lord Carrington, was anxious about Australian public opinion. 'I have just returned from Maralinga', he wrote on 29 May. 'There has been a good deal of comment . . . for some weeks past about nuclear tests. This has naturally been brought to a head by the explosion at Christmas Island' [actually off Malden Island, some 450 miles south of Christmas Island]. Public opinion, he thought, would find it hard to understand why atomic tests of this kind need continue after a high-yield bomb had been successfully exploded. There would be much opposition from Dr Evatt and the Labour Party—Evatt had recently challenged the government to conduct a referendum on the continuation of tests—and sensational and alarmist articles in the newspapers about radioactivity and strontium-90 were to be expected. It was difficult to see what could be done, and he had only one remedy to prescribe:

Sir William Penney has established in Australia a reputation which is quite unique . . . His appearance, his obvious sincerity and honesty, and the general impression he gives that he would much rather be digging his garden—and would be, but for the essential nature of his work—have made him a public figure of some magnitude in Australian eyes. If he can be persuaded to come out before the tests start, if only for a few days, to give one or two interviews and then hand over to his subordinates . . . a great deal of unpleasantness might well be saved.

This letter was passed on to the Minister of Defence, Duncan Sandys, but the suggestion was not adopted, partly because Menzies was confident that *Antler* would not give rise to any particular trouble but was anxious not to focus a spotlight on the trials. The policy was one of minimum publicity and a low profile.

The British government was considering issuing a statement about *Antler*, when it was overtaken by events early in June. Reports appeared in the Australian press that because of the Australian public opinion all the atomic testing facilities might be moved to Christmas Island. Beale, the Minister for Supply, denied these rumours and said that British scientists would shortly be arriving to prepare for a new series of tests at Maralinga later in the year. The explosions, he said, would be small compared with those taking place in the South Pacific and no hydrogen bomb would be tested.

The British decided that since Beale's statement had aroused no interest or comment, an announcement in the United Kingdom was unnecessary, but a draft statement was agreed with the Australians, for use if questions had to be answered, especially about the balloons. The obvious question was, what would happen if the balloon system escaped from its anchorages while carrying an atomic device? The answer was that the system included exhaustively tested safety devices that would eliminate the possibility; they would if necessary bring the balloons and the atomic weapon safely to the ground, in the highly unlikely event of a breakaway. Nevertheless as an extreme back-up measure an armed aircraft would stand by to shoot down the balloons before they could drift far.

The Australian authorities agreed with the draft announcement, except on one point. Titterton was anxious to avoid any reference to the use of aircraft to shoot down the system, even if a direct question were asked; he believed public fears would be enhanced rather than allayed by an admission that there was any possibility at all that the balloons might break loose and might then have to be shot down. If a question was asked, the possibility should be denied categorically, and if there was a leak about the armed aircraft on standby, the answer should be simply that this was a duplicate safety measure. Beale agreed with

Titterton, who produced an alternative draft that the British accepted. The statement never had to be used, no doubt to the relief of everyone concerned.

Press comments in Britain and Australia mounted during August. Penney, it was said, would be at Maralinga, but might not be director of the trials; four or five rounds would be fired, two of a type not previously tried; one of the rounds would be a 'simple triggering device for a pocket H bomb'. The *Adelaide Observer* carried a lengthy and accurate article on the use of balloons. In response to Press enquiries, Beale released part of the agreed statement about safety of balloons, but it attracted no publicity; the Prime Minister's Department apologized for not telling the British beforehand. A press announcement was released on 29 August[4]:

> The forthcoming tests of atomic weapons in the kiloton range which, with the cooperation of the Australian government, are being held at the Maralinga proving ground in South Australia, will begin in September. They will be directed by Mr C A Adams, chief of research at the Atomic Weapons Research Establishment. In agreement with the Australian government, facilities are being provided for the attendance of observers from Commonwealth and allied countries.
>
> Meteorological information to ensure safe conditions for the tests will be provided by the Australian meteorological service. Individual firings will take place only when the Safety Committee of the Australian scientists appointed by the Australian government have agreed that conditions are such as to ensure no risk to the people and stock of Australia.

With Australian agreement the British extended an unprecedentedly wide invitation to observers. NATO countries were invited to Round 3; Commonwealth countries that had defence relations with Britain—Canada, New Zealand, Pakistan, South Africa—to Round 2. As on earlier tests, six United States observers were asked as a reciprocal courtesy, and 24 Australian observers, besides 20 Australian Parliamentarians. A Press party of, say, 20 was to be accommodated. Although the Prime Minister, Harold Macmillan, thought the invitations 'an extraordinary proposal', the Defence Committee approved them. Fourteen countries (not including Australia) accepted, but Belgium, Canada, Greece, India and South Africa refused. The logistics for these observers were not easy; most of them had to be accommodated in Adelaide and flown to the Range just before the round was fired, and any postponed firings meant flights back and forth and much time spent waiting. Some of the observers found their visit well worthwhile, but some were disappointed or critical.

The balloon project

There had been mysterious indications from the United States during 1956 that ways had been found of firing test weapons so that fallout was much reduced; one way, it appeared, was to use balloons, which made it possible to detonate the weapons at a much higher altitude than if they were placed on a tower. Balloons for *Antler* were discussed in October 1956. Twelve hydrogen-filled balloons would be needed, able to lift loads of up to 9000 lb and to operate in wind gusts of up to 30 knots. RAE was to supervise procurement, while Aldermaston was to deal with development, and field trials were to be held at Cardington, Bedfordshire, in February 1957. A great deal of ancillary equipment—cargo cradles, pulleys, shackles, winches, etc—was needed. An RAF balloon unit would have to be trained for the job (which it was agreed would be carried out under the direction of the AWRE Range Facilities Section). Millions of cubic feet of gas would have to be procured from Australian industry and stored on the site.

A contract was signed for 110000 cubic foot balloons; but by July 1957 it was clear that the firm could not produce them in time, so that balloons of 70000 cubic foot capacity—modified versions of an existing type used in a project called 'Blue Joker'—had to be ordered. An attempt was made to modify the smaller balloons and uprate them to 110000 cubic feet, but they proved aerodynamically unsatisfactory.

Twelve 70000 cubic foot balloons were shipped to Maralinga, for use in firing the third round of *Antler* and for preliminary practice. But even before standby for round 1, there was trouble. The balloons when inflated were not kept in hangars, as at Cardington, but were moored in the open air. On 4 September there was a meteorological warning of lightning, and winds gusting up to 40 knots. The three inflated balloons were winched down to 100–150 ft; then an occluded front passed through the site and there was a violent increase in wind speed and turbulence. The balloon crews could hardly see the balloons through the swirling sand. One balloon burst into flames; a second, diving and turning in the wind, was too dangerous to approach, and then it, too, burst into flames. A third balloon was also destroyed. A fourth much smaller balloon was lost later; this small balloon was used for exercise purposes and was not fitted with the anti-escape devices used for the main balloons. An Inquiry was held and a report made to the Air Task Group Commander that same day.

Further bad weather losses might well occur and Adams asked

urgently for a spare balloon and rigging to be flown out from Britain. On 2 October, in good flying conditions, another balloon suffered an over-pressurization split during a practice hoist, because its vent valve failed in a closed position; this fault was corrected.

However great their advantages over towers in reducing fallout, balloons were not an easy option in adverse weather conditions, but they were used successfully for *Antler* and later at Christmas Island.

Firing the *Antler* shots

The three rounds

The three rounds to be fired were selected after various considerations had been most carefully weighed. The results of the first *Grapple* series in May and June made it possible to omit some *Antler* rounds originally planned, but since the overheads of the operation were high, it would be uneconomical to reduce the programme too drastically. Moreover, the prospect of a test ban on tests made it desirable to gain as much knowledge as possible without delay. However, fissile material was costly and Government pressure to make economies in research and development meant that a sound justification was needed for each shot. Further—apart from the cost—supplies of fissile material, as Penney warned urgently, were small and must be conserved; tests must not use up an undue proportion of the military stock. This meant that tests of a final design might have to be foregone for weapon designs that were well understood.

Three rounds were finally selected. The first round, to be fired at Tadje, was a *Pixie*, a light-weight device of small dimensions, with a plutonium core and an experimental, small-diameter implosion system. It had an expected yield of about a kiloton. The second, to be fired on a tower at Biak, was a larger plutonium device, *Indigo Hammer*, suitable either as a warhead for a surface-to-air missile or as a fission bomb to trigger a thermonuclear weapon; it was expected to yield about 6 kilotons. The third device, to be fired from a balloon assembly at Taranaki, contained a plutonium core in a highly enriched uranium shell, and was also intended as a trigger for a thermonuclear weapon; its expected yield was 25–30 kilotons, and its maximum was 50.

Standby

The first standby for Round 1 was declared on Thursday, 12 September, soon after midnight, and the complex routine of calculations, briefings and conferences began. Cloud heights were calculated, and fallout patterns predicted on the basis of the latest wind forecasts for the envisaged time of firing; they were presented at a pre-firing conference attended by the Trial Director, his Deputy, the Trial Superintendent, the members of the AWTSC, meteorological and theoretical predictions staff, the Services Commander and the Air Task Group Commander. Regular meetings were then planned for 0700 and 1900 hrs, when the meteorological outlook for the coming 24 hours would be studied; the earliest possible firing times would be, respectively, at 1400 hrs or 0700 hrs next morning.

If conditions remained promising, further meetings were arranged. At the first, more refined calculations of cloud height were presented, with predicted fallout safety contours. If the meteorological outlook was satisfactory, a second conference was held in 2 hours or so, to study recalculated cloud heights and fallout contours and to decide whether or not to declare Z hour—i.e., to begin the firing phase. If Z hour was declared, a third conference was arranged for 2 to 3 hours before the intended firing time (F hour). This conference—beginning at Maralinga Village and then moving to Forward Control at Roadside—would go on intermittently until half an hour before F hour, with updated predictions if any changing meteorological data were available, and with special attention to the forecasts of rain in regions over which the cloud would pass. So much meteorological material was flowing in, and so much effort was applied to analysing all the relevant data throughout the pre-firing period, that those responsible for firing were well supplied with information on which to make their decisions. The duties were shared between British and Australians, and the order to fire was not given unless and until all present—and in particular the AWTSC members—were satisfied.

Round 1—Tadje

The first standby for Round 1, on 12 September, was soon postponed; a second standby on 13 September was also cancelled for some reason—not apparently because of the predicted fallout contours. A conference at 2300 hrs that day predicted favourable conditions on 14 September, with upper winds improving during the afternoon. Z hour was declared at 0600 hrs on 14th, a further conference an hour later confirmed the firing time of 1430 hrs, and the final conference began at 1130 and continued until the weapon was fired at 1435 hrs (local time).

Conditions were almost ideal, with an intense anti-cyclone over the Great Australian Bight, and the cloud track did not enter the rain areas predicted in the east and south east of the Continent. The cloud-height, predicted first as 10 000 ft and then as 8300 ft, was actually 9500 ft; however the local fallout pattern was not exactly as predicted because of variations in the wind-field. The theoretical predictions staff concluded that an error of about 15 per cent must be expected, and that it was unlikely to be improved significantly by using more extensive forecasts.

A feature of this test that was later to cause concern and misunderstanding was the novel use of cobalt metal for so-called radiochemical 'diagnostic' purposes—i.e., as an aid to measuring the nuclear efficiency of the explosion. It was not a good idea and was not repeated. When the Australian range staff later found small pellets of radioactive cobalt scattered around the Tadje firing site, they were very puzzled. Besides causing an unforeseen type of surface activity, the pellets gave rise to a later, totally unfounded, suspicion that the British scientists had been working on a new type of nuclear weapon incorporating cobalt-60; this was not so, but the suspicion persisted.

Round 2—Biak

The first day of standby for Round 2 was a week later, on 21 September. Firing phases were cancelled on 21 September and again on 24 September because of likely rain areas. On the evening of 24 September it seemed that a brief opportunity would occur on the morning of 25 September but fog was forecast for the early morning, and about midnight hope of firing at 0700 hrs was abandoned. Another conference half an hour later was held to consider firing later in the morning; maps were prepared showing the fallout contours for a detonation of between 6 and 10 kilotons. There seemed a good chance of firing at 1000 hrs and Z hour was declared at 0330 hrs. The final meeting began at 0700 hrs in Maralinga Village, moved to Forward Control at Roadside, and continued till 0830 hrs. Wind forecasts then showed that the Taranaki site would probably have low levels of radioactivity deposited on it, but the decision was taken to fire at 1000 hrs (local time) as planned and to accept the difficulties that might arise.

The yield was about the expected 6 kilotons, but the cloud was much higher than predicted—up to 24000 ft instead of 14600 ft—and so some change in the direction of maximum fallout was likely. A secondary cloud was apparently formed at about 15000 ft. No rain had been forecast for any area within 300 miles of the cloud track, and the cloud did not pass through any rain area. The weather conditions were generally very good, except that winds at the lowest level were rather light and not very favourable in direction, and as expected they deposited low levels of radioactivity on the Taranaki site.

Round 3—Taranaki

The first day of standby for Round 3—the balloon round—was 7 October, but no attempt to fire was made for two days. From 6 October onwards the upper level winds were favourable but winds up to 1000 ft had too great a northerly component. By the early hours of 9 October, the upper wind structure was deteriorating. There was now a difficult problem of timing; the adverse low level winds seemed likely to improve soon but if firing was delayed too long the favourable upper winds would be lost, perhaps for several days.

A meeting at 0600 hrs on 9 October studied maps showing fallout contours assuming the maximum yield of 50 kilotons—a large safety margin as the probable yield would be up to 30 kilotons. The main cloud height was predicted as 28300 ft (for 30 kilotons) or 37000 ft (for 50 kilotons), with a secondary cloud at 13000 ft or 19000 ft. The upper winds that were forecast would not carry radioactive material into any of the expected rain areas in the south east of the continent. Z hour was declared and the firing phase began, with an expected firing time of 1600 hrs. A second meeting confirmed the decision and the final meeting began at 1300 hrs in Maralinga Village and then moved to Roadside. By F hour the lower wind directions were much improved, and when the weapon was fired at 1615 hrs (local time) the local contamination that had seemed possible did not occur. The near-calm conditions prevailing during the firing phase were not ideal from the point of view of fallout, but they greatly eased the difficulties of handling the balloons and hoisting the weapon, and the operation went very smoothly.

The yield was about 25 kilotons and the height of the cloud—23000 ft, with a secondary of cloud at 10000 ft—was rather less than expected. Cloud tracking showed that the main cloud moved rapidly away to the east; though at higher levels its course was less to the north than had expected, it was over rain-free areas.

Reporting on *Antler*

Operation *Antler* had gone very smoothly apart from the early troubles, and the balloons had performed well on the day. The briefing routines and pre-firing meetings were efficient and streamlined. All the meteorological arrangements had worked well although, surprisingly, the forecasting errors were greater than for *Buffalo*—perhaps because of the general atmospheric conditions in 1957 compared with those in 1956. Altogether 452 forecasts had been made. The RAF meteorological flights had been invaluable; some took place in appalling weather, and heavy demands were made on the aircrew, but they always completed their observations and the meteorologists had great confidence in them.

The RAF's low-level radiological surveys by Varsity aircraft and helicopters had been improved as a result of more reliable equipment. After *Buffalo*, better navigational equipment and a more accurate altimeter had been asked for, since the accuracy of aerial radiological surveys depended on the aircrew knowing precisely their position and altitude. The Decca navigator, introduced before *Antler*, proved excellent, though more accurate altimeters were still needed. Improved navigational equipment and more effective calibration techniques had enhanced the reliability of these surveys, and correlation with the results of ground monitoring by mobile units was good. However the relationship between air readings and the radiation dose-rate on the ground was complex and some uncertainties still existed.

Fallout

For Round 1, the varied direction of the upper winds had spread the radioactive material widely and thinly over the Continent to the north of Maralinga, and the fallout had not coincided with the rain areas in the south east coastal regions. For Round 2, again, windshear had dispersed the main cloud very widely to the north east and east of Maralinga. For Round 3, the main cloud moved east and then north east towards the Queensland coast, missing the rain areas in New South Wales and Victoria as predicted[5].

The network of fallout monitoring stations was in operation from 10 September to 24 October, and 12 stations—including Adelaide, Melbourne, Sydney, Brisbane and Darwin—collected rain samples, but no radioactivity above background level was detected. As a further check on fallout, measurements were made at intervals after each round on the thyroid glands of sheep grazing in various places up to 250 miles from the test site. Three radionuclides were found—iodine-133 and xenon-131 (detectable only in a few cases), and iodine-131, a radioisotope of iodine with a half-life of 8 days which, if ingested, concentrates in the thyroid. The highest concentration of iodine-131 found in the thyroids was negligible compared with the level considered by American and British agricultural scientists to be harmless to grazing sheep. (For H R Marston's report on radioiodine in thyroids of sheep and cattle, see below.)

Health and safety

Safety of test participants

Fifteen hundred test personnel at *Antler* were recorded as having been exposed to radiation; only 424 had exposures above the threshold level of detection. As Appendix H shows, 17 men received over 3 r. No civilians and no Australian citizens received more than 5 r during the trial: 5 members of the Defence Services did; two exceeded 12 r and one of them received 15 r, but all were within the special limit of 25 r. The two highest were the pilot and safety observer of the Canberra aircraft engaged on primary air sampling after Round 3. It was believed that for yields of less than 60 kilotons an aircraft could collect samples 30 minutes after the explosion without exposing the crew to more than about 3 r; this figure was slightly exceeded for Rounds 1 and 2, but for Round 3 an exposure of 10 r accumulated unexpectedly quickly and the pilot had to fly out of the cloud before completing a single pass. The observer described vividly the appearance of the fireball and the formation of the cloud, as seen from the Canberra orbiting at 30 000 ft. Flying into the cloud, he wrote, was like 'entering a reddish brown cloud of smoke which was at first very thick but rapidly thinned to a paler colour. During the first few seconds . . . the instruments indicated high activity, and almost before we had realized what had happened the "Charlie" meter was registering 10 r. We immediately took action . . . but it was more than 20 seconds before we got clear. However the time taken to clear the cloud added very little to the dose recorded . . .'

The health physicists had difficulty in obtaining the previous radiation histories of the crews, and some officers had apparently been employed as sampling crews on several trials; experience must have been invaluable in these specialized operations. Though they were apparently still within the limits set for the trials and within the lifetime limits shortly to be recommended by the ICRP, they were for the time being undoubtedly incurring a greater annual radiation exposure than most workers in the nuclear industry received in a year; however, it should be remembered that many radiation workers would continue to be exposed throughout their working lives.

Safety of the population

The theoretical radiation doses received by the population were again calculated by AWTSC using the fallout data from the monitoring stations. The highest cumulative dose of gamma radiation was 4 millirems, integrated over 50 years, as in previous calculations for *Mosaic* and *Buffalo*, and as before making no allowance for shelter or weathering. The four highest values, and the revised figures calculated by the Australian Ionising Radiation Advisory Council in 1983 (AIRAC No 9) are shown in Table 9.1. The AIRAC figures for *Antler*, as for *Buffalo* and *Mosaic*, are much lower than the AWTSC for the reasons previously explained (Chapter 7, p. 135).

Table 9.1

	AWTSC (millirems)	AIRAC (millirems)
Bourke	4	0.8
Mackay	4	0.2
Thargomindah	3	0.5
Townsville	3	0.2

The *Antler* doses—even the higher values calculated by the AWTSC— are clearly far below the "half level A" (equivalent to 1.5 r or 1500 millirems) that the AWTSC had stipulated before Round 1, and less than one-thousandth of the average Australian's exposure to natural radiation in 50 years.

However, higher exposures might well have occurred in places where there was no fixed monitoring station, so AIRAC calculated the radiation doses along the central fallout line from each of the *Antler* explosions. From Round 1 the fallout track, as determined by aerial survey, did not pass over any inhabited area, and the fallout would therefore have caused no radiation exposure.

After Round 2, the ARDU survey showed that the highest level at any inhabited place was at Coober Pedy, 146 miles north east of Maralinga. There the dose, integrated over six months, was 15 millirems (or 6 millirems allowing for shelter).

For Round 3—the balloon round—the close-in fallout, on the range and nearby, was very low; further out from ground zero it was more than expected, though not high. The ARDU survey found the highest level of fallout at any inhabited place at Mulgathing, 144 miles east of Maralinga. There the radiation dose, integrated over 6 months, was calculated at 13 millirems (or 5 millirems if an allowance was made for shelter). Wise and Moroney[6] assessed the population dose from *Antler* as 149 man-sieverts (14 900 man-rems) or about one-fifth of the total from all the tests in Australia. Most of the *Antler* dose was contributed by Round 3.

The last Maralinga trial

After the third *Antler* shot, on 9 October, the air task group moved without delay to Christmas Island, where preparations were being made for *Grapple X*, the next test in the Pacific area. The first three high-yield tests in the *Grapple* series had been in May and June; the fourth, *Grapple X*, was on 8 November, only a month after the completion of *Antler*.

A further substantial programme of tests in the Pacific was planned for 1958. Another kiloton series at Maralinga, Operation *Lighthouse*, was also contemplated, but 1958 was too full—five *Grapple* shots (*Grapple Y* in April, *Grapple Z* in August and September)—for another major trial to be carried out at Maralinga before 1959.

However, by November 1958 a moratorium on testing had been agreed by the three nuclear powers. It continued until September 1961, when the Soviet Union first resumed atmospheric testing, and then the United States followed suit. There followed two years of the most intensive atmospheric testing by these two powers, until the Partial Test Ban Treaty came into force in October 1963. The largest explosion was 58 megatons, made by the USSR on 30 October 1961. This was a version of their 100 megaton bomb where the yield had been kept 'low' for test purposes by replacing the uranium casing with some other material[7]. Britain made no attempt to develop such multi-megaton devices (see Chapter 12).

Britain's last *Grapple* series (*Grapple Z*) consisted of four shots in August and September 1958. She carried out no more tests in the atmosphere after the 1958–61 moratorium. Though the range at Maralinga continued in use for minor trials and experiments (see Chapter 10), *Antler* in 1957 was the last major trial there.

Postscript

A postscript to the major trials appeared as a paper by an Australian scientist, H R Marston, published in August 1958 under the sober title 'The accumulation of radioactive iodine in the thyroids of grazing animals subsequent to atomic weapon tests'[8]. It contained valuable new scientific information on iodine-131—an important constituent of fallout—and a great amount of meticulously researched data. It did not indicate high levels of iodine-131 contamination. Nevertheless the paper was very controversial at the time and later. Before it was published, it was described as 'dynamite to the uninformed'. Why was this? And why were attempts made—it was alleged—to suppress its publication?

It was controversial for two reasons: first, because of comments that Marston made, and did not make, on his data; second, because of the paragraphs he included on other fission products, especially strontium-90, in which he drew erroneous inferences from his iodine-131 results, with no supporting experimental data. These comments and these inferences sounded alarming. He wrote, for example, of 'heavily contaminated areas', 'repeated dressings' of radioactivity, and precipitations in 'areas more or less thickly populated'. Writing of strontium-90, he said that the contamination of any part of the earth's surface by fallout from the stratosphere was quite small when compared with the contamination of parts of Australia with fallout from the troposphere after recent weapon tests.

To understand the story of the Marston report it is necessary to go back to its origins, and also to look at the research on strontium-90 being done at the time.

Iodine-131

Iodine-131 is one of the most abundant fission products of an atomic explosion and though short-lived—with a half-life of 8 days—it is radiologically important. The thyroid glands of animals and human beings are avid for iodine and will absorb iodine-131 if it is present, with a consequent risk of thyroid cancer. Animal thyroid measurements by an American scientist, published in 1954[9], had indicated that, at existing levels, iodine-131 from weapon tests in the United States was no hazard to animals or human beings. The AWTSC, with the new permanent range being set up on the Australian mainland, wanted to be able to assess the Australian situation. They accordingly asked Marston to undertake a survey, starting well before trials began at Maralinga in order to establish a base line. He was to obtain the thyroid samples from sheep and cattle and to make iodine-131 measurements using scientific equipment supplied by Aldermaston.

Marston, of Adelaide University, was head of the Division of Biology and General Nutrition of the Commonwealth Scientific and Industrial Organisation (CSIRO); as we saw, he and his laboratory assisted in some of the biological experiments at *Buffalo*. A distinguished scientist in the field of animal health and nutrition, he was also by temperament controversial[10].

He began his survey at the end of April 1956, and by mid-December had measured more than 230 thyroid samples from 26 areas in northern and north eastern Australia that were likely to be traversed by plumes from explosions at Maralinga. When he began sampling he expected nil results until after the first *Buffalo* firing in September. At first, the iodine-131 content of all his samples was below the level detectable with his apparatus. But a few days after the first *Mosaic* firing (G1) on 16 May he found iodine-131 in many samples from across the country, and after G2 on 19 June the concentrations increased by a factor of 100 or more. Marston did not consider these levels dangerous, but he was surprised and angry because they showed that *Mosaic* had deposited radioactivity quite extensively on the mainland despite assurances that this would not happen and that the fallout would be blown out to sea.

After *Buffalo*, his iodine-131 measurements rose, predictably but less than he had expected. Meanwhile his laboratory in Adelaide, which had a long-standing interest in radioactivity in air caused by emanations of radon and thoron from rocks and soil, continued its periodic air sampling; this was unrelated to weapon tests and had never shown any response to them. However after the third *Buffalo* shot on 11 October an increase in radioactivity in the air suggested to Marston that the plume had passed close to Adelaide—a conclusion that authoritative evidence does not support (see Chapter 8). But even if it gave a correct picture of fallout over Adelaide, it was still irrelevant to a report on iodine-131 in animal thyroids.

The figures in Marston's 26 tables of thyroid measurements showed that the iodine-131 levels in inhabited and stock-rearing areas were all well below safety limits; the highest figure he recorded was about one-hundredth of the so-called 'Scott Russell' safety limit, which was based on the maximum iodine-131 concentration in milk for infants, the critical group. Yet Marston's paper did not say this, or compare his measurements with this or any safety standard.

Strontium-90

Another fission product abundantly produced in atomic explosions is strontium-90. It has a half-life of 28 years and (like calcium) is deposited in bone if taken into the body through the food chain; then, by irradiating neighbouring bone-marrow, it can cause leukaemia or aplastic anaemia, or may in the long term give rise to bone tumours. Strontium-90 was causing increasing concern to United States, Canadian and British scientists, and its significance was underlined in June 1956 by both the Bronk and the Himsworth reports on nuclear hazards (see p. 85).

The United States research programme on strontium-90 was known as *Sunshine*. In October 1956, American, British and Canadian scientists met in Washington to arrange to collaborate on Project *Sunshine*, by comparing strontium-90 levels in samples of soil, food, milk and animal and human bones in the three countries. Penney quickly suggested to Martin, as chairman of the AWTSC, that Australian samples should also be collected, from locations 150–200 miles from Maralinga, at regular intervals before and after weapon trials. Plans were worked out over the next few months; the collecting methods were specified by Scott Russell and the samples were to be despatched to AERE, Harwell, which had the necessary facilities and expertise for strontium-90 analysis, and where the techniques used had been standardized with those of United States and Canadian scientists. The results would be evaluated at Harwell by a group of biologists expert in internal radiation. Detailed arrangements were agreed at a meeting at Harwell at which Titterton was present for the AWTSC.

Meanwhile Marston, who was not involved in the strontium-90 work, used his iodine-131 results to make calculations about strontium-90 and included these vague, but somewhat alarmist, conclusions in his report on the iodine-131 survey. They were however not only unsupported by any experimental data but were based on faulty assumptions about the behaviour of strontium-90. A valid assessment of the strontium hazard could not be made in this way, but only on the basis of experimental data obtained from the assay of representative bone samples. Such an assessment was later published in *Nature*, in 1961 (see p. 198).

Open publication

Marston presented his paper to the AWTSC early in 1957, when a copy was sent to Aldermaston and was discussed with Harwell scientists, with Scott Russell, and with Loutit of the Medical Research Council.

Penney's chief comment, which he sent to Titterton as AWTSC chairman, was that the paper contained a small amount of technical matter, in two graphs, that could reveal weapon design information. If this was included, the whole document would have to have a high security classification; however these graphs were not essential to the text and if they, plus two sentences, were omitted, open publication would be possible. This condition was purely a matter of the security of weapon information, and had nothing to do with any debate on radiological safety. As for the paragraphs about strontium-90, etc, Penney said that if they were published they could be answered by scientific argument.

The AWTSC reconsidered the draft in August 1957 and referred it for an independent opinion to Sir Macfarlane Burnet, chairman of the new National Radiation Advisory Council (NRAC)[11]. An Aldermaston scientist visiting Melbourne in November saw the final version and confirmed that the security objections had been met. He said that 'unscientific assumptions' remained about strontium-90 in relation to iodine-131 measurements, but they were 'patently conjectural'; publication was not opposed.

The *Australian Journal of Biological Sciences*, after consulting independent referees, finally published the paper in August 1958. It still included four paragraphs on strontium-90, and argued that the ingestion of bone-seeking isotopes by grazing animals might be inferred directly from measurements of iodine-131 in the thyroid. These speculations were valueless compared with the mass of scientific data becoming available from the analysis of bone and other samples, and published in the first report of the United Nations Scientific Committee (UNSCEAR) which also appeared in August 1958. A 1961 report[12] on strontium-90 in Australia recorded an increase in late 1958 and early 1959, but noted that levels in bone were still one-third to one-half of levels in the United States and Britain.

The controversy generated much heat and publication was delayed by 18 months. Marston felt aggrieved and thought he was being muzzled. I have not seen the Australian documents, but I found no attempt in Britain to suppress his research results. It was unfortunate that he was determined to include, in his valuable report on iodine-131, extraneous passages about strontium-90 on which he had no experimental data and which was being extensively researched by many other scientists.

Notes and references

1 Herbert York: *Race to Oblivion* (Simon and Schuster, New York, 1971), p. 111.
2 AEC Minutes of February 1955 (declassified) record Strauss as mentioning, in a discussion of fallout, that the tests did repeatedly 'plaster' a few towns (The Public Historian, Vol. 8, No. 2, p. 118, Spring 1986).
3 J L Symonds: *A History of British Atomic Tests in Australia* (Australian Government Publishing Service Canberra, 1985), pp. 421–444, 465–467.
4 *The Times*, 30 August 1957.
5 *AWTSC Journal of Science*, September 1959.
6 Keith N Wise and John R Moroney: *Public Health Impact of Fallout from British Nuclear Weapons Tests in Australia 1952–1957* (July 1985).
7 Glenn Seaborg: *Kennedy, Kruschev and the Test Ban* (University of California Press), p. 114.
8 *Australian Journal of Biological Sciences*, Vol 11:3, August 1958.
9 L Van Middlesworth: *Nucleonics* Vol 12, p. 56, 1954; *Science* Vol 123, p. 982, 1956.
10 See *passim*, Stewart Cockburn and David Ellyard: *Oliphant* (Axiom Books).
11 J L Symonds: *Chronology of Events 1950–1968*, p. 63. I have found no indication of what Sir Macfarlane Burnet's comments were.
12 F J Bryant *et al.*: Strontium-90 in fallout and in man in Australia January 1959–January 1960 (*Nature*, May 27,1961).

10   *Kittens, Rats* and *Vixens*

The story of the atomic trials in Australia would be incomplete without an account of the supporting experimental work that began at Emu Field in 1953 and continued at Maralinga from 1958 until 1963, six years after the major trials ended. Five different kinds of experiment, involving some 550 events, were carried out during those ten years. They were not nuclear explosions, but they were an important element in the weapon programme. What was their nature and purpose? When and how were they conducted? What were their political and safety implications?

What the minor trials were for

The various minor trials were code-named *Kittens, Rats, Tims* (which were similar to *Rats*) and *Vixens*. The first three were purely weapon development experiments, and tests of components and materials; the *Vixens* were concerned with safety.

Kittens, the first experiments, were to develop and improve initiators. In an atomic bomb, an implosion system using conventional explosive is used to compress the fissile material in the core—plutonium or highly enriched uranium—very rapidly, and at the instant of firing a device called an initiator produces a supply of neutrons to initiate a chain reaction in the fissile material. The efficient functioning of the weapon depends on the timing, intensity and rate of neutron output from the initiator. In the *Kittens* experiments, small quantities of radioactive and other materials were mounted in an assembly of conventional (i.e. chemical) explosive. Various configurations and combinations of materials were tried, for example radioactive polonium and non-radioactive beryllium. The effect of the chemical explosion was to mix the polonium with the beryllium, thus allowing alpha particles to bombard the beryllium and so release neutrons. The output of neutrons after the explosion was measured by sensitive detectors coupled to oscillographic recorders. *Kittens* trials took place in 1953 at Emu Field, and in 1955,

1956, 1957, 1959, 1960 and 1961 at Naya, an area on the east of the Maralinga site.

Tims and *Rats* began later, in 1955 and 1956 respectively. They were experiments in which a conventional explosive was fired in a simulated weapon assembly; the resulting movement of the materials, and the passage of shockwaves through the assembly, were precisely measured and recorded. Natural uranium, which is non-fissile and only slightly radioactive, was used in the mock weapon to simulate the fissile material used in a real weapon. Though similar in purpose *Tims* and *Rats* used different techniques of measurement. For *Tims*, the methods—telemetry probes, high speed photography and radiography—were external. For *Rats*, an intense short-lived gamma-ray source, the size of a pea, was placed inside the non-explosive assembly; using gamma-ray detectors a picture of the event was obtained from the inside—Pilgrim said it was like taking an inside-out X-ray—and flux-time records were made at a nearby recording station.

Tims and *Rats* dispersed natural uranium locally, but the radioactivity was too low to be hazardous. These experiments took place in the Australian desert rather than in Britain, where they could have been safely conducted if necessary, because of a Ministerial undertaking made in 1954[1] that no experiments using fission products or any other hazardous material would be carried out at Aldermaston's range at Foulness. Though this statement referred specifically to Foulness, it was held to apply generally, and was re-affirmed in 1956.

Tims experiments took place on the Maralinga Range in 1955, 1956–61 and 1963 in an area called Kuli, and *Rats* each year from 1956 to 1960 at Naya and Dobo.

Vixens were safety experiments, which began in 1959. The first series was concerned with the consequences of accidents, especially fires, involving nuclear weapons, radioactive materials or reactors. It was important to know what would happen to the radioactive and toxic materials if a large fire broke out. Would they burn, and how widely would they be dispersed? Would they be carried downwind in the smoke, or would they remain in the debris of the fire? The burning experiments in this series were later called *Vixen A*, to distinguish them from the B series which began in 1960. *Vixen B* was a study of the inherent safety characterisitcs of nuclear warheads. The effects of detonating the explosive accidentally during manufacture, storage or transport had to be investigated however unlikely such accidents were. These *Vixen B* experiments were of serious practical importance, both for the armed services and for the public; they were also the most likely to cause significant contamination, especially by dispersing plutonium. *Vixen B* experiments differed from all the other minor trials since they used fissile material in a simulated weapon. The quantity was reduced and the experiment was arranged so as to limit the chain reaction to an amount of fission energy that was quite insignificant in comparison with the chemical explosive used. Nevertheless there was a fission reaction, and some fission products resulted; moreover plutonium debris was dispersed. These experiments had both political and safety implications, far more than any of the others.

There were *Vixen A* experiments in 1959, 1960 and 1961 at Wewak, and *Vixen B* in 1960, 1961 and 1963 at Taranaki, near the firing site of the third *Antler* round.

Kittens

The initiator experiments started very modestly with five shots at Emu Field in 1953 in an area ('K site') about eight miles from the *Totem* firing site and five miles from Emu Village. They began before the main *Totem* trial and were carried out on 26 and 30 September and 6, 14 and 17 October. Ground contamination was very light outside a 40 ft radius, though some radioactive debris was thrown up to 400 yards, but the maximum extent of the danger area, some 20 miles downwind, was well within the main *Totem* danger area.

The scientific results led to an improved design for a simpler and considerably smaller initiator. The scientists wanted to follow up with ten more shots in September 1954, perhaps in Australia again. However a site in the United Kingdom would doubtless save time and expense, and a third possibility was in Alberta, as suggested by Dr Solandt of the Canadian Defence Research Board. The best site found in the United Kingdom was in an area beyond Wick, in the far north of Scotland, where the bulk of contamination would be carried out to sea. One crofter would have to bought out if this site was to be used. Penney did not like the idea at all. The weather at Wick was unreliable; it rained constantly; the high humidity would be bad for electronic instruments. Contaminated debris would be a problem, and though the hazards of downwind contamination were probably acceptable he could not give the local authorities an honest assurance that they were zero. Besides, it would be difficult to get the site ready in time. Australian weather, by contrast, would be ideal. *Kitten* firings in the desert, far from the nearest people and stock, would be 'safe for certain'. A permanent range in Australia was intended in any case and, for the range staff, occasional minor trials would usefully fill in the gaps between major trials. There might not even be much difference in cost between Australia and the United Kingdom.

Proposals for *Kittens* in South Australia in September/October 1954 were approved, and Penney was instructed to discuss the technical aspects with Butement, the chief scientist of the Australian Department of Supply. But before the Australian government had been formally approached, Penney visited the United States and there acquired fresh information that made initiator tests unnecessary in 1954. They might be wanted in 1955, but even this was uncertain pending the results of new research work at Aldermaston. It was not until August 1954 that Penney confirmed the need for initiator tests the following May.

Meanwhile the Australian government seemed favourably disposed, but wanted safety data on the tests. Martin, the Australian defence scientific adviser, visiting London in the summer of 1954, had discussions with Penney which satisfied him on safety. Plans for the permanent proving ground, as we saw in Chapter 6, were worked out during November and December 1954 between the Australian authorities and the Wilson mission from the United Kingdom; these plans included arrangements for *Kittens* early in 1955, either at Emu Field or in a section of the Maralinga Range where they would not interfere with the main construction work. In December the Australian government confirmed its agreement to the tests, subject to detailed examination of the safety data, and promised the help of 20 Australian personnel for three months. Aldermaston produced a safety document in February, *The Scope and Hazards of Kittens 1955*, which the Australian government referred to Martin. He considered the hazards slight, but recommended that a standing committee should be set up to advise. This was the origin of the Australian Weapons Tests Safety Committee (AWTSC); though it was to be mainly concerned with the major programme of nuclear tests—*Mosaic, Buffalo* and *Antler*—it was first set up in connection with the small programme of much less hazardous minor trials, which were not nuclear tests.

The AWTSC recommended acceptance of the 1955 *Kittens*, and work began on the *Kittens* site at Naya to the east of what was to be the main range. A team of a dozen scientists arrived from Aldermaston in April.

With Australian agreement, on the advice of the new safety committee, the plan was extended to include some timing experiments of the type later called *Tims*, and the whole programme was completed successfully between May and July 1955.

The British asked for further *Kitten* tests in early 1956 and six were carried out uneventfully in March. After 1956 the *Kittens* experiments became only a small part of annual programmes of minor trials; *Kittens* featured in 1957, 1959, 1960 and 1961, and they ceased after 1961 when they were no longer considered necessary.

Tims

Penney explained the need for experiments of the *Tim* type to the Atomic Energy Authority board in April 1956. The success and inefficiency of nuclear weapons depended largely on the degree of compression of fissile material, and the synchronisation of the operation of the neutron initiator with the instant of maximum compression. These depended on several variables. As a guide to design, mathematically ideal circumstances could be calculated, but unless the theory was checked by controlled experiment, the calculations could not be confidently applied to practical designs. To obtain the design data needed for the weapons programme they were instructed to fulfil, the scientists required about 100 non-fissile firing trials.

The obvious site was Maralinga, but to save staff and time and to avoid delays in interpreting results, an alternative and nearer site was desirable. Aldermaston's range at Foulness (used for explosive firings) was out of the question. A suitable alternative to Foulness would be the range belonging to the Chemical Defence Experimental Establishment (CDEE) at Porton, less than an hour by road from Aldermaston. Here localized hazards could be confined well within the range which was fenced and controlled. Some radioactivity would, however, inevitably be carried beyond the boundaries, and Ministers would have to be consulted. One argument advanced in favour of Porton was the financial saving[3]. Another was that as the British tests in Australia gave rise to radioactivity there, it would be embarrassing to prohibit tests in the United Kingdom on the grounds that the British public could not accept 'the possibility of extremely small and quite safe exposures to occasional radioactive conditions of this kind'.

A hazard assessment was made jointly by the Harwell health physicists and the Medical Research Council's laboratory (the Radiobiological Research Unit, located at Harwell alongside AERE, the Atomic Energy Research Establishment). After consulting the Oxford agricultural scientist, Scott Russell, they concluded that the experiments could be safely undertaken at Porton, provided that there was detailed monitoring after each shot and that overlapping of contamination from various shots was avoided. However Ministers were adamant that the experiments could not take place in the United Kingdom; any publicity might have repercussions on the Atomic Energy Authority's other activities (the first civil nuclear power programme had been announced in February 1955). *Tims* experiments had to be in Australia. They duly took place at Maralinga, with AWTSC approval, during September and October 1956, in the intervals between the *Buffalo* shots.

Minor trials in 1957 and 1958

By 1957, minor trials had diversified and grown in scale since the 1953 *Kittens*, and some people thought that additions were made too readily and uncritically. The programme for 1957, approved by the Australian government in December 1956, included *Kittens*, *Tims* and *Rats*, up to 88 firings in all. It was carried out from March to November—21 *Kittens*, 44 *Tims* and 23 *Rats*. In 1958 there were 27 *Rats* and 71 *Tims* firings between April and November.

As the programmes became larger and more complex, there was increasing discussion and argument between the British and Australian authorities, largely for political reasons. The minor trials never attracted press or public attention in Australia, but international developments were taking place that were soon to put a temporary stop to major trials and to set a question mark against at least some minor trials.

Maralinga and the Moratorium

In April 1958 President Eisenhower had responded to a Soviet declaration—immediately after a series of H bomb explosions in Siberia—that the Soviet Union was suspending nuclear weapon tests unilaterally. Eisenhower, moving away from his previous insistence that nuclear weapons could only be discussed in the context of general disarmament, offered separate talks on the idea of a test ban, and suggested a technical conference on inspection and detection of tests. More United States H bomb tests—the *Hardtack* I series—began at once in the Pacific and lasted from the end of April to mid-August; Phase II continued from mid-September to the end of October. Meanwhile during July and August a Conference of Experts to Study the Possibility of Detecting Violations of a Possible Agreement on Suspension of Nuclear Tests met in Geneva. It included American, Russian, British, Canadian and French members. It considered four methods of detecting and identifying nuclear explosions: recording acoustic waves, locating and examining radioactive debris, recording seismic signals, and recording radio signals. By the end of August it reached the conclusion that it was technically feasible to set up a workable and effective control system for the detection of violations of an agreement to cease nuclear testing[2].

Early in August the United Nations Scientific Committee on the Effects of Atomic Radiation (UNSCEAR) had presented its first report. This report, compiled by scientists from fifteen nations, came to similar conclusions to those of the Bronk and Himsworth reports of June 1956. It found that the radiation received from fallout so far was slight—only 5 per cent of that from natural sources—but warned that even a small rise in environmental radioactivity in the world might eventually cause appreciable damage to large populations. It estimated the additional deaths from leukaemia due to fallout as between 400 and 2000 a year, world wide, but pointed out that even the higher figure was only a small fraction of the annual total of 150 000. The committee had voted down, by 9 votes to 5, a Soviet proposal to recommend suspension of all nuclear tests; the report did however urge member states to take steps to minimise the irradiation of human populations by nuclear weapon explosions as well as by medical and dental X-rays (the major source of man-made radiation exposures) and by atomic wastes.

Eisenhower proposed that test ban negotiations should begin on 31 October and pledged a one-year moratorium as soon as the talks began; the Russians agreed. The following month, September 1958, both sides mounted new tests, another H bomb series in Siberia and *Hardtack* II in Nevada which ended on 30 October. On 31 October a Conference on the Discontinuance of Nuclear Weapon Tests opened in Geneva. After the last Soviet firing was detected on 3 November, there begun a moratorium on nuclear weapon testing; it lasted for neary three years, until September 1961.

The latest British test series at Christmas Island, *Grapple Z*, had been completed in September 1958, and *Lighthouse*, a projected kiloton trial at Maralinga in 1959, had been cancelled. Britain was most anxious, however, to continue with minor trials, some of them essential to the next of the *Grapple* series. It could not then be foreseen that further *Grapple* trials would never take place and that *Grapple Z* in 1958 would be the last.

The minor trials were not nuclear explosions—they did not involve either significant fission or fusion—and they were considered by the British to be unaffected by the moratorium or by the Geneva negotiations. The Americans took the same view of their comparable experiments. However, in the circumstances the use of the term 'minor trials' might be misleading, and Penney decided that they must in future be called 'assessment tests'. 'We are changing the name', he told the Foreign Office, 'in order to prevent the possible interpretation that they are very small nuclear explosions'. At the same time, in order not to prejudice negotiations in Geneva, instructions were sent to Maralinga that all firings involving radioactive materials must cease by midnight on 31 October.

The new title was not at first introduced into correspondence with the Australians. Soon, however, it would be time to approach them about assessment tests in 1959. As a preliminary move, the British view of the tests and their exemption from the moratorium was disclosed to the Australian representative in Geneva. He seemed unsurprised.

The term 'assessment tests' only lasted a year, and by late 1959 another title, avoiding the word tests, became politically desirable. For the future, the work was to be known as 'the Maralinga Experimental Programme', or MEP, and the plan for each year was to be designated MEP 1960 (or MEP 60), MEP 61 and so on. The new title encapsulated a decision that the experimental work was to continue at Maralinga, but even this had come into question in 1958 during appraisals, at Aldermaston and in Whitehall, of future test policy. One possibility discussed was transferring the assessment tests to Christmas Island. Another was the use of the Nevada Test Site, which had been informally suggested by American scientists to a visitor from Aldermaston. (The bilateral agreement providing for technical cooperation in the uses of atomic energy for mutual defence purposes had been concluded in July 1958[3].) The Nevada idea had its attractions—an appreciable saving in staff, possibly some financial savings, and intangible gains in closer cooperation with the Americans. Practically, the chief disadvantage would be loss of independence and flexibility. Politically and strategically, Aldermaston felt that it might be inexpedient to withdraw all work from Maralinga.

To establish that these weapon experiments—and the safety experiments already contemplated—would be permissible under a test ban treaty, Aldermaston scientists were seeking for a definition of a nuclear explosion which would permit them while preventing even small-scale major trials. It proved extraordinarily difficult, scientifically and legally. Penney at first suggested that the term nuclear explosion should be held to mean 'explosions which are a consequence of the deliberate release of nuclear fission, or nuclear fusion, or both'. British and American scientists continued to seek a definition which could be included in a comprehensive test ban treaty, but the complex arguments about reaction times—10^{-6} seconds? 10^{-8} seconds?—and energy yields—10 tons TNT? 10lb TNT?—need not concern us here, as a comprehensive test ban treaty was never achieved. A definition was irrelevant to the Partial Test Ban Treaty eventually agreed in 1963.

New departures in the 1959 programme

The 1959 assessment tests were planned to take place from early March to November. Such programmes, lasting for nine or ten months of the year, meant that—even without major trials—the range was almost continuously operational. Three teams a year of Aldermaston staff, each of some 20 to 25 men, were engaged at Maralinga, apart from the numerous Australian and British staff permanently on duty there.

For 1959, there were to be 21 *Kittens* firings at Naya in March and May; 22 *Rats* firings at Dobo, a new site in the Naya area, from May to June; and about 64 *Tims* firings between May and December in the *Tims* areas TM100 and TM101 (see Map 5, p. 142). The approval of the Australian government was requested in January 1959 and a safety statement followed; approval was given six weeks later. Subsequently, as we shall see, experiments of a new type, the *Vixen* safety experiments, were added to the programme. The arrangements in the safety statement were based on the latest (1958) ICRP recommendations;

outside the safety boundaries for each firing site the radiation levels were not to exceed those for members of the general public, i.e., one-tenth of those recommended by ICRP for the protection of radiation workers in atomic energy establishments, universities and hospitals. The airfield and Maralinga Village were both well outside the safety radii. All the tests would create a local inhalation hazard around the point of burst and would leave areas of radioactive contamination out to about 60 yards. The scientists would take action to remove the worst contamination and would survey, mark and map the remaining con-taminated areas. Each team leader, before leaving Maralinga, would take all reasonable steps to make the areas and buildings safe and would give the scientific superintendent in overall charge of operations a map showing radioactive areas. He in turn would satisfy himself that every-thing required had been done, and finally would hand over to the Range Commandant (an Australian Army Officer) a composite map showing radioactive areas and buildings, with a signed statement detailing the residual radioactivity and specifying the precautions to be taken. Then, for the inter-trial period, these areas would become the responsibility of the Range Commandant, along with the remainder of the Range; he was assisted by the Australian health physics representative (AHPR) who would make regular surveys and some special measurements. The AHPR was accountable to the Commandant, but also was to make technical reports to Aldermaston and to the AWTSC.

The first *Vixens*

Hazards from accidents to nuclear weapons in transport or storage were much discussed during 1957/58. In March Penney called together sci-entists from Harwell, Risley and Aldermaston to consider them. In April, two Aldermaston scientists attended a conference in Washington and brought back information about American experiments that had been going on since 1955, and about accidents involving nuclear weapons that had already occurred. American data were still far from complete, especially on the dispersion of plutonium in a fire.

Experimental work at Maralinga seemed essential. However, burn-ing trials using plutonium and beryllium were unprecedented and could be open to political misrepresentation; 'a careful approach to Australia' would be needed. Three possibilities were suggested. First, Titterton might be told the reason for the tests, given estimates of the contamina-tion, and then asked how best to obtain political clearance. Second, the

Australian government might be approached directly through the normal channels, that is, through the Commonwealth Relations Office and the High Commission in Canberra. Third, the new tests might be assumed to be covered by the approval already received for the 1959 programme, and particulars might simply be forwarded to the AWTSC as an amendment—an unworthy suggestion. The first course was adopted and Titterton was asked for his advice on the best way of getting the Australian government's agreement to the *Vixen* shots. The object of the proposed *Vixen* experiments—'to study the dispersion of plutonium, uranium and beryllium when released in particulate form by explosions or fire, and to obtain information which will permit estimates of hazards downwind in case of accidental release'—was explained to him. Two trials were proposed, each using 200 g of plutonium metal, to be burnt in a controlled petrol fire. There would be no breathing hazard beyond 3600 yards and no deposition hazard beyond 2500 yards. Within a month, Titterton replied that the AWTSC recommended acceptance of the extended programme, and a formal request from London to Canberra was sent a few days later.

These *Vixen* experiments—later called *Vixen A* to distinguish them form the *B* type introduced in 1960[4]—had a special feature. They were the only experiments to use balloons—not to be confused with the balloon systems used for major trials. They were flown to carry meteorological instruments, especially anemometers, and radiological instruments for measuring radioactivities at high altitudes. These were needed in order to correlate the measurements of airborne and deposited radioactivity resulting from the fire with micro-meteorological conditions. Estimates of radioactive dispersal under various meteorological conditions, in case of a real accident or fire, could then be made.

Unfortunately, the unpredictable weather of Maralinga was bad for balloons, and in a violent storm during the *Vixen* series in 1959 two balloons tore their mooring cables apart and broke free. This was the first of three such occurrences.

MEP 60—the 1960 Maralinga experimental programme

General proposals for a 1960 programme, to include *Tims*, *Rats* and *Vixens*, were sent to Australia in October 1959, with the hope they would receive no publicity. Although the experiments were not nuclear tests, it would be embarrassing if they were talked about while test ban discussions were going on in Geneva.

During December 1959 plans for new safety experiments were being evolved at Aldermaston and discussed by officials and Ministers. The object was not, as in the 1959 *Vixens*, to investigate the hazards arising after an accident, but to study how the weapons themselves could be made accident-proof. A question of particular interest was 'one point safety'. For a nuclear weapon to operate properly, an accurately formed implosion was necessary, but an accidental initiation of the conventional high explosive at a single point would produce a very distorted implosion that would not create a full nuclear explosion but might trigger a limited, and small, fission reaction. The new *Vixen B* experiments were planned to produce design information to give assurance that this would not happen. Actual warheads were not to be used in the experiments and the amount of fission would be minimal, equivalent to grams, or at most a few pounds, rather than to tonnes of TNT.

United States scientists were planning similar experiments for 1960, but, it was argued, it would be wrong to rely entirely on American data. Nuclear weapons now being made in Britain to American designs—as a consequence of the 1958 bilateral agreement on collaboration in atomic energy for defence purposes—incorporated substitute materials of British origin, and some design modifications. Independent tests were therefore essential for safety during manufacture, transport and storage of the weapons; it was doubtful if such tests could be concealed.

Ministers considered the case for the new experiments and their implications for the Geneva Conference. They decided that the experiments would be necessary as long as Britain continued to manufacture, transport and store nuclear weapons, and Britain must try to make sure that they were not prohibited by any agreement to suspend tests. The United States authorities should be consulted about tabling a draft article defining nuclear explosions that would not preclude these safety experiments, and British representatives should be prepared to put the case frankly to the Soviet delegation at Geneva.

As for the Australian government, Ministers said that Titterton should be asked informally for his advice on the best approach, though the Commonwealth Relations Office would have preferred direct communication through normal channels. Two senior Aldermaston scientists, Newley and Pilgrim, left for Australia a few days later. They reported on their return that Titterton saw no objection in principle to the *Vixen B* proposals and would advise the Australian government accordingly if asked. He regarded the new experiments as a logical extension of *Vixen A*; the approval already given by the government for the 1960 programme would, he believed, adequately cover them, provided a satisfactory safety statement was submitted. He thought a formal approach undesirable; it would force the government to consider the specific nature of the experiments, and how they varied from those already approved. Then Newley asked him about the long-term radioactivity that the experiments would create on the Range. In Titterton's view it was acceptable provided it did not extend beyong the Range boundaries; in any case, Maralinga was being considered as a disposal ground for Australian radioactive waste.

Titterton's advice was well received in Britain and his help was much appreciated. The chairman of the Atomic Energy Authority, Sir Roger Makins, agreed that it was wise to avoid formal communications on 'these contentious experiments' and to proceed without going through formal channels. This, Makins conceded, involved a slight risk that the Australians might raise some objections later on. It had been suggested, he said, that instead of the usual channels the matter might be take up at the highest level, with Menzies, but this might lead to 'some danger of confusion and possibly irritation at the Australian end'.

Aldermaston despatched a safety statement for MEP 60 to Canberra, and Titterton replied in April that the AWTSC had accepted it, but would require advance notice of each *Vixen B* firing, and wanted more information about the contamination of the range. This was sent in May. A formal approach was made to Canberra in June, but the Australian government was slow in replying. Normally, Makins had commented, it did not enquire into details of British experiments, and approval was always given subject to AWTSC acceptance of a detailed safety statement.

If this had hitherto been the case, it was no longer so; the Australian authorities, especially the Department of Defence, were not happy. In August Titterton was astonished to learn that permission for *Vixen B* had not yet been sent. The situation—a silly one, he said—had developed without his knowledge, or he would have intervened earlier. The Department of Defence was demanding information to allow it to decide on the 'political safety' of the experiments, as distinct from the environmental safety which was the business of the AWTSC. Martin (Defence scientific adviser and former AWTSC chairman) 'spent a lot of time complaining that too little was put on paper beteen the UK and Australia'. If it was to be agreed between the two governments that information about present and future trials was to be given to the Department of Defence, as well as the AWTSC, Martin would insist on less discussion and more paper-work. He would want to know, for example, the total amounts of high explosive, fissionable and radioactive materials used in each round, the expected height of the cloud, and the fallout patterns.

At last, in September, news came from Canberra that the extended MEP 60 was approved and the four *Vixen B* firings could proceed at once.

More trouble with balloons

MEP 60 had more problems before it was completed in October. There was another loss of balloons. After the previous break-away, the design of the balloons had been modified, but in a thunderstorm on 23 September seven balloons broke loose simultaneously. Five were recovered on the range, but two were lost.

Titterton wrote Aldermaston a critical letter about this and other matters. The balloons did not concern the AWTSC, he said, except when they passed over the boundaries of the Range; it was to be hoped this would never happen again, but some level must be set for the permissible level of radioactivity on any balloon that was to be flown. Apart from safety, if anyone were to identify a lost balloon, or if a small child were to pick up a piece of balloon fabric, the Australian government could be politically embarrassed.

The AWTSC asks more questions

Titterton's letter continued with a list of questions. In the *Vixen B* experiments, had there been an approach to criticality in any round? What information about the results could be given to the AWTSC? What did the residual radioactivity consist of? The committee felt strongly that the materials ought to be named; vague descriptions like 'fissile material of long life' and 'toxic material' were unsatisfactory. The committee had complete confidence in the safety assessments, but it wanted to be able to reject criticisms from elsewhere about insufficient information, and to regularize the difficult position in which it found itself after the 'recent fuss', especially about balloons. Could general descriptions be given of the various types of experiment—*Tims, Kittens* and *Vixens*—and the radioactive clouds associated with them? Until it had received Aldermaston's views on these matters, the committee felt that it should not make a recommendation to the Australian government about the next programme.

Pilgrim replied fully on each point, giving a summary of the purpose and method of each of the five types of experiment. He enclosed a detailed technical note on the meteorological conditions required for firing, and on how the safe distances were calculated using the latest ICRP recommendations. He promised reports on the 1959 *Vixen A* burnings very soon, and on the 1960 *Vixen B* firings in a few months. The latter had gone very much as predicted; the small controlled amount of fission which occurred was adequate for experimental purposes but radiologically insignificant. It was agreed that in order to provide the fuller information which the AWTSC was now asking for, safety statements would be more detailed and explicit and therefore highly classified. The safety statement for the 1961 programme, already sent, was being revised accordingly.

MEP 61

Plans for MEP 61 were in hand well before MEP 60 finished. MEP 61 was expected to be similar but on a rather smaller scale. It was to run from March to November or December. Some Aldermaston scientists would arrive in February, and the number on site would rise to about 100 during April, when *Kittens* and *Vixen A* and *B* firings would be in progress. About 250 range staff would also be needed, with a contingent of Royal Engineers who had taken part in the 1960 *Vixen* series, and a few RAF personnel for decontamination duties. The numbers engaged in these programmes, though nothing like those at major trials, were considerable, and *Vixen* firings were said to have something of the appearance and atmosphere of a small major trial.

A request for approval was sent to Canberra in late September. The safety statement followed and, under a new arrangement agreed between Ministers in the summer, a copy was sent to the Department of Defence, as well as to Titterton for the AWTSC. But when scientists began arriving at Maralinga in February to start firings in March, MEP 61 had not yet been approved. The Australian Department of Defence, inspired by Martin, wanted further information, and more was sent, but it did not satisfy the Minister, Athol Townley. He had specific instructions from the Prime Minister to satisfy himself about the Maralinga experiments from the political as well as the safety point of view. Especially since the balloon incident of 23 September, the Australians had become extremely sensitive about Maralinga; they felt that they really did not know what was going on there and now they were determined to do so. If it was believed that nuclear weapons were being tested there during the moratorium, public opinion in Australia would be united against the government and it would be accused of opposition to disarmament—and this in a general election year.

At the beginning of March the Prime Minister's Department (said to be 'plainly embarrassed' by it) despatched a strongly worded letter, in terms personally approved by Townley, protesting about inadequate information. He was anxious not to delay the programme but could not agree to it on the strength of the two documents received from the United Kingdom. A senior British officer familiar with the trial programme should visit Australia at once to brief him and his departmental advisers, and should be authorized to disclose any information—other than on weapon design—needed to enable the Minister to fulfil his responsibilities to his government.

The British Minister (Peter Thorneycroft, the Minister of Aviation) replied affably, and Dickins, the Director-General of Atomic Weapons, accompanied by Pilgrim from Aldermaston departed promptly for Australia. Their visit produced instantaneous results. They had long meetings with Martin and Defence Department officials—during which Martin disconcerted them by asking why implosion experiments could not be done in Britain if they were so safe—and two meetings with Townley. He quickly agreed to advise approval of MEP 61, subject to satisfactory precautions for balloons and to the omission from the *Vixen A* series (the burning experiments) of a device that looked like a real bomb; he was understandably afraid its appearance might lead to false rumours. (Devices externally resembling bombs had been used in the 1959 *Vixen* series).

All difficulties appeared to be resolved. Townley and Thorneycroft exchanged friendly, and grateful, messages. But within a few days, on 22 March, a thunderstorm struck Maralinga. Ten balloons, all inflated, were bedded down; fortunately all were clean of surface radioactivity. Four broke loose in the fierce gusts of winds; on three the safety devices worked, but the fourth escaped, leaving a broken ripcord and trailing 600 ft of flying cable. A search for it began in the darkness. A report of the incident reached Ministerial level within hours and Townley was furious. A board of enquiry was set up at once, and balloon flying and

Vixen A firings were suspended. It seemed that balloons might be banned for the future, but the embargo was lifted three weeks later and the *Vixen A* series was completed. There were no more after 1961.

Another, much less serious, problem arose over *Vixen B*. Titterton, as AWTSC chairman, complained that the 1961 *Vixen B* firings had violated the western boundary of the permitted firing sector in a minor way and had spread radioactivity outside the area agreed with the AWTSC. There was a good deal of internal argument at Aldermaston as to whether the alleged violation had actually occurred, but all the senior Aldermaston scientists, including the Director, found even the possibility of a minor violation disturbing and insisted that every effort must be made to avoid the slightest infringement of agreements between Aldermaston and the AWTSC.

MEP 61 ended in December, and the same month an Australian general election returned Menzies and his government to office with the slenderest of majorities. A different result would probably have meant very different nuclear policies.

MEP 62

In August 1961, while MEP 61 was still in progress, British intentions for 1962 were conveyed to Canberra. Beginning in March, up to 10 *Vixen B* shots, 30 *Kittens* and 80 *Tims* were planned. The full costs of the experiments and any subsequent safety arrangements would be borne by the United Kingdom. As usual, publicity should be avoided. There would be the usual health physics precautions, and a safety statement was coming. One novel safety feature of MEP 62, code-named *Waterlily*, was a large steel vessel, like a small gasholder, that was to be used to contain *Vixen B* explosions.

The AWTSC accepted MEP 62 with slight reservations; firing arcs must be strictly observed, and more restrictive conditions should be applied to firings at Taranaki. Formal approval was given by Australia in November.

By January the programme had to be reviewed. Circumstances had radically changed since it was planned. The Geneva negotiations had broken down and the moratorium had ended. The Soviet Union had resumed nuclear testing in the atmosphere in September 1961, and had detonated a 58 megaton device in October. The United States had also resumed underground testing later in September; atmospheric tests in the Pacific came later, in April 1962. In March a joint Anglo-American test (*Pampas*) was to be carried out underground in Nevada, and the British were also to participate later in the year in the American *Dominic* series, for which the United States would use Christmas Island as one of their bases. The original MEP 62 was obsolete, and furthermore British resources would be heavily engaged in *Pampas* and also in Operation *Dominic* (in which the United Kingdom support task was code-named *Brigadoon*).

A modified programme (incidentally dropping the *Waterlily* idea) was sent to Canberra. The *Vixen B* series would now be only three or four shots, and not before October; a reduced *Tim* series would begin in September; *Kittens* would take place concurrently. After all the build-up for a programme starting in March or April, the British authorities were very apologetic about the last minute change, but Maralinga could expect a full work-load in 1963. No one, however, could clearly foresee the course of nuclear weapon development or nuclear testing and the future of the Range was undeniably in question. British officials found the situation vis à vis Australia uncomfortable, and the High Commission staff in Canberra tried hard to find some way of presenting the Australians with less embarrassingly laconic statements.

By the time *Pampas* had taken place, the technical position had changed again. The analysis of results would take time, and firm decisions about MEP 62 could not be made before the end of May, if then. Probably MEP 62 would not be required at all; it was an embarrassing position. The Australians were told without delay and were very understanding, albeit concerned about the 80 or so Range staff whom they maintained. It was agreed that Australian and British manpower at Maralinga would have to be run down, and the Range put on a care and maintenance basis, but more work was likely in 1963 and subsequent years, and no satisfactory alternative site existed.

The Australians asked for definite information about 1962, 1963 and the long-term prospects, and an appreciation was given to them in June. There would now be no MEP in 1962, but as long as nuclear weapons were in service, experiments at Maralinga would be necessary. Planning for 1963 would begin shortly; MEP 1963 would contain no new types of experiment.

The Maralinga staff position was inevitably fluid. It was difficult for the Range Commandant to maintain morale throughout 1962, but the time was profitably used for a much needed tidying up exercise, which greatly improved the appearance of the place.

MEP 63

Originally, plans for 1963 included only *Tims*—about 12 shots, beginning in October—and up to six *Vixen B* shots, beginning in March. No *Vixen A* experiments were intended, and so no balloons (other than small meteorological balloons) would be used. Proposals were sent to Canberra in September 1962, but were soon modified to include extra *Tims*. The actual programme—16 *Tim* shots and 5 *Vixen Bs*—was all in March and April.

When Pilgrim, together with a new DGAW, L T D Williams, visited Australia in December they found the Australians anxious on two counts. First, they clearly wanted a tighter Australian control in the future. Martin emphasized that though he was recommending approval of MEP 63 he would not agree to a programme in 1964 without more information about what was being done; he seemed uncertain about what further information he would be seeking but his attitude was suspicious. The Minister for Defence, Athol Townley, could not resist the opportunity of referring again to the balloon incidents of 1960 and 1961, which had not been serious in themselves but which had eroded confidence. However, he was not so much worried about safety at Maralinga—he was content to leave the details to the AWTSC—as about political embarrassment. The government was constantly aware of its narrow majority, and was sensitive to the slightest possibility of trouble at the Range. An untoward incident there might create a public impression that the government had little control over events on Australian territory.

The second anxiety of the Australian authorities was about the future of the Range. They felt that Australia got nothing for her contribution and indeed that neither side was getting value for money; the cancellation of MEP 62, and the very few firings proposed for 1963, prompted doubts as to whether the continued existence of the Range was justified. Williams apologized again for MEP 62 and explained the reasons for cancellation, unforeseen when MEP 62 was planned. But he assured the Australians that Britain would need a facility like Maralinga as long as she had a nuclear deterrent.

The Australians reassured Williams and Pilgrim that approval for

MEP 63 would be forthcoming. Discussions then touched on what might happen to Australian nuclear policy if Menzies were to retire soon, as seemed likely. (He did not, and continued as Prime Minister until 1966.) A Labour government might even want a nuclear-free zone.

The visitors also had talks with Titterton who suggested that the political worries of the Defence Department should not be taken too seriously. But the general view in Australia was he had overplayed his hand and that he had by this time little influence except on matters of safety.

The 1963 experiments took place uneventfully. There were 16 *Tim* firings, all in April, and five *Vixen B* shots were fired in March and April, with such success that Aldermaston notified the Australians in June that no more would be needed that year. Nor would a second series of *Tims* in the last quarter of the year. MEP 63 was over by the end of May and—though it was not realized at the time—it was the last ever at Maralinga.

The minor trials in retrospect

The minor trials did not deploy ships, aircraft and large numbers of men as did the twelve nuclear tests. But they were a continuing and very considerable commitment for Aldermaston for ten years, and were an important and integral part of the weapons research and development process (especially the *Kittens*, *Tims* and *Rats*.) Minor trials, especially the *Vixens*, were the justification after 1957 for the continuation of the Maralinga Range, which had after all only accommodated two major trials.

There had been a certain amount of publicity for the nuclear tests and a great deal of press and public interest in them in Australia. It was not so with the minor trials (under their various titles). Outside official circles, very few people apparently realized that Maralinga was used for these experimental programmes, and that it continued to be used after *Antler*. The two *Vixen* series—which were on a much larger scale and involved more people, including Australians—were more likely to attract notice. But the British authorities were particularly anxious to avoid any publicity about the *Vixen B* series during the Geneva negotiations, since there was no agreed definition of nuclear explosions which would specifically exclude *Vixen B*.

Rules for the radiological protection of the minor trials participants were the same as those for major trials ('The Maralinga Radiological Safety Regulations'). Exposures were kept very low. In 550 events, 1120 men were exposed to radiation: no one received more than 5 r, and only five of them exceeded 3 r; for nearly 800, exposures were at or below the threshold of detection. The public health hazards of the minor trials were non-existent at the time. Unlike the nuclear tests, they produced no fallout beyond the Range boundaries. However they caused greater residual surface radioactivity, some of it extremely long-lived owing to dispersed plutonium around, and downwide of, *Vixen A* firing sites at Wewak and *Vixen B* sites at Taranaki. Thus it was the minor trials, not the nuclear tests, which had the more significant long-term effects—though limited to Range areas—on the Australian environment.

Notes and references

1 H L Deb, 7 April 1954, Vol. 186, cols 1134–5.
2 Glen T Seaborg: *Kennedy, Kruschev and the Test Ban*, p. 12.
3 Cmnd 537 (HMSO, July 1958).
4 The names *Vixen A* and *Vixen B* were adopted in March 1960. Previously, *Vixen A* was simply *Vixen*, and *Vixen B* went under the names *Salt Cellar* and *Hamster*.

11   Closing Down

The Maralinga range, created in 1955/56 at a cost of some £10 million, covered 20000 square miles which included a test area of some 100 square miles. Maralinga Village, built on high ground in thickly wooded country, consisted by 1959 of aluminium huts providing accommodation for some 750 men, and with kitchens catering for up to 1600. There were well equipped laboratories and workshops. There were also a church with resident chaplain, a power station, a small, well equipped hospital, a well stocked and comfortable mess, a library, a bank, a post office, a shop, a cinema, a swimming pool, and facilities for tennis, cricket, football and golf.

The Range had an excellent internal road system, and over 400 vehicles. There was an airfield with a single runway, and a tented airfield camp for 450. Another camp for Service personnel was near the Forward Control at Roadside. From Forward Control an elaborate network of underground cables—several hundred miles—ran to the Village and various sites on the Range. Camera towers, 65 ft high, were permanently installed at various vantage points. There were special areas and buildings for storage of explosives, storage of radioactive materials, and decontamination. A self-contained mobile health physics unit of nine fully equipped caravans was known as 'the HP circus'. Sites on the Range used for different operations—Naya (*Kittens* firings), TM 100 and TM 101 (*Tims*), Dobo (*Rats*) and later Wewak and Taranaki (*Vixen A and B*)—each had their own facilities, such as mobile generators, subsidiary laboratories (in caravans), and recording shelters.

The staff of the Range, the Maralinga Range Support Unit (MARSU), was drawn from six armed services, 70 per cent from the United Kingdom and 30 per cent from Australia[1]; it totalled about 120 between trials and 450 during a major trial and was under a commandant from the Australian army.

Maralinga was a large commitment for the Australians. For the British it was a considerable investment and an essential facility for the nuclear weapons programme. In 1956, the Ministry of Supply expected no major trials there in 1957, but looked forward to regular, perhaps annual, trials from 1958 onwards. There was after all a major trial,

Antler, at Maralinga in 1957, but no more after that, for within two years of its completion three important factors altered the position of Maralinga.

The first factor was an Anglo-Australian one. Australian public opinion was increasingly restive; the Menzies government, anxious as it was to be fully cooperative, could not ignore the political implications. A Gallup poll in 1952 had shown a majority in favour of the tests (58 per cent, with 29 per cent opposed). However opinion moved steadily against them, until in 1957 the poll showed a majority of 49 per cent against the tests and 37 per cent in favour. The British were well aware of what the Australian public opinion could mean for Maralinga, especially if there were to be a change of government; there were general elections in 1954, 1955, 1958 and 1961. However, after Maralinga was established, the new test range at Christmas Island had been acquired. Though set up expressly for high-yield trials, which were impossible at Maralinga, its use if necessary for kiloton and minor trials as well was an option which was seriously considered. Christmas Island had some disadvantages, but the decided advantage that its geographical position and the prevailing north-easterly winds meant that fallout would not be a problem.

The second factor bearing on the future of Maralinga was an Anglo-American one. The bilateral agreement of July 1958 created a fundamentally new relationship between the United States and Britain in the nuclear weapons field. It made possible the sharing of weapons data and designs, and radically changed the British weapons programme. By 1962 it led to joint weapon tests, underground, at the Nevada Test Site and to cooperation in atmospheric testing in the Pacific.

The third factor was an international one. In 1957, the future of all atmospheric nuclear weapon testing had become uncertain, with international discussions of a possible scheme to limit nuclear tests. The object of this scheme was to reduce global fallout in view of increasingly powerful public opinion all over the world. The British government's position was clear; it was prepared to discuss limitation of tests, but not suspension—a quite separate issue that it would only consider as part of a comprehensive disarmament agreement. At the Anglo-American Bermuda conference in March 1957, Eisenhower was concerned about public anxiety over nuclear tests, but believed it essential that the tests should continue. The British Prime Minister was no less concerned about public opinion. A public statement was made from Bermuda that the United States and British governments would conduct their tests so that radiation would be kept well below dangerous levels. It proved impossible to agree on an international scheme for limitation, but then events took a new turn and, as we saw in the previous chapter, the test ban question was disengaged from that of comprehensive disarmament, and negotiations began in Geneva that resulted in the nuclear test moratorium that lasted from November 1958 to September 1961.

Besides planning for the assessment tests (or minor trials) which they intended to continue during the moratorium, the British made provisional plans for major trials, since no one knew how long the moratorium would last or what would be the results of the Geneva Conference on the Discontinuance of Nuclear Weapons Tests which opened on 31 October 1958. During 1958 some thought was given to the possibility of underground testing at Maralinga, if atmospheric tests only were banned. (The United States had carried out two underground tests in Nevada in March 1955, three in 1957 and eleven in 1958.) But the idea did not seem promising; the only suitable site was 250 miles from Maralinga, and in an Aboriginal reserve.

The British thoroughly reviewed their test policy in December 1958 and Duncan Sandys, the Minister of Defence, advised the Prime Minister in January 1959 that no further high yield tests were needed until the spring and no kiloton tests until the autumn of 1960, depending on the outcome of the Geneva Conference. It was decided for planning purposes to assume the indefinite suspension of all British nuclear tests—atmospheric, underwater or underground. This decision would be reconsidered if the Geneva Conference failed to reach a comprehensive agreement for the cessation of all nuclear tests. Neither the Australian nor the United States governments were to be informed until Ministers had been able to consider the results of the Geneva negotiations.

Apart from its use for assessment trials, Maralinga was still important to the British authorities; in case the Geneva Conference failed, they wanted the option to resume major trials there. The Director of Aldermaston argued that the cessation of major trials even accentuated the importance of Maralinga for minor experiments to support weapon development and safety research. Meanwhile it was staffed and run at a reduced level, to support the assessment tests and MEPs, but requiring long notice for preparation for any possible major trials in future.

In September 1961 the moratorium ended and, as we saw, the USSR resumed atmospheric tests at once. The United States, too, began testing, but underground in Nevada; then from April to November 1962 they carried out an extensive programme of atmospheric testing—the *Dominic* series—in the Pacific. No American detonation was as large as the 15 megaton *Castle Bravo* shot of 28 February 1954, but the USSR detonated a 58 megaton device in 1961 and two 30 megaton devices in 1962; 1962 was the year of the largest total yield—108 megatons. More global fallout was created between September 1961 and October 1963, when the Partial Test Ban Treaty came into force, than in all the previous years of atmospheric testing. However British atmospheric testing was not resumed, either at Maralinga or Christmas Island, after the moratorium ended.

The situation changed again in 1962 when the British had the opportunity of a joint major trial (*Pampas*) underground, at the Nevada Test Site. This, and the Anglo-American cooperation in *Dominic*, made the function of Maralinga more uncertain. But the Range was still needed for minor trials, and as an insurance against the possibility that the Nevada Test Site might not be open to the British for major trials if they were required later; the 1962 arrangement had been *ad hoc*, with no guarantee for the future.

The following year, 1963, the Partial Test Ban Treaty was signed in August, and came into force in October. It prohibited atmospheric but not underground tests so, although it ended the worst fears of fallout, it did not halt nuclear weapons development. The British authorities again reviewed the future of Maralinga during the summer, in the light of the treaty, which Australia as well as the United Kingdom had signed. It was agreed that Maralinga was the best site for the experiments involving nuclear materials that would still be needed, and that the Australian government should be asked that the Range should be kept on a care-and-maintenance basis, ready to come into operation at 6 to 9 months' notice.

Discussions went on in 1964 between Britain and Australia, and in the Maralinga Board of Management, and there was some suggestion of a further programme in 1966 (MEP 66), but the Memorandum of Arrangements was due to expire in March that year unless extended by mutual agreement (see Appendix C). Meanwhile cleaning up operations continued. Where possible radioactive debris was collected and buried in pits in special disposal areas; chain mesh fences with posts set in concrete were erected; all the fences carried durable warning signs. The clean-up culminated in an operation, code-named *Hercules V*, by an Aldermaston team. After its completion, the Range was considered safe on a care-and-maintenance basis, with reduced staffing and no health physicists present.

In 1965 the feasibility of using Maralinga for underground testing, if the Nevada Test Site was not available, was again considered; however it would have been very expensive to develop an underground test facility there and the political as well as the geological and engineering problems were formidable. There seemed no further justification for maintaining the Range, even at the minimum level, just to accommodate an occasional *Vixen B* experiment, and the British government finally informed the Australian government that the Range would no longer be required after the expiry of the Memorandum of Arrangements.

The AWTSC was asked to advise on any additional measures that ought to be taken before the Range was closed down. The detailed requirements that they laid down were carried out in 1967 at Maralinga and Emu Field by an Aldermaston team, in Operation *Brumby*. Debris and pieces of glazing from sites of the major trials were collected and buried, where the soil surface was contaminated with plutonium that could not be removed it was ploughed into the earth, and in some cases clean soil was spread over as a top cover. The AWTSC reported that their requirements had been fulfilled. At the ground zeros of the major trials, radioactivity was low enough to meet ICRP standards for continuous exposure of members of the public (0.5r a year), but at two areas used for minor trials there were still appreciable levels of plutonium contamination in the soil. The AWTSC considered that unrestricted access could be allowed to all but a few small areas, and they could be occupied on a short term basis without risk; however patrols at regular intervals would be advisable, for general surveillance and to dissuade any visitor from staying too long in areas unsuitable for permanent occupation.

The British authorities formally withdrew from the Range, and a Memorandum respecting the Termination of the Memorandum of Arrangements (see Appendix D) was signed on 23 September 1967. As from 21 December the United Kingdom was released from all liabilities and responsibilities except for certain claims covered by clause 11 of the original Memorandum. This was confirmed in January 1979 after the British had agreed to an Australian request for the 'repatriation' of half a kilogram of recoverable plutonium buried at Maralinga.

There were to be two further investigations, in 1977 and 1985. The first arose out of a proposal in 1972 that the Australian government should relinquish control of Maralinga. The Australian Ionising Radiation Advisory Council (AIRAC) was asked for its views on what restrictions, if any, were still necessary. The Council saw no reason why the greater part of the range should not be relinquished at once, but recommended a field study of the whole range. This study was eventually carried out in 1977 by Australian scientists and published by AIRAC in January 1979 as AIRAC 4. It recommended that an area sufficient to include the sites of major and minor trials, and the burial ground and airfield 'cemetery' where radioactive material was buried, should remain under government administration; the remainder of the range could be released. A further survey should be carried out not later than 1987.

This survey was done in 1985[2]. The major trial sites were re-examined, all the experimental sites were re-surveyed, and the sites at which plutonium had been used were studied in much greater detail. The results showed that at the sites of the major trials (including the *Totem* sites at Emu Field) radioactivity would have decayed in the next 40 years sufficiently to allow continuous occupation. The main hazard remaining on the range was from the plutonium and associated americium (a daughter product of one of the plutonium isotopes) dispersed over comparatively large areas by the minor trials; if the plutonium-239 in the most contaminated area at Taranaki were air-borne in 'dust raising activities', long-term occupation would entail radiological risks from inhaling or ingesting the dust. This survey, using more sophisticated portable instruments than those available earlier, drew attention to the widely scattered plutonium-contaminated fragments, distinguishable from the finely divided material and present in varied concentrations—from a few to less than one per square metre. These could be dangerous if found and picked up by, for example, souvenir hunters. The amount of plutonium buried in shallow pits and spread around an area of approximately one square mile at Taranaki—and smaller areas at Wewak, TM 100 and TM 101—was substantial. 'Disposal of radioactive waste of this nature in this manner', the report concluded, 'cannot be considered acceptable current practice'.

The minor trials had left more trouble behind them than the big explosions.

Notes and references

1 I have found many varying figures from time to time, some with a higher Australian component.
2 ARL/TRO 70, April 1985 (Ed. Lokan).

12   In retrospect

In retrospect, the 1950s saw nuclear weapons developments that might lead to the destruction of civilization, or even the extinction of the human race and many other forms of life. The technology of thermonuclear explosives was being developed by the United States and the Soviet Union, who were about level, and by the United Kingdom, four or five years behind on a more limited programme.

While the weaponeers were developing thermonuclear technology, great changes were happening in other areas of military engineering. Rocketry was making sensational advances, pointing towards missiles with ranges varying from a few hundred miles to many thousands of miles. Electronics, computers and instrumental advances generally indicated that it would be possible to deliver a missile accurately within a distance less than the radius of destruction of a nuclear explosion. The combination of thermonuclear warheads with precise rocketry, counter-measures notwithstanding, have by today produced the military situation where East and West could destroy each other, whichever fired first.

All of these things were foreseen in the 1950s by some politicians, military men and scientists, but only dimly. The continuing policy of the West was to be one of deterrence, and within that policy the United Kingdom so far has always insisted on having an independent component judged by the government of the day to be sufficient 'to deter'. France took an even stronger line in regard to nuclear weapons, and now has a nuclear arsenal and delivery system at least as powerful as those of the United Kingdom.

The international and political aspects of the military balance of power in the world are outside the scope of this book, but it must be noted that it was the British perception of military nuclear power that led to the British nuclear weapon programme, with its constant updating. However, the United Kingdom gave up the attempt to develop its own rockets and control systems. But it did share in the advances in electronics and computers that are an essential part of nuclear weapons systems.

The main task, therefore, seen by the British governments in the

1950s was, first, to build an atomic bomb and then to develop the technology of thermonuclear explosives in sufficient detail to make possible the manufacture of nuclear warheads. The means of delivery were to be the V bombers; later, the Polaris missile bought from the United States and carried in British nuclear submarines.

The need for tests was implicit in the political decision to produce nuclear weapons. Looking back at the test programme from the vantage point of 1986, our perspective must be different from what it would have been at the time of the tests. Were the trials worthwhile, and what did they achieve? At what cost? Were they conducted with due care for the safety of the men taking part and of Australian and world populations? And if so, were they really safe or did they cause illness and death?

The nuclear task

Hurricane in 1952—three years after the first Russian atomic explosion—was a successful test of a plutonium device, but it was not a weapon and needed further work to develop it into an atomic bomb for the RAF. If some of the British scientists had thought of this bomb as 'the deterrent' and their definitive goal, they soon found new objectives before them. For some, there was the challenge inherent in the very nature of nuclear energy. For all, there were new requirements from the Services to be met—for smaller and lighter bombs, for bombs of high, low and intermediate yields, and for varied designs for different purposes. But, above all, within a few weeks of *Hurricane* came the world's first thermonuclear explosion—an American test of a 10-megaton device[1]—and a Russian thermonuclear weapons test followed a few months later[2]. Just as Britain was acquiring an atomic bomb capability, the Americans and Russians were acquiring infinitely more powerful hydrogen weapons, and the whole strategic scene was changed. In the summer of 1954, the British government decided that British scientists too should develop and manufacture hydrogen bombs. It was a race of the Red Queen's variety[3], in which 'it takes all the running you can do, to keep in the same place. If you want to get somewhere else, you must run at least twice as fast as that'.

The programme of research and development of a thermonuclear weapon (as well as the production of a stockpile of A-bombs) was daunting, though it started with one immense technological advantage—knowing that it could be done. But Penney's scientific staff, by United States standards, was very small indeed, and he had persistently worrying staff shortages in some skills and disciplines. Some of the scientists he most wanted were impossible to recruit; even within the atomic project, the work lacked the appeal of Harwell, partly because the weapon scientists—instead of attending conferences, publishing reports and building up scientific reputations and career prospects—had to hide their lights under a bushel of super-secrecy.

Penney had to face several other difficulties. The intrinsic scientific research problems were formidable. His computing facilities were inadequate, hardly one-tenth of those Los Alamos commanded. Supplies of fissile material were also a cause for anxiety, since the growing demands for it on Hinton's industrial group could scarcely be met, and material used on tests was at the expense of the stockpile. Thinking had to take the place of experiment as far as practicable. Other supplies besides fissile material were sometimes scarce, or late in delivery, because of production problems; this was especially true of the special materials needed for the hydrogen bomb, for which novel production processes had to be designed and new plant built at great speed. A trial planned many months ahead might depend crucially on whether a small quantity of some essential material was delivered on time.

The achievement

The weapon tests were implicit in the postwar defence policy of both Labour and Conservative governments. They were essential to the acquisition of a British nuclear deterrent, and as such they were highly successful. The first British test had been seven years after the first American and three years after the first Russian atomic test. But within five years of *Hurricane* the British had progressed from a clumsy atomic device to a megaton hydrogen bomb, and had developed a range of atomic weapons that Britain thought would meet her needs. The timescale, as has recently been emphasized[4], was short compared with that of the United States and Russian hydrogen bomb programmes. From the Defence White Paper in February 1955, to the first megaton-range airdrop at Christmas Island in May 1957, was only 27 months; even from the Cabinet decision of mid-1954 it was only 34 months. By either figure, it compares with 76 months for the United States and 60 months for the Soviet Union. Britain's entire programme of major trials was compressed into less than 6 years compared with 17 (postwar) years for the United States and 14 years for the Soviet Union[5], up to the Partial Test Ban Treaty of 1963. Of course, the United States and the Soviet Union developed a much wider range of nuclear warheads and delivery systems than did the United Kingdom. Then too the British had brought back from Los Alamos the earliest United States ideas about the 'super'—the H bomb.

These few years of intense and unremitting effort produced much more than a small stockpile of British-made military hardware. Ever since 1946, when the United States had so abruptly ended the wartime atomic partnership and agreements, Britain had striven to renew them and had made some promising but unsuccessful attempts. During the years of nuclear independence, restoration of interdependence had been a primary aim of Labour and Conservative governments; it had taken priority over relationships with European and Commonwealth friends and allies. The weapons trials, leading up to the trials at Christmas Island, demonstrated Britain's nuclear competence, and her value to the United States as a partner. They showed that cooperation with the British would no longer be—as an American senator had once said—like trading a horse for a rabbit[6].

American perception of the advantages of partnership was enhanced by the launching of Sputnik I in October 1957, which aroused American fears that the Soviet Union was overtaking the United States in technological achievement. President Eisenhower invited Prime Minister Macmillan to Washington for talks about cooperation on the military applications of nuclear energy, and at the conclusion a Declaration of Common Purpose was issued, in which the President committed himself to seek the amendment of the Atomic Energy (McMahon) Act[7] so as to 'permit close and fruitful collaboration of scientists and engineers of Great Britain, the United States, and other friendly countries'. The McMahon Act, which had prevented collaboration on nuclear weapons for twelve years, was amended on 2 July 1958, and the very next day a comprehensive bilateral defence agreement was signed[8]. In May 1959, a further agreement placed Britain in a highly favoured relationship by enabling her to buy component parts of nuclear weapons and weapons systems (but not nuclear warheads) from the United States[9].

These agreements effectively pooled the two countries' scientific expertise in nuclear weapons where both had a requirement, adding Aldermaston's knowledge and skills to those of Los Alamos and Livermore. What the Americans wanted was not actual British designs but another source of ideas, access to the brains of Penney and his scientists, and the capacity of another weapons laboratory that could make independent and original contributions.

They got a better bargain than they expected, when to their surprise it became clear that during the years of separate development the two countries had reached very much the same understanding of the physics involved (though the Americans were clearly ahead, especially in engineering design). Moreover they soon realized that the British scientists had developed some techniques that they did not possess and were anxious to share[10]. They were 'amazed to learn how much we already know', the Prime Minister wrote, and 'this was a major factor in convincing them that we could be trusted with more information than they probably intended originally to give us'[11].

Circumstances were favourable for a bilateral agreement in 1958, but negotiations—even with Sputnik assistance—could not have succeeded without Britain's proven achievements in nuclear energy and especially in nuclear weapons. Penney and his men provided Macmillan with a powerful case, and he gave credit to them for a 'tremendous achievement', of which they had 'every right to be proud', enabling Britain 'to keep virtually abreast of the United States in this complex and intricate business of nuclear weapons development'[11]. To this 'tremendous achievement', and all that it implied, Australia had made a most generous—and indispensable—contribution.

Besides their primary purpose, the weapon trials had served as convincing demonstrations to the United States of Britain's scientific and technological status, and the resulting agreements of 1958 and 1959 created a unique relationship of nuclear interdependence, which—with periodic renewals—has lasted 28 years, and has powerfully shaped post-war British history. For the British, the new relationship gave access not only to American data and experience, but also to materials such as uranium-235 which could be supplied by the United States much more cheaply than they could be produced in British plants. It increased the potential of both countries and optimized the use of resources. The aims of British post-war nuclear policy had been triumphantly achieved, but the achievement of interdependence meant that the independent deterrent was no longer truly independent.

Costs

Though small by American and Russian standards, the major British trials were large and costly operations. Six of the nine series involved long-distance naval expeditions[12]; all nine involved, in total, hundreds of aircraft and thousands of civilian and Service personnel; massive amounts of money were spent on engineering and construction work in remote and inhospitable areas, to be written off in a few years at most.

No estimate of the total expenditure on weapon tests is attempted here. The costs were small in relation to the results achieved with so few trials and so few shots—only 21—and Macmillan, Chancellor of the Exchequer before he was Prime Minister, certainly considered them very cheap. Financial statements showing total expenditure on trials are unlikely to be found, since the costs were shared among various Service and civilian departments and the Atomic Energy Authority, and were sub-divided among general departmental expenditure on salaries, Service pay, travel, civil engineering and supplies. Moreover figures for the cost to the British Treasury would still give an incomplete picture, since they would not include that borne by Australian government departments.

Estimates made in February 1957 for the Lord President of the Council give a round figure of £39 million for four trials (presumably *Hurricane*, *Totem*, *Mosaic* and *Buffalo*), but it is not clear exactly how the total is made up. Including fissile materials, the cost is put at £15 million a year, declining after 1957/58 to £10 million a year or less. These annual costs were less than 10 per cent of the £150–160 million a year estimated for development and production of nuclear weapons and delivery systems, and that figure was itself only 10 per cent of the defence budget.

Whitehall officials noted approvingly how cost-conscious the scientists were. Even so, as we have seen, the scientists were always under pressure to reduce expenditure and pare down their requirements. At all the trials, resources were barely adequate and insufficient allowance was made for contingencies or for the breakdown of equipment. It was a strangely parsimonious attitude on the part of a government that attached overwhelming importance to the independent nuclear deterrent.

In relation to the magnitude and the momentous consequences of the trial programme, it was undeniably cheap. Its objectives were quickly fulfilled, with only 21 shots fired. The tenth, at Christmas Island in

May 1957, was a thermonuclear bomb dropped from a V bomber. In comparison, the Americans' first airdrop (at Bikini in 1956), was their 67th shot.

The tasks assigned to the scientists had been carried out rapidly, effectively and with a minimum of testing. The small number of shots meant huge savings. Costs were low not only in terms of logistics, but in scarce and costly fissile material. Britain had ordered a nuclear arsenal with the approval of the majority of the public, for even after 1958, when CND was most active, opinion polls showed consistent support for the nuclear deterrent. Britain's scientists and engineers had delivered it promptly, and a bargain price.

Health and safety allegations

It has frequently been suggested recently that the weapon trials were conducted without regard for health and safety. All kinds of accusations, have been made, both in the media and in evidence to the Australian Royal Commission. The evidence is anecdotal, and it is impossible to discuss numerous individual stories, but criticism follows several general lines. It includes allegations that international radiation protection standards were flouted, and that the trials staff drew up their own more accommodating rules; that safety rules and procedures were inadequate or were not enforced, and test personnel were not warned of radiation hazards; that film badges were not issued, or were not collected, and exposures were not recorded; that protective clothing and respirators were not provided when they were necessary. Stories have been told of men being used as guinea pigs and deliberately exposed to danger to study the effects of radiation. It has been suggested that the Australian population was put at serious risk from fallout and that some people were harmed as a result; that shots were fired in unsafe weather conditions, either through error, or deliberately because time was too pressing to wait for safe opportunities; that insufficient care was taken to protect people, especially Aboriginals, from wandering into danger areas; that when things went wrong, the facts were suppressed and the public was deceived.

If all these accusations were true, the scientists must have been guilty of ignorance, incompetence, or a cynical disregard for safety, or all three, and there must have been a gigantic secret conspiracy among many scores of them. I have tried to consider without prejudice as much of the evidence as I could[13] and before coming to any conclusions, to weigh up its credibility bearing in mind the state of knowledge at that time.

Health and safety of test personnel

Radiation standards

The radiation protection standards used at the trials were based on the recommendations of the International Commission on Radiological Protection. Penney said: 'ICRP was our bible'. However in 1950, the postwar ICRP was just resuming its interrupted work, with a brief set of Recommendations on the protection of workers routinely exposed to radiation for a working lifetime. It did not deal—as it was to do later—with 'one-off' special emergency exposures, or with compensatory lay-off periods after a higher dose, nor did it differentiate between occupational and non-occupational standards, either for individuals or populations.

The ICRP maximum permissible dose (MPD) of 0.5 roentgen (r) a week, equivalent to 25 r in a year, was exactly reflected in the normal working rate of 0.5 r a week applied to trials personnel and, like ICRP, the trial orders emphasized also that radiation exposure should be kept as low as possible (see Appendix G). The integrated doses approved for use at the trials in certain circumstances were not set by the weapon scientists themselves, but by an independent Medical Research Council panel; the panel included members of ICRP, and was *au fait* with research and clinical data, with ICRP thinking and with current American standards and experience. Integrated doses did not at this time appear in ICRP Recommendations but were to do so well before the end of the decade. It may be worth noting here that ICRP Recommendations embodied an extremely wide international consensus of scientific opinion, and were not handed down from the mountain engraved on tablets of stone. Ideas were discussed for months or years before they appeared in a formal report, and the initial input into ICRP was from United States, British and Canadian scientists and scientific committees and from tripartite conferences on radiological protection. There is therefore nothing surprising or suspect in the adoption by the

United States or Britain of radiological protection rules in advance of publication by ICRP.

ICRP occupational standards developed during the decade; by 1958/59 there was no weekly MPD but, instead, limits of 3 rems a quarter or 12 rems a year (subject to a limit on accumulated dose which was related to age and which averaged 5 rems a year)[14]. The considerable changes since the early 1950s in ICRP Recommendations on occupational exposure, reflecting increased knowledge of radiation effects, have not invalidated the basic standards of that time. Judged by those standards, the documentary evidence shows that the rules adopted for trials personnel were completely acceptable. The record of radiation exposures indicates that the standards were met (see Appendix H); most test personnel received much less radiation than the normal working rate, and only a small number (six) received the higher exposures that were authorized to facilitate certain tasks such as ground surveys, collection of crater samples, and special flights.

To say this is not to prove that the trials were necessarily safe. It may be argued that the standards, the ICRP's Recommendations, were inadequate. There is a body of scientific opinion today that believes that existing ICRP standards are insufficiently rigorous and should be tightened up, perhaps by a factor of 10; however, most scientists believe equally strongly that ICRP standards are sound and are not in error by so much as a factor of two. This debate is undecided, and will remain so until further and conclusive evidence is available, perhaps from the current reassessment of data from the continuing study of Japanese atomic bomb survivors. Meanwhile, what ICRP may or may not decide in the future is irrelevant in judging how the weapon trials were conducted.

Safety in practice

Standards are necessary but not sufficient to give assurance of safe operation, since they have to be embodied in rules, procedures, organization and discipline, and put into effect by staff with adequate resources. Information and instructions have to reach all parts of the organization; all concerned need to know and understand the rules and to comply with them. Standards, plans, rules and procedures for the trials are all well documented, but in the nature of things there is more uncertainty about application and compliance—how it all worked out in real life. It would be miraculous if everything had gone perfectly according to plan; some things certainly went wrong, and are so recorded.

In addition to the records, there are numerous anecdotes. Although it would be wrong to ignore or dismiss them without investigation, accounts of events 30 years ago, told in good faith, may be unreliable. (This is especially so if they are second-hand accounts, or related by people only slightly involved who may not have understood the events well at the time). This is not the place to discuss individual stories, but rather to try to form a general picture from the available information, in particular from contemporary records. The mass of the evidence shows that the health and safety of the trials participants were regarded very seriously and that a great deal of trouble was taken over radiological protection. Film badges were duly issued and collected and doses recorded; movements were effectively controlled and men did not wander at random within danger areas; monitoring and decontamination of personnel was careful and systematic; protective clothing and respirators were available and were issued for work in contaminated areas. Undoubtedly some film badges were lost, as happens even in routine factory operations, but it is believed that losses were few in the case of people entering contaminated areas. It is possible, but unlikely, that some film badges supplied for Service officers to issue to their men may not all have been handed out and returned. A few people may have broken rules, ignored instructions, or cut a corner. Some men, especially perhaps young Servicemen, may have had a cavalier attitude to safety, out of ignorance or bravado. The scientists' familiarity with radiation sometimes bred contempt and a few were scornful of the stringent precautions; Penney had a 'black list' of them. But most of them had too much respect for radiation hazards to be careless, and they included men with many years of experience in high explosives research, who were habitually cautious. The men who incurred the highest exposures were themselves highly qualified scientists and doctors; for example the *Hot Box* pilot and observer at *Totem*, and the various scientists who collected crater samples at *Totem* and *Mosaic*. They took small calculated risks themselves for scientific purposes, voluntarily and in full knowledge of the radiation hazards.

The few deficiencies that existed in the health and safety arrangements were mainly due to weaknesses in overall organization of the operations or to failures of communication between the main elements engaged. Especially in the earlier trials, the different elements were run almost independently, and Captain Cooper, Penney's technical aide, commented (as we saw) on the need for stronger headquarters control. The most obvious example was the lack of radiological protection for the air and ground crews of the RAAF Lincolns used at *Hurricane* and *Totem* in Harwell's programme of long-distance air-sampling flights.

Radiation limits at the trials were adequate by the standards of the time, and stand up well even by today's standards. Whether these standards were maintained in the actual operations cannot be established with the same certainty, but the radiation records show exposures of test personnel that compare very favourably with those of radiation workers in the atomic laboratories and factories. No one received a recorded dose anything like large enough to cause immediate physical or health effects, such as radiation burns or radiation sickness, and these do not appear in any of the medical reports. As for the suggestion that men were used as guinea pigs, it is untrue (see Chapter 8).

The health record

Did radiation exposures at the trials nevertheless cause illness many years later? Most of the men at the trials were young, and indeed many of them were doing their two years' National Service. The scientists were mostly young, too, and since the conditions were physically tough they had to be fit. In all, there were about 20000 Servicemen from Britain, plus civilian scientists, 8000–10000 Australians, and a small number of Canadians, making a grand total of about 30000 participants. These young men are now middle aged or elderly. Some have died. Cases of illness, especially cancer, have been reported, and radiation exposure at the atomic weapon trials has been blamed.

It is generally accepted that levels of radiation exposure too low to have any immediate effect may lead to long-term damage to health, notably cancer; the latent period may be only a few years for leukaemia or up to 30 years for solid tumours. These long-term effects are 'stochastic'; that is, the amount of the radiation dose does not affect the severity, only the probability, of the damage. For radiological protection planning purposes the ICRP assumes that risks can be extrapolated to lower doses in direct proportion to the dose, and that the risk is linearly related to exposure. However radiation is not the only cause of cancer and radiation-induced cancers cannot generally speaking be distinguished from others. In the western world more than 20 per cent of all deaths are due to cancer. There are in all 130000 cancer deaths a year in the United Kingdom of which, it has been postulated, 1250 may be due to natural sources of radiation[15]. Many of the British test veterans would by now be suffering from cancer or would have died if they had never been at the trials. But it is inevitable that some, knowing that radiation can cause cancer, should associate their illness with the trials.

The total radiation—i.e., the 'total collective dose equivalent'—received by the 30000 or so test participants[16] is about 16 man-sieverts (1600 man-rems). On the basis of ICRP and UNSCEAR figures for dose-risk relationships, the number of extra cancer deaths that might be expected is 0.2, or may be zero; the estimate is considered unlikely to be too low by more than a factor of two.

Since it is generally impossible to distinguish between radiogenic and other cancers in individual cases, whether the trials have caused cancer must be a statistical question to be answered by the epidemiologists. A study is being undertaken by the National Radiological Protection Board[17] (NRPB) to compare mortality—perhaps also cancer morbidity—in United Kingdom test veterans with that in a control group of men not involved in the trials but otherwise closely matched (e.g. as to date of birth, Service, rank, and tour of duty in the tropics.) The NRPB mortality study is being carried out to see whether there are differences between the two groups, in cause of death, and age at death. The morbidity study, if it proves feasible, will be based on cancer registrations. It is further intended to correlate the mortality rates with the known radiation exposures. The whole investigation is to be conducted as a soundly based epidemiological study as quickly as practicable, in order to answer the concern raised by allegations that the health of participants has been affected. Completion is expected in 1987, but the work may continue after 1987 so as to derive maximum value from all the data.

The Australian Commonwealth Department of Health also undertook a survey in 1982–83 of the health of Australians who had participated in the tests[18]. It was done under considerable pressure and was something of a rush job. From Maralinga security records and Department of Defence data, nearly 15000 men who might have been involved were identified including many construction workers who left the sites before any trials began. A further 472 were 'self-identified'. Over 8000 were traced and questionnaires were sent to them; 2536 replies were received and analysed. Every effort was made in the time available to collect and examine radiation records, but it could not be claimed that complete lists or exact individual exposures were obtained. In particular there were some gaps in the information on RAAF air and ground crews[19]. Nor was the control group well defined. The report concluded, after comparing test participants and controls, that the study did not support the view that there was evidence of increased mortality that might be attributable to radiation[20].

NRPB's more comprehensive epidemiological study will provide very full coverage of the British participants, and will be able to compare them both with the relevant control groups and with the male population in general. It will be interesting to see how its results compare with the Australian conclusions, and also whether they bear out UNSCEAR, ICRP and other risk estimates—such as those by the United States Biological Effects of Ionising Radiation (BEIR) Committee—based on collective dose. When the NRPB investigation is completed in 1987, it may be possible to answer the question whether or not the weapons trials may have caused illness later in life to those who took part.

Safety of the Australian population

Trials personnel were a small and special population—male, mostly young, passed medically fit for service in arduous conditions. All were under health physics and medical supervision. Protection for members of the public was quite another matter: any risks they ran were involuntary; they included vulnerable groups, such as children and pregnant women, and they could not be individually monitored. They had to be protected from radiation hazards in the first place by keeping them out of the danger areas, and then by seeing that fallout did not harm them outside those areas.

No entry

The regions of the tests—the Monte Bello Islands, Emu Field and Maralinga—were so barren that they were uninhabited and the only problem in excluding people from them was the reputedly small number of Aboriginals travelling across the Maralinga Range. Penney had enquired particularly about the Aboriginals when Maralinga was first being considered and had been reassured. The Australian security authorities were given the task of controlling access to the Range and warning the nearest Aboriginal communities. Patrolling the Range was undertaken by Aboriginal welfare officers and Commonwealth 'peace officers', with the help of land searches and low-flying RAF air searches before firings.

There have been various stories of Aboriginals on the Range. One well documented instance was in May 1957 (between *Buffalo* and *Antler*) when an Aboriginal family named Milpuddie—husband, wife, little boy and baby girl—walked across the Range and were discovered at a place called Pom Pom near the health physics control unit. They were monitored and the boy was found to be very slightly contaminated, so they were all showered. The radiation dose they had received during the walk and while camping at Pom Pom was estimated at 6 to 7 millirems (60 to 70 microsieverts) or about one-seventieth of the present ICRP short term non-occupational limit of 0.5 rem in a single year. It is impossible to prove conclusively that the Pom Pom incident is the only one, despite the efforts made to ensure that no one strayed into the prohibited area. The AWTSC believed at the time, and reported to the Australian Prime Minister, that these efforts were effective, and that no Aboriginals were nearer than 170 miles. AIRAC later[21] came to a similar conclusion. Many people present at the time, and working in areas where intrusions were likely to have been observed, still maintain that there were no other events, though there have been various stories of Aboriginals wandering or camping on the range.

Fallout

Protection of the public against fallout beyond the danger area depended on firing criteria and meteorology, as we have seen repeatedly. Weather data had to be combined with theoretical calculations of bomb yield, cloud height and particle distribution, and confidence established that favourable conditions would persist for long enough to permit preparation, firing and subsequent safe dispersal of radioactive debris—ideally giving 24 hours of stable conditions after firing, to allow the cloud to disperse. At any point in this process there was room for uncertainties and for the unforeseen. Meteorology was as much an art as a science, and still is an inexact science. Before the trials, not much was known about the weather patterns of either the Monte Bello Islands or the Central Australian Desert; much was learnt in the course of them, but, in the earlier trials especially, there were some meteorological problems, partly due to having too few weather stations. Cloud heights were sometimes predicted incorrectly, winds changed direction unexpectedly, or the expected shear pattern failed to materialize. Even so, no catastrophes such as the 180° change of wind direction at Bikini in March 1954 occurred (see Chapter 5). Meteorological facilities and methods improved during the decade, and by the time of *Mosaic* the network of weather ships, weather stations and long-range reconnaissance flights extended from the Cocos Islands in the west to Christmas Island in the east and from the Equator to Antarctica. I have seen no evidence of pressure being exerted on the trials staff to fire in meteorologically unsafe conditions, for political or any other reasons. Errors occurred, as at *Totem*, but there is no indication, in the records of any of the trials, that the trial director ordered a firing in conditions that he believed to be unsatisfactory, against his better judgment and that of his colleagues (including Australian and British meteorologists and members of the AWTSC).

Before *Mosaic*, as we saw, fallout monitoring stations were set up and were soon increased to provide an extensive monitoring network all over the Australian Continent. Evidence from these stations was that radiation exposure of the population due to fallout from the 1956 and 1957 trials was slight. As we saw in previous chapters, from the readings at these stations the AWTSC calculated the lifetime radiation doses to people in these locations from each of the *Mosaic, Buffalo* and *Antler* shots, and in 1983 AIRAC revised the calculations on what it considered a more realistic basis. (All the figures were, of course, theoretical doses, not measured doses to actual persons.) A possible weakness of both assessments was that they only used readings from the monitoring stations; these were widely distributed, and were planned to give representative coverage, but fallout can be patchy and some higher readings might have been found at other places.

Then in 1985 a new appraisal of the fallout and its public health impact was made by two scientists of the Australian Radiation Laboratory, Wise and Moroney[22], whose work has been mentioned earlier in connection with the individual trials. Wise and Moroney take into account not only the data from the monitoring stations and the AWTSC and AIRAC work, but all the other information available on yields, radiological air and ground surveys, cloud trajectories and meteorological conditions. For *Hurricane* and *Totem*, before the monitoring stations were set up, they make conservative calculations based on all the available information and extrapolation from later trials. They apply more recent worst case assumptions about the pathways by which radioactivity may reach man, and because of the consequent large additional contribution from internal radiation their figures are generally a good deal higher, thus more pessimistic, than AIRAC's. They stress that the emphasis on external radiation at the time of the tests was consistent with the best contemporary practice and reflected the limitations of the knowledge available then of the environmental transport of radionuclides.

Because their appraisal is the most recent, the most comprehensive and the most pessimistic, it is reasonable to accept their view of the health impact of fallout on the Australian population and now to leave the AWTSC and AIRAC figures aside. Wise and Moroney—who warn that their figures may be ten times too high, or too low by a factor of 2—calculate the population dose[23] from all twelve shots in the major trials as 700 man-sieverts (70000 man-rems) or about one-sixtieth of the natural background dose over the same period of time. This extra dose averages 70 microsieverts—0.7 millirem—per person. The statistical result of applying the ICRP's risk coefficient to the population dose of 700 man-sieverts may be a total of seven fatal cancers and seven serious hereditary effects expressed in the first two generations—probably fewer. For individual people the numerical risk of serious detriment to health was higher in those population centres which received greater fallout than elsewhere, but within such a small overall figure was obviously still very low. Even if the Wise and Moroney figures, and the ICRP estimates of risk, are too low by factors of 2, the effect of the atomic weapon tests on the health of the Australian population appears to have been very minimal. The estimate of perhaps 7 (or probably fewer) cancer deaths may be compared with over 500000 cancer deaths in Australia since the early 1950s, of which total, background radiation and medical uses may account for 5000.

The Aboriginals and the land

Months before *Hurricane*, the British Prime Minister was asked in the House of Commons what steps were being taken to protect from harm the Australian Aboriginals likely to be in the neighbourhood of the impending atomic bomb test. He replied that there was no danger whatsoever to the health or safety of the people of Australia[24]. The planners did not know of the whereabouts of any Aboriginals in the northwest of Australia, within 200 miles or so of the Monte Bello Islands, but in any case it was intended to fire only in conditions that would prevent fallout reaching the mainland.

Penney was anxious about the safety and welfare of Aboriginals around Maralinga and as we saw in Chapter 6 he was given assurances by Butement. Measures were taken to warn homesteads and Aboriginal communities and to patrol the Range—particularly in areas in the direction in which the fallout was destined to occur—before firings. But the two Native Welfare Officers had an impossible task; their function was to do everything practicable to persuade natives to keep out of the way of operations, but they had no vehicles of their own, no radio communications, and a vast area to cover.

The health effects, if any, of the tests on the Aboriginals are difficult to establish because of the lack of health and other records, and because of the general background of ill-health; the condition of the Aboriginals in the 1950s was very poor, suffering as they did from malnutrition and recurrent severe epidemics, especially of measles and influenza. If the Wise and Moroney estimates are accepted, of perhaps seven fatal cancers and seven serious hereditary effects in a population of ten million, the incidence in the Aboriginal population—even if disproportionately high—must have been very small. In the group that probably incurred the highest exposure, at Wallatinna, the estimated dose indicated a probability of much less than one fatal cancer[25].

However the test programme undoubtedly had an adverse effect on the Aboriginals' lives. Howard Beale, the Australian Minister for Supply, asserted that the natives were not deprived of their tribal grounds. The area over which watch was kept for native movements during test periods was, he said, very arid and was uninhabited, no natives had been found there and so none had been interfered with[26]. It is true that there was no forced removal of communities, as occurred at Bikini and Eniwetok. A decision had been taken some time earlier to move the tribes associated with the Ooldea Mission, before a permanent proving ground was in question. Having already removed the Aboriginals, the Australian government was not averse to using the deserted region, and acceded to the British request. Some care was taken not to encroach on reserves or tribal hunting grounds. But to the Australian authorities the deserts were simly vast, empty, useless spaces. They did not appreciate the Aboriginal's attitude to the land, and had little understanding of their social organization or of their journeyings to visit relatives and sacred sites and to attend ceremonial gatherings. The decisions were taken by people with little or no knowledge of the Aboriginals; they wanted to ensure that the Aboriginals did not come to harm by wandering into danger areas, but there was to be no question of 'placing the affairs of a handful of natives above those of the British Commonwealth of Nations'[27].

This is hardly surprising. At that time Aboriginals had no rights as citizens; they did not, for example, get the right to vote until 1967. The Constitution expressly stated that 'in reckoning the numbers of the people of the Commonwealth . . . Aboriginal natives shall not be counted'[28]. For years it had been expected that they would solve the dilemma of a property-owning advanced society confronting nomadic people without a sense of individual property, by dying out or being assimilated; in the 1920s and 1930s there were said to be only a few thousand left who preserved some semblance of their tribal culture[29]. When in 1972 a committee of enquiry recommended land grants for Aboriginals forced off their customary hunting grounds by pastoralists in the Northern Territories, there was still opposition[30]. The Whitlam government proposed extensive welfare measures, and the suspension of grants of mining leases on Aboriginal reserves, but these policies were reversed by the Fraser administration which followed.

When the Range was established at Maralinga, its long-term future was hardly considered. The Memorandum of Arrangements made no stipulations abut the condition of the area when no longer required, beyond saying that the United Kingdom government 'accepted liability for such corrective measures as may be practicable in the event of radioactive contamination resulting from tests on the site' (see Appendix C). When the Range was closed down the United Kingdom, as we saw, undertook various cleaning-up operations, culminating in Operation *Brumby* in 1967. Long-term or permanent habitation of contaminated areas was considered unlikely by the AWTSC, though they thought that short-term occupancy by itinerants passing through was possible and ought to be taken into account[31]. These assumptions formed the basis for the cleaning-up operations.

In December 1967 the Range was relinquished by the United Kingdom and became the responsibility of the Australian Federal government. It remained to be decided how long the Federal government would have to retain control of it; how long it would have to be fenced, guarded and supervised; and when it could be released for possible other uses. Maralinga was surveyed in 1974 and again (together with Emu Field) in 1985[32]. In 1984 a Land Rights Act passed by the

Australian Parliament gave Maralinga to the Tjarutja tribe; but what use would they be able to make of it? By early 1985, residual fission product radioactivity at six of the seven major trials sites (Tadje was the exception) was low and, by 1977 ICRP standards, would decay sufficiently in 50 years to permit 'continuous occupancy'—an interesting term that no one would have applied to these arid regions 30 or 40 years earlier, and one that some old Maralinga hands would find it difficult to view as realistic today.

In four other areas—Taranaki, Wewak, TM100 and TM101—there were still significant surface densities of plutonium, resulting from the minor trials and especially from the *Vixen* safety experiments (see Chapter 10). Taranaki is the largest and most heavily contaminated. There are also various sites where radioactive materials are buried in shallow pits, a manner of disposal that some experts do not regard as acceptable current practice in an area where access and habitation are unrestricted. A decision by the Australian government on what further remedial work is needed will be based on a study conducted jointly by Australian and United Kingdom experts.

The people most affected by the atomic weapon tests programme of the 1950s were the Aboriginals, because of damage to their way of life rather than directly to their health. They had no rights and their interest in the land was not realized or respected; but this was, and had been, their general situation and was neither new nor peculiar to the weapons trials.

The atmosphere

Finally, what did Britain's tests in Australia add to the global fallout? Besides close-in and intermediate fallout in Australia, British weapon tests contributed to the global fallout that occasioned worldwide anxiety in the 1950s and early 1960s—between *Castle Bravo* in 1954 and the Partial Test Ban Treaty in 1963. Up to the time the treaty came into force, there were nearly 400 nuclear detonations in the atmosphere, 212 by the United States, 161 by Soviet Union, 21 by Britain—twelve in Australia and nine at Christmas Island—and four by France[33]. The total fission yield[34] has been estimated at about 195 megatons (111 megatons from Russian, 72 from American, 11 from British, and less than 0.2 from French tests[35]). Thus British tests contributed just over 5 per cent of the pre-1963 fallout; slightly over 4 per cent of that from all atmospheric tests up to 1980. The scale of the British programme kept environmental costs, as well as financial and resource costs, low.

The biggest detonations were by the Soviet Union—one of 58 megatons in 1961 and two of 30 megatons in 1962—and the total fission yield for 1961/62 is estimated at about 85 megatons. The biggest American shot was the 15-megaton *Castle Bravo* in 1954; American shots were smaller, but more numerous, than the Russian, and after 1957 a high proportion were carried out underground (and a few at high altitudes) to minimize fallout.

Global, or long-range, fallout is deposited in a band of latitudes around the world, centred on the latitude where the explosion occurred. (The smaller the explosion, the narrower the band of latitudes containing the fallout.) It is true that high-yield explosions, made a mile or more above ground level, produce a cloud that rises well into the stratosphere; the radioactivity is contained in very fine particles that remain in the high atmosphere for a considerable time, and the radioactivity therefore has time to spead over the whole hemisphere. Some is taken into the other hemisphere by the slow exchange of air across the Equator, but by the time some radioactivity has moved into the other hemisphere the activity has been greatly reduced by natural decay. It is therefore a good approximation to assume that the fallout from any explosion takes place only in the hemisphere where the explosion occurred.

Fallout from the British tests in Australia therefore remained in the southern hemisphere, where there was a high probability of its being deposited in the oceans and harmlessly dispersed. It did not add to the heavy contamination of the densely populated countries of the northern hemisphere, where by 1958 the United States, Britain and Japan had three times the world average of accumulated fallout[36]. By early 1959 the level measured in Britain rose for the couple of months to almost one-third of the natural background[37].

The current figure for all cancers in the United Kingdom is 130 000 a year, of these perhaps 1250 may be attributed to natural sources[38], 330 to medical exposures, seven to fallout, six to occupational exposure, two to nuclear waste and five to miscellaneous sources; the actual numbers are probably smaller. Britain, as we saw, has received decidedly more fallout than the world average, but even so the cancers due to fallout are about one-fiftieth or less of those due to medical exposures, and one-eightieth of those due to natural sources of radiation. The risks associated with medical radiation were, and still are, much higher statistically than those of fallout; though they are not perceived as such, since medical radiation is largely non-controversial, and the patient receiving radiation does so voluntarily and stands to benefit personally.

Radiation doses from fallout have seldom exceeded a few millisieverts, but have been delivered to very large populations. Fallout from past atmospheric detonations will continue to irradiate the peoples of the world for very many generations, but at an extremely low rate. The total dose—past, present and future—is estimated to be about 4 millisieverts (400 millirems) for each member of the world's present population; this is equivalent to two years' exposure from natural sources. The present annual dose is about 0.01 millisieverts (1 millirem), compared with about 2 millisieverts (200 millirems) from natural sources. The best estimate is that fallout increases the risk of dying from cancer by, at worst, about one chance in 40 000. There is probably a real risk, although it is not exactly known and individual cases are not identifiable. Fallout is not a substantial hazard to human health. But it might have raised the levels of environmental radioactivity to a serious extent if testing had continued for some years at the 1961/62 rate. In Britain, for example, consideration was given on at least one occasion to stopping supplies of fresh milk for children because of increasing levels of radioiodine[39].

The 1963 decision to end atmospheric tests, by the United States, the Soviet Union and Britain, was indeed highly desirable, and was universally welcomed; it ended a period of intensive testing which produced 85 per cent of the world total of fallout.

Three thoughts on fallout

Paradoxically, the Australians received far less fallout from all atmospheric weapon tests, including the twelve British shots in Australia, than did the British themselves, with no weapon tests in their own islands. Up to 1963, when the Partial Test Ban Treaty ended Russian, American and British atmospheric tests, the population of the British Isles was exposed to levels of strontium-90 three times greater than was the Australian population. In the years following the Treaty, however, the ratio changed slightly because of French atmospheric tests in the southern hemisphere.

Australia willingly accepted the British weapon test programme and cooperated generously and effectively in it. But the Australian continent has been subject involuntarily to fallout from tests carried out by other countries as well, and it is ironical that the Australian population received seven times as much fallout from other nuclear tests as it did from the British tests on Australian territory.

As to the worldwide effects of fallout, it is impossible to estimate realistically what harm might result over thousands of years from that ten-year period of heavy testing by the United States, the Soviet Union and Britain. However, effects on the health of large populations can be very approximately assessed from the collective dose. For example, as we saw, it has been estimated that, out of 130000 cancer deaths a year in the United Kingdom, 7, or probably fewer, may be due to fallout. Worldwide, although individual instances cannot be identified, many cases of injury to health must have been caused by global fallout, and to these injuries the British tests must have made some contribution; although a very minor one since they created a small fraction of the total fallout, and moreover in the less populated hemisphere. 'Statistical deaths' may often be implicit even in the most humdrum and everyday of government decisions. But the British decision to possess, and therefore to test, nuclear weapons was not an everyday decision; it was a most momentous one. It was made, as Penney said, in the sober hope of bringing nearer the day when world war was universally seen to be unthinkable. Whether it justifies the possibility of additional cancer deaths or genetic defects—however unforeseen, unintended and few—must be a matter of opinion. Those who think the possibility was not justified, should nevertheless look at the tests—and the defence decisions that led to them—in the light of the times and not only in today's light. Those who think it was justified must accept that some unknown, but relatively small, degree of harm was part of the cost of Britain's nuclear policy.

Notes and references

1 *Mike*, the first shot in the *Ivy* series at Eniwetok, 31 October 1952.
2 12 August 1953.
3 M Gowing: *Independence and Deterrence* (Macmillan, 1974), Vol. 1, p. 450.
4 J Simpson: *The Independent Nuclear State* (Macmillan, 1984), p. 104.

5 These periods would be 14 and 11 years respectively, if the years of the moratorium (November 1958–September 1961) are excepted.

6 Growing: *Independence and Deterrence*, Vol. 1, p. 450.

7 The United States Atomic Energy Act 1946 as amended in 1951 and 1954.

8 *Agreement for Cooperation in the Uses of Atomic Energy for Mutual Defence Purposes* (HMSO, Cmnd 537).

9 Cmnd 859.

10 H Macmillan: *Riding the Storm* (Macmillan, 1971), p. 500.

11 *Ibid*, p. 566.

12 *Hurricane* (1952) and *Mosaic* (1956) at Monte Bello; *Grapple* and *Grapple* X (1957) and *Grapple* Y and Z (1958) at Christmas and Malden Islands.

13 In particular from the transcripts of evidence given to the Australian Royal Commission on British Atomic Tests in Australia 1984–85.

14 $D = 5(N-18)$, where D is the accumulated dose in rem and N is the age in years. This worked out at an average of 5 rems a year over a working lifetime. The present ICRP occupational limit is 5 rems a year (50 milli-sieverts) effective dose equivalent; and 50 rems per annum to individual organs other than the eyes, for which it is 15 rems per annum.

15 E Pochin: *Nuclear Radiation: Risks and Benefits* (Clarendon Press, 1983), p. 173.

16 W N Saxby: *Radiation Exposures at United Kingdom Overseas Atmospheric Nuclear Tests* (to be published – 1986).

17 See NRPB – R 154 (September 1983): *Protocol for a Study of the Health of United Kingdom Participants in the United Kingdom Atmospheric Nuclear Weapon Tests* (ed. J A Reissland). Note that this study covers the Pacific tests as well as the Australian ones.

18 The Donovan Report: *Health of Atomic Test Personnel* (1983).

19 These gaps were discussed in detail by the Australian Ionising Radiations Council (AIRAC) which studied the contemporary records and made estimates of the exposures incurred by RAAF personnel (AIRAC 9, Chapter 15).

20 This report and AIRAC 9 have been criticized as unreliable on epidemiological grounds and because of (a) inadequate instruments and (b) the suggestion (unsubstantiated) that the position and the radiation exposures of large numbers of people were either not measured or not recorded.

21 AIRAC 9 (1983).

22 Keith N Wise and John R Moroney: *Public Health Impact of Fallout from British Nuclear Weapon Tests in Australia 1952–1957.*

23 Wise and Moroney[22] use 'population dose' as a convenient shorthand term for the formal 'collective effective dose equivalent commitment'. The population doses they calculate for each of the atomic tests, and the health impact, are given on p. 249.

Series	Round	Collective dose equivalent (man-sieverts)	Stochastic effects	
			cancer deaths	serious hereditary consequences*
Hurricane	1	110	1	1
Totem	1	70	1	1
	2	60	1	1
Mosaic	1	10	<1	<1
	2	52	<1	<1
Buffalo	1	83	1	<1
	2	11	<1	<1
	3	56	<1	<1
	4	101	1	1
Antler	1	3	<1	<1
	2	28	<1	<1
	3	118	1	1
Total		700	7	7

* Expressed in the first two generations

24 H C Deb., Vol. 449, Col. 1658, 1 May 1952.
25 AIRAC 9 (1983).
26 Final submission to the Australian Royal Commission on behalf of Aboriginal groups and individuals (16 September 1985), p. 295.
27 *Ibid*, p. 64.
28 Russel Ward: *The History of Australia in the Twentieth Century*, pp. 319, 372.
29 *Ibid*, pp. 132–133.
30 *Ibid*, pp. 372, 397.
31 Final submission to the Australian Royal Commission on behalf of Aboriginal groups and individuals (16 September 1985), p. 386.
32 AIRAC 4 (1974) and ARL/TR 070 (1985).
33 These figures are taken from SIPRI Year Books 1974–85 and the US publication *Announced Nuclear Tests July 1945 to December 1984* (US Department of Energy).
34 These figures are taken from the 1982 UNSCEAR Report.
35 Atmospheric tests were discontinued by the United Kingdom in 1958, and by the United States and USSR in 1963, but were continued by France till 1974 and by China into the 1980s.

36 Southern hemisphere countries had much less than the world average. See UNSCEAR Report 1958, p. 100 and map No 1. Figures for strontium-90 deposits up to 1980 still show the southern hemisphere levels to be one-third of those in the northern hemisphere (UNSCEAR Report, 1980).

37 *Second Report on Hazards to Man of Nuclear and Allied Radiations* (HMSO, Cmnd 1225, 1960), pp. 46–50 and Appendix F.

38 Pochin: *op cit.*, p. 173.

39 *The Times*, 3 September 1963. Sir John Cockcroft: *Gains from nuclear test ban treaty*.

Appendix A Chronology

Date	Nuclear weapon events	Other events
1945 April		President Roosevelt dies—succeeded as US president by Truman
May		War with Germany ends (7th)
July	*Trinity* test in New Mexico (16th)	In UK Labour government elected; Attlee Prime Minister
August	Hiroshima and Nagasaki bombed (6th and 9th)	Japan surrenders (14th)
October		United Nations comes into being. UK government announces plans for atomic energy research organisation
November		Washington declaration (US/UK/Canada) on atomic energy and international control
1946 January	British Chiefs of Staff report on atomic bomb requirements	First UN meeting, in London, sets up UN Atomic Energy Commission to consider international cooperation and control (UNAEC—wound up in May 1948)

Date	Nuclear weapon events	Other events
February		Britain sets up atomic energy organization to produce fissile material
March		Arrest of British atom spy, Alan Nunn May
June/July	US tests at Bikini—*Crossroads* (2 shots)	
August	British Air Ministry sends requisition for atomic bomb to Ministry of Supply	In USA, Atomic Energy Act (the McMahon Act) ends Anglo-American atomic cooperation
November		UK Atomic Energy Act places atomic energy project in Ministry of Supply
1947		
January	British Ministers decide on production of atomic bomb	
March		USA takes over British commitments in Greece and Turkey
May	First meeting of British atomic bomb staff under Dr Penney	
June		Partition of India and Pakistan announced. USA puts forward European Recovery Program (Marshall Plan)
July		USSR rejects Marshall Plan

Date	Nuclear weapon events	Other events
August		India and Pakistan become independent
September		Sixteen nations accept Marshall Plan. Britain announces withdrawal from Palestine
December		Tripartite discussions (US/UK/Canada) in Washington on atomic cooperation
1948 January		Tripartite agreement on atomic cooperation—'modus vivendi'. Gandhi assassinated
February		Communist regime established in Czechoslovakia
April/May	US tests at Eniwetok—*Sandstone* (3 shots)	
May	British atomic bomb decision disclosed to Parliament	UNAEC (set up January 1946) wound up having failed to achieve anything
June		Soviet blockade of Berlin (until May 1949). Berlin airlift
July		US bombers based at British airfields
November		Truman re-elected US President

Date	Nuclear weapon events	Other events
1949		
April		North Atlantic Treaty Organisation (NATO) set up
May		Berlin blockade ends
August	First Soviet atomic weapon test	
September		Communist People's Republic of China created. Tripartite talks (US/UK/ Canada) in Washington on closer atomic collaboration
October		German Democratic Republic (GDR) established
December		Tripartite talks in Washington continue. Robert Menzies elected Prime Minister of Australia (in office until 1966; re-elected 1951, 1956, 1958, 1963)
1950		
January	Truman orders US development of the H bomb	Washington talks break down after arrest of Harwell scientist Klaus Fuchs for spying
February		Anglo-American agreement on guided missiles. In UK, general election returns Attlee government with much

Date	Nuclear weapon events	Other events
		reduced majority. 30-year Sino-Soviet alliance
April	Aldermaston taken over as main British atomic weapon establishment	
June		Korean War begins (ends July 1953)
July	Menzies is asked to agree to atomic weapon test in Australia	
September	British Chiefs of Staff ask for US bomb testing facilities. Formal request to Menzies for test in Australia if US site is unavailable; he agrees in principle	Britain undertakes general rearmament. Harwell scientist Bruno Pontecorvo defects to USSR
October	US test facilities for British test refused	
November	Preliminary survey of Monte Bello Islands, Western Australia	
December	Order placed for British V-bombers (to carry atomic bombs)	Attlee flies to Washington to see Truman about Korean War and atomic weapons

1951

Date	Nuclear weapon events	Other events
January/ February	US shots in Nevada— *Ranger* (5 shots)	
February	British Chiefs of Staff agree on shipborne test at Monte Bello in late 1952	

Date	Nuclear weapon events	Other events
March	Attlee askes Menzies to agree Monte Bello plan (*Hurricane*)	
April/May	US tests at Eniwetok— *Greenhouse* (4 shots)	
May	*Hurricane* Executive set up in London. Task Force Commander and scientific director appointed for *Hurricane*	Foreign Office officials McLean and Burgess defect to USSR. Menzies re-elected Prime Minister of Australia; agrees to Attlee's March request
July	*Hurricane* panel set up in Australia	
July/ August	Survey of Monte Bello Islands	
August	US offer of facilities for British test—refused as conditions unacceptable	
October	Soviet atomic tests	In UK, general election returns Conservative government under Churchill
October/ November	US tests in Nevada— *Buster-Jangle* (7 shots)	
November		British government introduces retrenchment programme
December	British Ministers make final decision on Monte Bello Islands for *Hurricane*	

Date	Nuclear weapon events	Other events
1952 February	Britain announces forthcoming *Hurricane* test. First ships of *Hurricane* flotilla sail	King George VI dies and is succeeded by Queen Elizabeth II
April/ June	US tests in Nevada— *Tumbler-Snapper* (8 shots)	
June	Australian reconnaissance of possible mainland test-sites	
July	Main *Hurricane* party arrives in Australia	
September	Penney and Butement visit possible test site at Emu Field	
October	*Hurricane* device exploded in HMS *Plym* (3rd)	
October/ November	US tests at Eniwetok—*Ivy* (2 shots). First shot, *Mike*, is first full-scale thermonuclear explosion in history	
November		US election—Eisenhower elected President in Republican landslide
December	British Ministers approve test at Emu Field in 1953 (*Totem*)	

Date	Nuclear weapon events	Other events
1953 February	Australian team visits UK for *Totem* planning	
March	British team visits Australia for *Totem* planning and reconnaissance	Stalin dies
March/ June	US tests in Nevada—*Upshot-Knothole* (11 shots); one shot, 61 kT, is biggest ever in Nevada	
May	British Chiefs of Staff consider permanent test site	
July		Korean War ends (began June 1950)
August	Soviet tests, including first H bomb test	
September	US aircraft to take part in monitoring *Totem*. Minister of Supply Sandys visits Australia; discusses permanent proving ground	In USSR, Kruschev succeeds Stalin as First Secretary
September/ October	Minor trials (initiator tests) at Emu Field	
October	*Totem* at Emu Field—2 shots (15th and 17th)	
November	Scientific survey of Monte Bello Islands	
December		Meeting in Bermuda,

Date	Nuclear weapon events	Other events
		Eisenhower and Churchill stress NATO as foundation of Western policy
1954 February/ March	US tests at Bikini and Eniwetok—*Castle* (6 shots). *Bravo* shot on 28 February (15 MT) contaminates Marshall Islands and Japanese fishing vessel *Lucky Dragon*	
March		Committee for Abolition of Nuclear Weapon Tests formed in north London (precursor of CND)
April		United Nations sets up 5-nation disarmament committee
May	USSR announces it will soon have intercontinental ballistic missile (ICBM) Britain asks Australia for agreement to minor trials in 1955	
June		United Kingdom Atomic Energy Authority Act creates UKAEA. UN Disarmament Conference opens in London with Anglo–French proposals for arms limitations and abolition of nuclear weapons

Date	Nuclear weapon events	Other events
August	Menzies informed of Britain's needs for 1956 trials and permanent proving ground	UKAEA comes into being
September/ October	Soviet test series	
December	British team visits Australia to discuss permanent proving ground and minor trials	
1955 February	British government announces decision to develop H bomb. US government releases report on fallout from *Castle Bravo* (February 1954)	British government announces first civil nuclear power programme
February/ May	US tests in Nevada— *Teacup* (14 shots)	
April	Australian Weapons Tests Committee (AWTC) set up	Australian troops to be stationed in Malaya. Churchill resigns; succeeded as Prime Minister by Anthony Eden. Eisenhower writes to Kruschev proposing test ban
April/ June	Minor trials at Maralinga	
May	US test (underwater)— *Wigwam*, in the Pacific. Permanent proving	Warsaw Pact formed. UK general election— Conservative government

Date	Nuclear weapon events	Other events
	ground at Maralinga announced	returned
June	Australian Atomic Weapons Tests Safety Committee (AWTSC) formed. Menzies accepts 1956 trials in principle. Task Force Commander appointed for Operation *Mosaic* at Monte Bello	US/UK bilateral agreement on exchanges of information on cooperation regarding atomic information for mutual defence purposes (Cmd 9555)
July	British team visits Australia to discuss *Mosaic*. Minor trials at Maralinga	Russell-Einstein manifesto calls on world scientists to work for peace. Eisenhower proposes 'open skies' plan (aerial inspection to monitor an arms control agreement)
August		First Geneva Conference on Peaceful Uses of Atomic Energy
August/ November	Soviet test series, including megaton shot in November	
September	AWTSC meteorological study of Monte Bello	
November	USSR launches first long-range ballistic missile from submarine	
December		UN sets up Scientific Committee on Effects of Atomic Radiation (UNSCEAR)

Date	Nuclear weapon events	Other events
1956 January		Menzies re-elected as Prime Minister of Australia
March	Memorandum of Arrangements regarding Maralinga. Minor trials at Maralinga	
March/ April	Soviet tests—including shots in megaton range	
May/ June	*Mosaic* in Monte Bello Islands—2 shots (16 May and 19 June)	
May/ July	US tests at Bikini and Eniwetok—*Redwing* (13 shots)	
June		US National Academy of Sciences report on radiation hazards and British MRC report (Cmnd 9780) both conclude fallout not yet dangerous but give warning for future. USA begins U-2 reconnaissance flights over USSR
July	US bomber crashes at RAF Lakenheath; nuclear weapons involved but do not explode	Egypt nationalizes Suez Canal
August/ November	Soviet tests	
September		Suez dispute referred to UN by Britain and France

Date	Nuclear weapon events	Other events
September/ October	*Buffalo* at Maralinga—4 shots (27 September and 4, 11 and 22 October) Minor trials at Maralinga	
October		International Atomic Energy Agency formed with 72 member countries. Calder Hall, 'world's first nuclear power station', opened in Cumbria
October/ November		Suez operation—British, French and Israeli forces enter Egypt
November		Eisenhower re-elected US President. Soviet forces enter Hungary
December		British and French forces withdraw from Egypt
1957 January		USA presents 5-point disarmament proposals to UN. Eden resigns; Macmillan becomes Prime Minister
January/ April	Soviet tests (including shots in megaton range)	
March		UN Disarmament Committee resumes talks in London. Euratom Treaty signed in Rome

Date	Nuclear weapon events	Other events
March/ November	Minor trials in Maralinga	
April		In UK, Defence White Paper emphasizes dependence on the nuclear deterrent and end of conscription. Albert Schweitzer appeals for test ban
May	AWTSC reconstituted	USSR appeals to USA and Britain to cease tests. Britain proposes limitation and registration of tests. Eisenhower approves temporary test ban proposals
May/ June	*Grapple*—off Malden Island to the south of Christmas Island area—3 shots (15 and 31 May, 19 June)	
May/ December	US tests in Nevada— *Plumbob* (28 shots, 2 underground)	
June		IAEA comes into being. Linus Pauling presents scientist's test ban petition to Eisenhower. Joint Western proposals for suspension of tests as part of disarmament agreement

Date	Nuclear weapon events	Other events
August/ December	Soviet series of 6 H bomb tests	
September	US first underground test (*Ranier*) in *Plumbob* series. USSR tests first ICBM successfully	
September/ October	*Antler* at Maralinga—3 shots (14 and 25 September, 9 October)	
October		USSR launches first space satellite, Sputnik. Windscale accident—fire in No 1 plutonium production reactor
November	*Grapple X* off Christmas Island—1 shot	

1958

Date	Nuclear weapon events	Other events
January		Scientist's petition for test ban presented to UN by Linus Pauling. CND formed in UK. First US satellite (Explorer I) in orbit
February/ March	Soviet tests (including 6 shots in MT range)	
March		First Aldermaston march by CND. Kruschev announces unilateral Soviet test suspension

Date	Nuclear weapon events	Other events
April	*Grapple Y* off Christmas Island—1 shot (28th)	US Scientific Advisory Committee recommends comprehensive test ban to Eisenhower. Eisenhower separates test ban issue from general disarmament in message to Kruschev
April/ November	Minor trials at Maralinga	
April/ August	US tests in the Pacific— *Hardtack I* (31 shots, several in MT range)	
July		US/UK bilateral agreements on collaboration in atomic energy for defence purposes (Cmnd 537). Soviet and American scientists meet in Geneva to discuss detection and inspection of nuclear tests
August		Geneva meeting of experts agrees on extensive inspection system. Eisenhower proposes test ban negotiations to begin 31 October and pledges one-year test moratorium. UNSCEAR makes first report on radiation hazards
August/ September	US high altitude tests in South Atlantic—*Argus* (3 shots) *Grapple Z* at Christmas Island—4 shots	

Date	Nuclear weapon events	Other events
September		Kruschev accepts Eisenhower's proposals. Second Geneva Conference on Peaceful Uses of Atomic Energy
September/ November	Soviet tests, some in MT range. US tests in Nevada— *Hardback II* (32 shots)	
October		3-Power Conference on Discontinuance of Nuclear Weapons Tests begins in Geneva (31st)
November	Last Soviet test detected (3rd)	Test moratorium begins (lasts until September 1961)
December		Menzies re-elected as Australian Prime Minister
1959 March		US/UK bilateral defence agreement July 1958 (Cmnd 537) amended (Cmnd 859). Macmillan visits Eisenhower to discuss test ban problems
March/ December	Minor trials at Maralinga— first *Vixen A* trials begin	
April		Eisenhower proposes to Kruschev interim atmospheric test ban

Date	Nuclear weapon events	Other events
June/ July		Technical working group in Geneva discusses detection of high altitude tests and explosions in space
July		Kruschev proposes European nuclear-free zone
September		10-Power Disarmament Conference set up by Britain, France, USA and USSR
October		UK general election—Conservatives returned with increased majority
November/ December		Second technical working group in Geneva falls to agree on test detection
1960 February	First French nuclear test (atmospheric) in the Sahara	Eisenhower proposes ban on all atmospheric tests and large underground tests
March		USSR accepts ban conditionally
April	Second French nuclear test (atmospheric) in Sahara. Britain cancels *Blue Streak* (IRBM) programme	
April/ October	Minor trials at Maralinga—first *Vixen B* tests	

Date	Nuclear weapon events	Other events
May		Soviet missile brings down US U-2 spy plane. Summit conference in Paris broken up by Kruschev because of U2 incident. New report by US National Academy of Sciences on radiation hazards concludes fallout danger is still small
October		In Britain, Labour Party Conference votes for unilateral nuclear disarmament. First British nuclear-powered submarine, HMS *Dreadnought*, launched
November		John F Kennedy elected President of United States. In Britain, activist group (Committee of 100) formed within CND
December	Third French test (atmospheric) in Sahara	British MRC's second report on radiation hazards (Cmnd 1225) agrees generally with US May 1960 report

1961

Date	Nuclear weapon events	Other events
March/ December	Minor trials in Maralinga	CND demonstrations throughout the year
April	Fourth French test in Sahara	Manned Soviet spaceship orbits earth
May		Manned US spaceship makes suborbital flight

Date	Nuclear weapon events	Other events
July/August		Berlin crisis—Berlin wall erected between East and West Berlin
August		Britain applies to join EEC
September	USSR resumes atmospheric tests (1st). USA resumes testing	
September/ December	US underground tests in Nevada—*Nougat* (8 shots). Soviet tests—15 in MT range, one of 58 MT (30 October)	
October		In Britain, Labour Party Conference reverses 1960 vote for unilateral nuclear disarmament
November	Fifth French test in Sahara	Kennedy and Macmillan meet in Bermuda
December	Kruschev announces USSR has nuclear weapons of 100 MT plus	
1962 January		3-Power test ban conference in Geneva finally breaks down
January/ June	US underground tests in Nevada—*Nougat* (continued) 36 shots	
February	Soviet underground test	

Date	Nuclear weapon events	Other events
March	Joint US/UK underground test in Nevada—*Pampas*	17-nation Disarmament Conference opens in Geneva
April/ November	US atmospheric tests in the Pacific, in Christmas Island and Johnston Island areas—*Dominic* (36 shots, 7 over 1 MT). UK assistance, code-named *Brigadoon*	
May	Sixth French test, underground	
July/ December	US tests in Nevada—*Storax* (19 shots). Soviet atmospheric tests (39 shots, one 30 MT, several in MT range)	
October		Cuban missile crisis
November		Soviet missile sites in Cuba dismantled and bombers withdrawn
December	Second joint US/UK test in Nevada	*Skybolt* (US air launched ballistic missile) cancelled. Kennedy and Macmillan meet at Nassau—agree USA will provide Britain with Polaris missiles
1963 January		Britain's EEC application fails

Date	Nuclear weapon events	Other events
February/ June	US underground tests in Nevada—*Storax* (continued) (11 shots). *Blue Steel*, British stand-off bomb, comes into service	
March	French tests (2 shots) underground	
March/ April	Minor trials at Maralinga	
April	France announces new test site in Polynesia—New Zealand protests	Polaris agreement between USA and Britain
August		Partial Test Ban Treaty (banning atmospheric tests) signed in Moscow
August/ December	US underground tests in Nevada—*Niblic* (15 shots)	
September	AWTSC reviews Maralinga contamination	
October	French test—one underground shot	Partial Test Ban Treaty in force. Macmillan resigns as Prime Minister for health reasons; succeeded by Lord Home (Sir Alec Douglas-Home)
November		President Kennedy assassinated; succeeded by L B Johnson
December		Menzies re-elected as Australian Prime Minister

Date	Nuclear weapon events	Other events
1964 January		President Johnson proposes nuclear freeze at 18-nation Disarmament Conference
January/ June	US underground tests in Nevada—*Niblic* (continued) 13 shots	
February	French test—one underground shot	
April		Britain's second civil nuclear power programme announced
June	Closure of Christmas Island announced. French test—one underground shot	
July	Joint US/UK underground test in Nevada—*Cormorant*	
July/ December	US underground tests in Nevada—*Whetstone* (15 shots)	
August		3rd Geneva Conference on Peaceful Uses of Atomic Energy. Kruschev retires—succeeded as Soviet Premier by Kosygin, and as Party Secretary by Brezhnev

Date	Nuclear weapon events	Other events
October	First Chinese test (atmospheric)	UK general election returns Labour government under Harold Wilson
November	French test—one underground shot	Democrat landslide in US election gives Johnson victory
December		Heavy fighting in Vietnam
1965 January	Soviet underground test	Churchill dies
January/ June	US underground tests in Nevada—*Whetstone* (continued) 18 shots	
February	French underground test	
March		3500 US marines land in Vietnam. Vietnam war lasts until 1973
April		Australia sends troops to Vietnam
May	Chinese atmospheric tests (2 shots) French underground test (1 shot)	
July/ December	US underground tests in Nevada—*Flintlock* (10 shots)	
August		17-nation Disarmament Conference reconvened after 10-month recess.

Date	Nuclear weapon events	Other events
		USA presents draft non-proliferation treaty
September	Fourth joint US/UK underground test in Nevada—*Charcoal*	
October	French underground test	
December	French underground test	
1966		
January	4 US nuclear bombs accidentally released at Palomares, Spain; none explode, widespread contamination	Menzies resigns as Australian Prime Minister—succeeded by Harold Holt
January/ June	US underground tests in Nevada—*Flintlock* (continued) 29 shots	
February	French underground test	In UK, general election returns Labour government under Wilson
March	Soviet megaton test detected	Expiry of Memorandum of Arrangements (1956 agreement on Maralinga)
May	Chinese atmospheric test	
July/ October	French atmospheric tests at Mururoa—5 shots	
July/ December	US underground tests in Nevada—*Latchkey* (11 shots)	

Date	Nuclear weapon events	Other events
October/ December	Chinese atmospheric tests—2 shots. Soviet underground tests	
December		In Australia, election victory for Holt and Liberal Party
1967 January/ June	US underground tests in Nevada—*Latchkey* (continued) 16 shots	
April/ July	Operation *Brumby*—clean up at Maralinga and Emu Field	
May		Britain applies again for EEC membership
June	Chinese atmospheric test	Arab–Israeli conflict at its height
June/ July	French tests at Mururoa (3 shots in atmosphere)	
July/ December	US underground tests in Nevada—*Crosstie* (12 shots) (continued during 1968)	
September		Termination of agreement on Maralinga
November		British EEC application refused
December	Maralinga Range relinquished	

Appendix B   Modus Vivendi 1948 (Annex 2)

Areas of Co-operation between Members of the British Commonwealth

(Approved by the Combined Policy Committee at its meeting on 7 January 1948)

Apart from the arrangements which already exist between the United Kingdom and Canada, the question has arisen of co-operation between the United Kingdom and other members of the British Commonwealth.

As a part of the combined effort during the war years, assistance to the British atomic energy project was given by scientists from New Zealand, Australia and South Africa. Some of these have worked in Canada and some in United States and from there have moved to Harwell. Several of them will shortly be returning to New Zealand and at a later stage—one year or more—there will be a similar return to Australia. It is intended to admit further scientists from these Dominions to work at Harwell.

The three CPC governments are also actively co-operating with the Dominions in the field of raw materials. South Africa in particular is likely to become an important source of raw materials and is carrying out active work on benefication of ores. In due course South African interests may be expected to extend.

With a view particularly to making secure the information held by Dominion scientists on their return to their respective countries, and of furthering full co-operation in the field of raw material investigation and supply, it is recommended that the areas of co-operation outlined below should be recognised:

(a) The subjects covered in Sections I and II of the proposed Declassification Guide and which are listed as 'Topics for immediate declassification'.

(b) *The field of health and safety*, including
1. Experimental work from which radiation tolerances may be established.
2. Genetics.
3. General medical and biological studies.
4. Instruments, laboratory design and techniques of this field.

(c) *Research uses of radioactive isotopes and stable isotopes, including* preparation, techniques for handling, instruments, mutual availability for research purposes.

(d) *Detection of a distant nuclear explosion*
Operation of recording stations.

(e) Survey methods for source materials.

(f) Benefication of ores—co-operation with South Africa and with other Dominions of (sic) the work developed there.

(g) Extraction of low-grade ores—within the fields defined by the ores locally available.

(h) *Design information on research reactors*
Design information on the low-power graphite reactor build at Harwell (Gleep) to be communicated by United Kingdom to New Zealand. It is recognised that this information will be effectively available to the New Zealand Government on the return of its staff in early 1948.

(i) *General research experience* with the following reactors
Harwell, Gleep, to be communicated by United Kingdom to New Zealand.

Co-operation within the above classified fields will be subject to an understanding between Governments to adopt common standards in holding information secure. Transmission would also be subject to the principle of current usability.

Appendix C Memorandum of arrangements between the United Kingdom and Australian Governments

Atomic weapons proving ground—Maralinga

Introduction

1 The Australian Government and the United Kingdom Government being agreed on the desirability of establishing a proving ground for atomic weapons and the Australian Government having offered to make a site available for this purpose in South Australia, this Memorandum sets out the principles which the two Governments agree shall govern the establishment of this site as a proving ground and its use for atomic weapon trials.

Conditions as to occupancy of site

2 The Australian Government will make the site at Maralinga in South Australia as defined in the annex to this Memorandum available to the United Kingdom Government as a proving ground for atomic weapons for a period of 10 years which may be extended by mutual agreement.

3 The use of this site by the United Kingdom Government in accordance with this agreement shall be free from all rent and similar charges.

4 During the currency of this agreement the Australian Government will take such steps as may be necessary in accordance with the laws and regulations in operation in Australia to proclaim the area defined in the annex as a prohibited area.

5 On the termination of this Agreement the United Kingdom Government shall have the right to remove and dispose of all movable facilities and equipment provided at the expense of the United Kingdom Government.

Nature of the tests to be carried out

6 No thermo-nuclear (hydrogen) weapon will be tested on the site.

7 An agreement of the Australian Government will be obtained before any atomic test is carried out on the site. For this purpose the United Kingdom Government will provide the Australian Government with sufficient information about the nature of any proposed test to enable the Australian Government to satisfy itself that the test can safely be carried out on the site. Such information shall be made available only to properly authorised persons in accordance with the security arrangements agreed between the two Governments.

Safety

8 The United Kingdom Government will be responsible for undertaking all practicable measures on the site to ensure that any tests carried out there do not cause injury or damage to persons or property.

9 In collaboration with the United Kingdom Government the Australian Government will set up and operate a chain of fixed monitoring stations at agreed sites in Australia and will make the information from these measurements available to the United Kingdom Government.

Claims for compensation

10 The Australian Government will take all reasonable steps to exclude unauthorised persons from the prohibited area.

11 The United Kingdom Government undertakes to indemnify the Australian Government in respect of all valid claims arising out of the death or injury of any person or any damage to property due to tests carried out on the site, except for claims made by any employee or servant of a Government other than the United Kingdom Government authorised to be within the prohibited area specifically in connection with tests on the site.

12 The United Kingdom Government accepts liability for such corrective measures as may be practicable in the event of radioactive contamination resulting from the tests on the site.

Australian access to the site

13 Subject to such safety and security arrangements as are agreed by the United Kingdom Government authorised officers of the Australian Government will be allowed access to the site.

14   By agreement with the United Kingdom Government the Australian Government will have the right to construct and/or install facilities and equipment for tests in the course of atomic weapon trials on the site and to send official observers to be present at any test on the site.

Information and effects

15   The United Kingdom Government will provide the Australian Government with all the data compiled as a result of the tests on the site about the effects of atomic weapons for both civil defence and military purposes. Such data shall however only be made available to properly authorised persons in accordance with the security arrangements agreed between the two Governments.

16   The Australian Government will similarly make available to the United Kingdom Government information about the results of tests of Australian facilities or equipment tested on the site.

Control of the project

17   A Joint Committee of Australian and United Kingdom representatives under the chairmanship of a representative of the Australian Department of Supply will be set up in Australia to consider all matters of joint concern in relation to the establishment and maintenance of the proving ground and to the arrangements for any trials thereon as may be approved from time to time and to advise the responsible departments through their respective representatives. The functions of the Committee will include the co-ordination of all activities within Australia of the United Kingdom and Australian Government Departments and Authorities, and their agents concerned with the project, and such executive action in matters of joint concern in Australia as may be agreed by the representatives of both parties.

Financial arrangements

18   A separate financial agreement will be negotiated between the Australian and the United Kingdom Governments in regard of costs of this project.

19   Nothing in this agreement shall be regarded as precluding the participation in atomic tests on the proving ground of other members of the British Commonwealth of Nations as may be mutually agreed by the Australian and United Kingdom Governments.

20 Unless provided to the contrary in any separate financial agreement which may be made between the two Governments, this agreement shall be deemed to be made on the understanding that all costs will be to the account of the United Kingdom Government.

Memorandum of Arrangements between Australian and United Kingdom Governments in regard to allocation of the costs of establishing and maintaining a proving ground for Atomic Weapons in South Australia, and for any tests carried out thereon.

1 This document is intended to be read in conjunction with the Memorandum of Arrangements between the Australian Government and the United Kingdom Government concerning the establishment in South Australia of a proving ground for atomic weapons.

2 Complementary to the arrangements outlined in that document regarding the terms and conditions on which the Australian Government agrees to make the site at Maralinga available to the United Kingdom Government for use as a proving ground for atomic weapons, this Memorandum sets out the financial obligations of the respective Governments in respect of the establishment and maintenance of the proving ground and of the arrangements for holding such tests thereon as may from time to time be approved.

Allocation of costs

3 It is agreed that subject to paragraphs 4 and 5 hereunder, the United Kingdom Government will bear all costs in connection with the establishment and maintenance of the proving ground and of any tests carried out thereon.

4 The Australian Government will bear—

(a) the cost of any agreed target response or other tests carried out specifically at the request of any Australian Government Department or Authority;

(b) the expenses of any Australian personnel authorised at the request of the Australian Government to attend any trials held on the proving ground; and

(c) the costs of providing such Australian Services personnel as are agreed upon by the Australian Government from time to time for specific tasks at the Maralinga Proving Ground.

5 The Australian Government will, through appropriate Departments and organisations, provide such administrative assistance as is practicable in directions appropriate to their functions without cost to the United Kingdom Government. Where, however, such assistance cannot be rendered without additional cost to the normal functioning of such Departments, the additional cost concerned will be met by the United Kingdom Government.

6 The Australian Government agrees that any installation or facility provided at the expense of the United Kingdom Government in Australia will remain the property of the United Kingdom Government and, as provided for in Clause 5 of the Memorandum of Arrangements, be subject to removal or disposal on termination of the main agreement.

7 If it is mutually agreed between the Australian and United Kingdom Governments that another member of the British Commonwealth of Nations should participate in tests on the site, the allocation of any expenses of personnel authorised to be present at the request of the said member government and of any costs of agreed tests carried out specifically at the request of the said member government will be separately arranged between the United Kingdom and Australian Governments and the other Government concerned.

8 The cost of fares of United Kingdom personnel travelling to and from Australia and whilst in Australia, and the cost of Australian personnel travelling to and from the United Kingdom and whilst in the United Kingdom, will be borne respectively by the United Kingdom and Australian Governments.

9 The provisions of this Memorandum of Financial Arrangements may be altered by mutual consent between the Australian and United Kingdom Governments.

7 March 1956.

Appendix D Memorandum respecting the termination of the memorandum of arrangements between the United Kingdom and Australian Governments of 7 March 1956 concerning the Atomic Weapons Proving Ground—Maralinga

The Government of the United Kingdom of Great Britain and Northern Ireland and the Government of the Commonwealth of Australia, desiring to terminate the arrangements set out in the Memorandum of Arrangements of 7 March 1956 between them concerning the Atomic Weapons Proving Ground—Maralinga (the "Memorandum of Arrangements") and the Memorandum in regard to allocation of costs of the same date, hereby record the following matters:

(a) The United Kingdom Government have completed decontamination and debris clearance at the Atomic Weapons Proving Ground Maralinga to the satisfaction of the Australian Government.

(b) On 21 December 1967, the United Kingdom Government relinquished to the Australian Government the site at Maralinga, as defined in the Annex to the Memorandum of Arrangements, and transferred without charge to the Australian Government certain installations and movable stores in accordance with detailed arrangements agreed between the British Defence Research Supply Staff and the Australian Department of Supply.

(c) With effect from 21 December 1967, the United Kingdom Government are released from all liabilities and responsibilities under the Memorandum of Arrangements save that the United Kingdom will continue to indemnify the Australian Government in accordance with Clause 11 of the Memorandum in respect of claims for which the cause for action occurred after 7 March 1956 and before 21 December 1967.

Signed at Canberra this twenty-third day of September 1967.

For the Government of the United Kingdom of Great Britain and Northern Ireland.

For the Government of the Commonwealth of Australia.

Appendix E   Major Trials in Australia

Summary

Date	Operation	Location	Service Commander	Director	Deputy	No. of AWRE personnel
Oct 1952	*Hurricane* (1 shot)	Monte Bello Islands	Rear Admiral A D Torlesse, RN	Dr W G Penney	Dr L C Tyte	99
Oct 1953	*Totem* (2 shots)	Emu Field	Brig. L C Lucas*	Sir Wm Penney	C A Adams	158
May/June 1956	*Mosaic* (2 shots)	Monte Bello Islands	Commodore H Martell, RN	C A Adams	I Maddock	53
Sep/Oct 1956	*Buffalo* (4 shots)	Maralinga	Air Commodore C T Weir, RAF	Sir Wm Penney	R Pilgrim	224
Sep/Oct 1957	*Antler* (3 shots)	Maralinga	Air Commodore W P Sutcliffe, RAF	C A Adams	Dr J A T Dawson	195

* Australian Department of Works

Appendix E (2)

United Kingdom Atmospheric Nuclear Weapons Tests in Australia, October 1952–October 1957

Operation and location	Date and time (GMT)	Site	Type*	Height (m)	Approx Yield (kT)	Yield range
Hurricane Monte Bello Is, WA	3 Oct 1952 0000Z†	Lagoon of 12 m depth	CSB: in HMS *Plym*	−2.7	25	Kiloton, or low intermediate
Totem Emu Field, SA	14 Oct 1953 2130Z	T1	NSB: MS Tower	31	10	Kiloton, or low
	26 Oct 1953 2130Z	T2	NSB: MS Tower	31	8	kiloton, or low
Mosaic Monte Bello Is, WA	16 May 1956 0350Z	G1: Trimouille Is.	NSB: Al Tower	31	15	Kiloton, or low
	19 June 1956 0214Z	G2: Alpha Is.	NSB: Al Tower	31	60	Kiloton, or low intermediate

Buffalo Maralinga Range, SA	One Tree	27 Sept 1956 0730Z	NSB: Al Tower	31	15	Kiloton, or low
	Marcoo	4 Oct 1956 0700Z	CSB: at ground surface	0.2	1.5	Kiloton, or low
	Kite	11 Oct 1956 0557Z	Airburst: freefall	150	3	Kiloton, or low
	Breakaway	21 Oct 1956 1435Z	NSB: Al Tower	31	10	Kiloton, or low
Antler Maralinga Range, SA	Tadje	14 Sept 1957 0505Z	NSB: Al Tower	31	1	Sub-kiloton, or very low
	Biak	25 Sept 1957 0030Z	NSB: Al Tower	31	6	Kiloton, or low
	Taranaki	9 Oct 1957 0645Z	Airburst: balloon system borne	300	25	Kiloton, or low intermediate

* NSB: Near surface burst
  CSB: Contact surface burst
  MS: Mild steel
  Al: Aluminium alloy
† For clarity, this time is conventionally quoted as 0001Z on 3 October 1952 (GMT): the firing time was almost exactly midnight 2/3 October 1952 (GMT).
Source: SFS, AWRE, Aldermaston

Appendix F   Published figures of nuclear explosions between 1945 and 1984

Year	USA a	USA u	USSR a	USSR u	UK a	UK u	France a	France u	China a	China u	India a	India u	Total
1945	3	0											3
1946	1	1/1											2
1947	0	0											0
1948	3	0											3
1949	0	0	1	0									1
1950	0	0	0	0									0
1951	15	1	2	0									18
1952	10	0	0	0	1	0							11
1953	11	0	2	0	2	0							15
1954	6	0	2	0	0	0							8
1955	16	2/1	4	0	0	0							22
1956	18	0	7	0	6	0							31
1957	27	5	13	0	7	0							52
1958	60	17/2	26	0	5	0							108
1959	0	0	0	0	0	0							0
1960	0	0	0	0	0	0	3	0					3
1961	0	10	30	2/1	0	0	1	1					44
1962	38	58/1	41	1	0	2	0	1					141
to 5 Aug 1963	4	25	0	0	0	0	0	2					31
Total pre PTBT*	212	119	161	3	21	2	4	4					526

	USA		USSR		UK		France		China		India		Total
Year	a	u	a	u	a	u	a	u	a	u	a	u	
5 Aug to end 1963	0	14	0	0	0	0	0	1					15
1964	0	29	0	6	0	1	0	3	1	0			40
1965	0	28	0	9	0	1	0	4	1	0			43
1966	0	40	0	15	0	0	5	1	3	0			64
1967	0	28	0	15	0	0	3	0	2	0			48
1968	0	33	0	13	0	0	5	0	1	0			52
1969	0	29	0	15	0	0	0	0	1	1			46
1970	0	30	0	12	0	0	8	0	1	0			51
1971	0	12	0	19	0	0	5	0	1	0			37
1972	0	8	0	22	0	0	3	0	2	0			35
1973	0	9	0	14	0	0	5	0	1	0			29
1974	0	7	0	19	0	1	7	0	1	0	0	1	36
1975	0	16	0	15	0	0	0	2	0	1	0	0	34
1976	0	15	0	17	0	1	0	3	3	1	0	0	40
1977	0	12	0	16	0	0	0	6	1	0	0	0	35
1978	0	12	0	27	0	2	0	7	2	1	0	0	51
1979	0	14	0	29	0	1	0	9	0	0	0	0	53
1980	0	14	0	21	0	3	0	11	1	0	0	0	50
1981	0	16	0	21	0	1	0	11	0	0	0	0	49
1982	0	18	0	31	0	1	0	5	0	0	0	0	55
1983	0	15	0	27	0	1	0	7	0	1	0	0	51
1984	0	15	0	27	0	2	0	7	0	2	0	0	53
Total post PTBT	*0*	*414*	*0*	*390*	*0*	*15*	*41*	*77*	*22*	*7*	*0*	*1*	*967*
Total	212	533	161	393	21	17	45	81	22	7	0	1	1493

a = atmospheric
u = underground + underwater (number of latter indicated after oblique)
* Partial Test Ban Treaty
Sources: *SIPRI Yearbook 1974–1985*, consolidated with *Announced United States Nuclear Tests, July 1945 to December 1984*, published by the US DOE.

Appendix G Some Notes on Ionizing Radiations and Radiation Safety Standards

These brief notes are in nine sections:

- Types of ionizing radiations
- External and internal radiations
- Units of radiation
- Effects of high doses of radiation
- Effects of low doses of radiation
- Maximum permissible levels or limits
- Radiation limits for trials personnel
- Measurement of radiation exposure
- Radiation limits for population exposure used in determining criteria for safe test-firing conditions

Types of ionizing radiations

1   Everyone is exposed to one or more man-made sources of ionizing radiation, from medical X-rays to fallout, as well as to natural sources (mainly cosmic rays and terrestrial radiation from rocks and soil). Ionizing radiations include high-energy subatomic particles, and electromagnetic radiation such as X-rays and gamma rays (which are of shorter wavelength and higher energy than ultraviolet or visible radiation.)

2   It is the ability of these forms of radiation to ionize atoms in biologically important molecules that leads to their various health effects (see paras 14–19). These biological effects have been more extensively studied than those of any comparable environmental agents that affect large numbers of people.

3   The five types of ionizing radiation are:

Particulate radiation

(1) *Alpha particles*—these relatively heavy, positively charged particles are the nuclei of helium atoms. They have so little penetrating power that they can be stopped by a sheet of paper; they are only a hazard to health if alpha-emitters (e.g., plutonium) are taken into the body, but can then cause extremely localised but very damaging irradiation of the tissues.

(2) *Beta particles*—these are electrons and are very light particles. They are more penetrating than alpha particles, but from an external source, they only reach the surface tissues of the body; thus they are a hazard to the skin, and to immediately underlying tissues to a depth of the order of 10 mm, but not to deep tissues. Beta particles can also be hazardous if beta-emitters are taken into the body.

(3) *Neutrons*—these uncharged particles are about one quarter the mass of an alpha particle. They are penetrating, and can be very damaging biologically. Fortunately the circumstances in which people are likely to be exposed to neutron radiation are rare; it invariably irradiates the body from external sources.

Electromagnetic radiation

(4) *Gamma radiation*—these photons are electromagnetic rays originating in the atomic nucleus; they are extremely penetrating and can affect the whole body, including the internal organs, when the source is external to the body. They are less effective when their parent material is inside the body.

(5) *X-rays*—these result from bombarding a metallic surface by energetic electrons; they are otherwise similar to and behave like gamma rays.

4   In the context of weapon trials, gamma rays were significant, with beta particles and X-rays less so. Neutrons can be ignored, as no one at the trials was exposed to them in other than trivial amounts. Alpha emitters, though potentially hazardous as internal sources, were not of any importance as a result of the nuclear tests.

External and internal radiations

5   The predominant potential hazard to atomic test personnel was from external irradiation of the body by gamma rays from radioactive

fallout; not by radiations from the actual nuclear explosions, since the safety distances adopted provided protection against this hazard as well as against blast and thermal effects. An American handbook published in 1950 indicated that radioactive material entering the body after an atomic explosion was not a significant problem (*Effects of Atomic Weapons*, p. 358); in the United Kingdom trials, protective measures were taken to provide assurance that there were no intakes of radioactive materials by trials participants.

Units of radiation

6   The units used to measure radiation in the 1950s were the roentgen, the rep, the rad and the rem, and these are the units that appear in all the contemporary documents; other units are in use today (see para 12).

7   *The roentgen* (abbreviated as r and later as R) was first defined in 1937. Named after the discoverer of X-rays, it correctly applied only to a specified range of X-rays, but subsequently was used as a practical way of quantifying gamma rays (but not other types of ionizing radiation). It was a measure of radiation *exposure* measured in air, or more usually as measured by a film-badge worn on the torso.

8   *The rep* ('roentgen-equivalent-physical') was a unit of absorbed radiation dose that, by comparing the absorption in tissue of alpha and beta particles with the absorption in tissue of energy corresponding to that from one roentgen of gamma rays, could express a radiation dose consisting of mixed types of radiation.

9   *The rad and the rem* replaced the rep by the late 1950s and early 1960s. Both were units of absorbed radiation dose, i.e., energy absorbed in a small mass of material, and the rad ('radiation absorbed dose') was for most practical protection purposes numerically equal to the roentgen. The rem ('roentgen-equivalent-man') was a more sophisticated unit of 'dose equivalent'; it took account of the differing capacity for biological damage of different types of radiation by using a modifying factor—the 'relative biological effectiveness' (RBE) or an average 'quality factor' (Q). Thus rem = rad × Q. For gamma radiation Q is 1, and therefore 1 rem = 1 rad. But some ionizing radiations have a higher Q, e.g., for fast neutrons it is 10 and for alpha particles it is 20.

10   *The curie* (Ci) was a measure of radioactivity, i.e., of the disintegration rate of radioactive material. (It was not a measure of radiation

dose.) Named after Marie Curie, the discoverer of radium, it was based on the radioactivity of radium. One gram of radium decays at the rate of 3.7×10^{10} disintegrations per second (dps), and any quantity of a radioactive substance that produces 3.7×10^{10} dps exactly constitutes one curie. Multiple units were often used—e.g., megacurie (one million curies), millicurie (one-thousandth of a curie), microcurie (one millionth of a curie).

11 During the 1950s, radiation exposures were measured in roentgens, and doses in reps, rads and rems. (For exposure to gamma radiation, roentgens, reps, rads and rems were all about the same.) Multiple units were used as appropriate—e.g., 1 millirem (mrem) was one-thousandth of a rem.

12 The historical units have recently been superseded by new international units—the gray (named after an eminent British radiologist), the sievert (named after a Swedish scientist who was a pioneer of radiological protection) and the becquerel (named after the French scientist who discovered radioactivity). The old and new units are related as shown below:

(1) *Units of dose*
    1 gray (Gy) = 100 rads
    1 rad = 0.01 Gy

(2) *Units of radiation exposure*
    There is no special new name for the roentgen (r or R) which is obsolete. Radiation exposure is now expressed in coulombs per kilogram.

(3) *Units of dose equivalent*
    1 sievert (Sv) = 100 rems
    1 rem = 0.01 Sv

(4) *Units of activity*
    The curie (Ci) has been replaced by the becquerel (Bq). As 1 Bq = 1 dps, the equivalent of the curie is 3.7×10^{10} Bq exactly.

13 Because grays and sieverts are very large units for practical use in expressing radiation doses and dose equivalents, the sub-units milligray, millisievert and microsievert are often used (mGy, mSv, and μSv). Because the Bq is so small, multiple units are used; the prefix giga indicates 1000 million, thus 37 gigabequerel (GBq) is equivalent to one curie (Ci) exactly.

Effects of acute radiation exposures to the whole body

14   The so called 'median acute lethal dose' of radiation—i.e., that which will cause the death within 30 days of 50 per cent of the people so exposed—is estimated at 3 to 4 sieverts (300 to 400 rems) delivered to the whole body over a short time, generally less than 24 hours. At a dose of 1 sievert (100 rems) deaths would be unlikely. These estimates are based on the total of some seventeen immediate or early deaths known to have occurred throughout the world as a result of radiation accidents before 1986. Where exposures are prolonged, over days and weeks rather than hours or minutes, the dose required to produce an equivalent amount of damage or risk of death would be greater, perhaps by up to a factor or 2 or 3 (Pochin, 1983, p. 99).

15   Below 25 rems, there would probably be no obvious immediate effects of acute radiation—say up to 24 hours in duration—to the whole body. At 25–100 rems, some blood changes and some slight nausea might be expected. Then up to 200 rems there would be in increasing possibility of nausea, vomiting and diarrhoea, and a small chance of permanent injury. Ill effects would increase with higher doses, until at very high prompt doses within a few minutes, say 600 rads in air (or 450 rems to the bone-marrow) death would occur within about 60 days in 50 per cent of those exposed.

Effects of low doses of radiation

16   For a few, non-stochastic*, effects of radiation (such as eye cataracts) a threshold dose exists. For most long-term effects of low radiation doses (such as leukaemia and other cancers) it must be assumed for protection purposes that there is no threshold; they are stochastic† and the risk of damage—on the linear (non-threshold) assumption—is taken to be proportional to the exposure, however small. This assumption may overestimate the risks when people are exposed to very small

---

* *Non-stochastic* effects are those for which (a) the severity of the effect varies with the size of the dose causing it, and (b) the likelihood of the effect is high once a threshold dose is exceeded.

† For *stochastic* effects it is the probability of the effect occurring, rather than its severity, that varies with the size of the dose.

amounts of gamma radiation.

17   The latent period between radiation exposure and the onset of disease averages about 12 years for leukaemia, and even longer—over 20 to 25 years—for most other forms of cancer. Since between one quarter and one third of all people develop cancers during their life time, individual cases of cancer can seldom be shown to be causally related to a small radiation exposure perhaps 20 years or more earlier. But if a collective dose to a population can be calculated, an upper estimate of the health impact may be made by applying a risk factor. Much work has been done in this field in recent years by various scientific bodies, in particular the International Commission on Radiological Protection (ICRP—see para 20), the United Nations Committee on Effects of Atomic Radiation (UNSCEAR) and the United States Committee on Biological Effects of Ionizing Radiations (BEIR). A great deal has been learnt since the 1950s, and the risks of radiation-induced cancers developing after long latent periods are now much better appreciated than they were at that time.

18   The risk factor of 0.01 cancer death per sievert, which until recently has been generally accepted, was applied in 1985 to the estimated radiation exposure of the whole Australian population resulting from the British atomic tests. Wise and Moroney, two scientists from the Australian Radiation Laboratory, estimated the population dose as 700 man-sieverts (70 000 man-rems), an average of 70 microsieverts (7 millirems). On the linear dose-risk hypothesis of ICRP and UNSCEAR, such a dose indicates that there may be up to a maximum of seven fatal cancers and less than seven serious hereditary defects (see Chapter 12). Even if the risk factor is 0.1 excess cancer per sievert, as new data suggest, this would mean, say, 70 excess cancers in total. (This figure refers to *incidence* not cancer fatalities; the latter figure would be lower). The excess cancers would not be evenly distributed over the population, but would occur chiefly in a much smaller population of those who received the higher doses.

19   The complex problems of genetic (or inheritable) effects of radiation exposure have been much studied for some 60 years, and ample evidence has been obtained in different animal species—particularly the mouse—on the frequency with which radiation induces various types of genetic abnormality. For man, no reliable data exist. However, it is estimated that if one million people of all ages in England and Wales each received 1 millisievert (0.1 rem) six hereditary defects might be expected. (Pochin, 1983, p. 124).

Maximum permissible levels or limits

20 Maximum permissible levels (MPL) and maximum permissible doses (MPD)—old fashioned and misleading terms, now replaced by 'limits'—were recommended by the International Commission on Radiological Protection (ICRP), an international scientific body responsible to the International Congress of Radiology. It was originally set up in 1928 to advise on safe use of X-rays and radium. After the Second World War, it was reconstituted in 1950, with enlarged advisory functions which were widely accepted by national authorities. Up to 1958, ICRP limitations on radiation exposure were purely occupational. In 1950 the Commission set an occupational limit of 0.5 r a week. This referred to the whole-body external radiation, measured in air; an exposure of 0.5 r per week as measured in air at the body surface was equivalent to about 0.3 r per week measured in the deep tissue of the body. (The other 1950 recommendations are omitted here for simplicity, and for the reasons given in paras 2 and 3).

21 In 1956 ICRP set a weekly limit of 0.3 rem—an apparent reduction but, since 0.3 rem in deep tissue (para 20) was equivalent to the previous 0.5 r measured in air, it is not actually a change.

22 In 1958 new ICRP recommendations replaced the weekly limit of 0.3 rem by a quarterly limit of 3 rems, i.e., up to 12 rems per year, but with an over-riding age-related limit on the radiation dose that might be accumulated. (This was based on a formula $D = 5 (N - 18)$, where D was the accumulated dose in rems and N was the year of age. It amounted in practice to an average annual limit of 5 rems over a working life time.) ICRP also published recommendations for the general public for the first time; because pregnant women, children, the sick and the elderly were included, these levels were lower by a factor of 10 than those for occupational exposure. As the Commission's views were under discussion continuously in between the appearance of its reports, the Medical Research Council and other British scientists concerned were aware of forthcoming changes well in advance of publication.

23 The ICRP emphasized from the beginning that all radiation exposures should be kept as low as reasonably practicable, since no radiation level higher than the natural background could be regarded as absolutely 'safe'. The values that ICRP recommended as limits were, in its judgment, such as to involve a risk 'small compared to the other hazards of life'; ICRP emphasized that 'limits' did not represent the

upper bound between safety and danger, but rather a level at which procedures should be reviewed with the objective of reducing the exposures.

Radiation limits for trials personnel

24   The limits for penetrating radiations for trials personnel were approved by the Medical Research Council before *Hurricane*. In brief they were:
(1)   Normal working rate—0.1 r a day (gamma radiation)
(2)   Lower integrated dose (LID)—3 r (gamma radiation)
(3)   Higher integrated dose (HID)—10 r (gamma radiation).
   The integrated doses applied to the duration of the trial. All three values were for exposures measured by a film-badge worn on the torso; thus the limits for deep tissue were about ⅔ of these values in rems.
25   It is sometimes believed that these levels were more permissive than the ICRP standards then current, and even more so than later ICRP standards. This was not so. *The normal working rate* of 0.1 r corresponded to ICRP's 1950 limit of 0.5 r a week for routine exposure of occupational radiation workers. *The LID* of 3 r corresponded almost exactly to ICRP's later recommendation of 3 rems in 13 weeks (see para 21). It also corresponded closely to the level of 3 rems in 10 weeks (or 3.9 in 13 weeks) adopted for United States weapons trials in the period 1950 to 1952. The current (post-1977) ICRP limit is 50 mSv per annum effective dose equivalent (5 rems) which may be received in any period, from fractions of a second to a year; this corresponds to an exposure limit, as in the trials, of about 7.5 r per annum. *The HID* of 10 r, and the special limit of 25 r introduced subsequently, anticipated later ICRP recommendations about permissible levels for special emergency exposures (1958) and for planned special exposures (1977). In the trials, the LID and HID were for planned exposures governed by strict rules, and the HID required the advance approval of the Task Force Commander. (Rules for United States weapon tests did not specify a limit corresponding to the HID, but they allowed exposures higher than 3.9 r without any specific limit, at the sole discretion of the Test Commander).

Measurement of radiation exposure

26 At the atomic weapons trials there were two means of monitoring individual personnel exposure. Film badge dosimeters (FBD) measured gamma radiation exposure of the badge with considerable accuracy (about ± 20 per cent) but beta radiation exposure less accurately; the latter could, however, be assessed from the gamma readings by knowing the ratio of the two. All trials personnel actively involved in the tests were issued with film badges; for most, exposure was so low that usually the badge could be worn from beginning to end of the trial period before being read. For all personnel working in radioactive and radiation areas, film badges were issued before, and worn during, each sortie; they were developed and read and the exposures recorded daily.

27 Useful but less accurate was the quartz fibre dosimeter (QFD or QFE). It was issued, as well as a film badge, for certain operations where its capability of being read while at work was useful as a control measure, although the total it finally recorded could be very unreliable. QFD or QFE readings were never sufficiently certain for personal dosimetry and record purposes.

28 Information about exposures was additionally provided by the monitoring instruments carried by health escorts who accompanied working parties into radioactive areas and who controlled their movements so as to keep within prescribed exposure limits. The monitoring instruments were for operational purposes and were not a substitute for individual film badges.

Radiation limits for population exposure used in determining criteria for safe test-firing conditions

The basic requirement—limits on radiation exposure

29 The basic requirement for safe firing conditions was that fallout should not cause people to receive radiation exposures greater than the currently acceptable standard. In the period 1950–1958 ICRP recommended dose limits of 0.3 r a week for gamma radiation to deep tissue, and for beta radiation 0.6 or 1.5 rep (according to the energy of the particles); ICRP at this time, as we saw, did not differentiate between members of the public and radiation workers (i.e., those occupationally exposed at nuclear sites, in hospitals, or in laboratories).

Secondary standards—limits on levels of surface radioactivity

30 Secondary standards were established for the trials. They defined fallout deposition in terms of radioactivity per unit of area (microcuries per cubic metre) such that, if the level of activity determined as the limit was not exceeded, the primary requirement—the limit on radiation exposure—would not be exceeded either.

31 Various names were used for these secondary standards. Before *Totem, zero risk* was defined as 'that quantity of fission products which will cause no measurable effect on the body'. *Slight risk* was defined as 'that quantity of fission products which may cause some slight temporary sickness to a small number of people who have a low threshold sensitivity to radiation'.

32 In 1955 (between *Totem* and *Mosaic*) these terms were replaced, respectively, by *Level A* ('that level which will not give rise to any observable effect on the body') and *Level B* ('that level which could cause a slight sickness, in a few people if they had a low threshold sensitivity to radiation. The proportion of such people in a population would only be a fraction of one per cent'). [Recent information suggests that the proportion may be higher—perhaps 5 per cent or more.] The change from zero and slight risk to levels A and B was only one of terminology, not of substance.

33 Before *Antler* in 1957, the secondary standards were revised. New levels of density of deposited radioactivity were derived for four levels $(A, A^1, B$ and $B^1)$, defined as follows:

A   is that level which will not give rise to any observable effect on people living under 'civilized' conditions, 'i.e., wearing footwear and some clothing.

A^1 is that level which will not give rise to any observable effect on people living under 'primitive' conditions, i.e., with no footwear or clothing and sleeping in the open.

B   is that level which may give rise to a slight observable effect such as temporary slight sickness in a small percentage of 'civilized' people if they had a low threshold of sensitivity to radiation.

B^1 is the corresponding level for 'primitive' people.

34 Though these (secondary) levels changed, the corresponding primary values remained the same:

For zero risk, level A and level A^1: external gamma radiation, 3 r; external beta radiation, 15 rep.

For slight risk, level B and level B^1: external gamma radiation, 25 r; external beta radiation, 50 rep.

35 The approved standards varied. For *Hurricane* and *Totem*, firing requirements had been stated in meteorological terms (see Chapters 2 and 4). After 1955, to meet acceptable firing conditions, the predicted fallout patterns had to conform to an agreed level, or fraction of a level, of surface activity; only for the two later rounds of *Antler* in 1957 was the requirement expressed directly in terms of exposure.

36 The levels approved for determining safe firing conditions were:

Mosaic

Half level B—predicted surface activity corresponding to 12.5 r (gamma) and 25 rep (beta)

Buffalo

Level A—predicted surface activity corresponding to 3 r (gamma) and 15 rep (beta) with no overlapping of fallout contours from successive shots

Antler Round 1

Half level A—predicted surface activity corresponding to 1.5 r (gamma) and 7.5 rep (beta)

Antler Rounds 2 and 3

After the first round of *Antler*, the Australian Weapons Tests Safety Committee (AWTSC) asked for conditions to be expressed not in terms of surface radioactivity but of radiation exposure, i.e., 0.5 r (gamma) and 2.5 rep (beta), plus 0.5 rep for internal radiation.

Appendix H   Distribution of radiation exposures—United Kingdom atmospheric nuclear tests and experiments in Australia, 1952–1957

	Hurricane 1952				*Totem* 1953			
	C	DS	A	T	C	DS	A	T
No. of participants with exposure data	117	1275	126	1518	89	19	78	186
At or below threshold	33	1107	123	1263	30	2	27	59
Above threshold	84	168	3	255	59	17	51	127
Above 0.5 R	49	98	1	148	32	13	16	61
Above 1 R	42	69	1	112	25	13	15	53
Above 1.5 R	28	49	1	78	17	10	11	38
Above 3 R	6	25	0	31	3	8	8	19
Above 5 R	0	0	0	0	0	5	1	6
Above 10 R	0	0	0	0	0	2	0	2
Above 12 R	0	0	0	0	0	1	1	1
Above 15 R	0	0	0	0	0	0	0	0
Above 20 R	0	0	0	0	0	0	0	0

C: civilians, other than those in DS and A below
DS: members of Defence Services, mainly in HM Forces but including a few civilians
A: Australian citizens
T: total

Source: SFS, AWRE, Aldermaston

Mosaic 1956				Buffalo 1956				Antler 1957			
C	DS	A	T	C	DS	A	T	C	DS	A	T
61	586	81	728	288	749	213	1250	234	692	574	1500
34	441	70	545	133	403	119	655	103	440	533	1076
27	145	11	183	155	346	94	595	131	252	41	424
7	22	0	29	65	128	23	216	27	66	8	101
6	20	0	26	35	70	3	108	10	44	6	60
5	15	0	20	22	51	3	76	4	31	5	40
4	9	0	13	5	19	0	24	0	14	3	17
2	6	0	8	2	1	0	3	0	5	0	5
2	0	0	2	0	0	0	0	0	2	0	2
2	0	0	2	0	0	0	0	0	2	0	2
1	0	0	1	0	0	0	0	0	1	0	1
0	0	0	0	0	0	0	0	0	0	0	0

Appendix I Fallout

Immediate effects of a nuclear weapon test explosion

When a nuclear bomb or device is detonated, it releases vastly more energy per unit mass than the most powerful chemical explosion, accompanied by intense light and heat and highly penetrating ionizing radiations. An expanding fireball—an incandescent mass of debris from the device, and air—is created in a few thousandths of a second; in it the nuclear bomb or device and its container are almost completely vaporized, at a temperature of some 1 000 000 °C. It expands very rapidly, and by the time the fireball from a 20-kiloton burst is 90 ft across, the temperature is about 300 000 °C and the luminosity is a hundred times that of the Sun seen from the Earth. In less than a second, the fireball attains its maximum diameter of some 900 ft.

Besides intense light and heat, the other immediate effects of the explosion are blast and the prompt (or initial) ionizing radiations already mentioned. For a 20-kiloton airburst, the safety distance is dictated by the thermal effects; moderate skin burns would result within a radius of about 10 000 ft from ground zero, a much greater distance than that required for protection from severe blast (6500 ft) or immediate radiation effects (4500 ft).

The protection of test participants therefore depended on distance. They had to be far enough from ground zero to be safe from flash burns, blast and ionizing radiations from the detonation. To protect their eyes from the intense light, which could cause temporary blindness, they had to face away from the explosion, or to use dark glass shields or goggles.

The remaining hazard to test personnel—on-site fallout (see below)— was avoided by positioning them upwind of ground zero and well away from it.

Delayed effects of nuclear weapon test explosion—fallout

What fallout consists of

The luminosity of the fireball of a 20-kiloton burst in air dies out in about 10 seconds and a radioactive cloud forms and rises rapidly. It is lighter than the surrounding air and rushes upward at a speed of some 200 miles an hour. In a few minutes it spreads out into the characteristic mushroom cap. The cloud, which may remain visible for an hour or more before being dispersed by the winds, is mainly air and water droplets condensed from water vapour in the air, but it also contains the vaporized materials of the bomb or device—the fission products, the unconsumed uranium and plutonium (or either of these), and the casing and components. Below the cloud is the stem of the mushroom. Both cloud and stem contain considerable quantities of dirt and debris, unless the explosion is above 500 to 600 ft (in the case of a 20-kiloton burst); if the explosion is at 450 ft or less, the fireball may actually touch the ground. In this case soil becomes contaminated with radioactivity, or is made radioactive by neutron induction, and is carried up into the cloud.

The contents of the radioactive cloud depend therefore on the size and make-up of the bomb or device; its efficiency—i.e., what proportion of the fissile material is used in the chain reaction and what is left; and the amount and nature of the extraneous material drawn up into the cloud. These latter depend on the height of burst, the yield, the nature of the soil, and the support structure (e.g., a steel or aluminium tower).

The particles are very variable in size and weight, and the fission products are a mixture of more than 200 isotopes (mostly radioactive) of 36 different elements. The range of half-lives is enormous, from fractions of a second to many years, and the pattern of radioactive decay is extremely complex; overall, radioactivity decreases by a factor of 10 after every multiplication by 7 of the elapsed time (i.e., by 10 in the first 7 hours, by 100 in 49 hours and so on. This is called 'the rule of seven').

After an underwater detonation—like the *Baker* shot in the United States' 1946 trials at Bikini (Operation *Crossroads*)—seawater and material from the seabed are drawn up into a spray dome which, as it falls back into the sea, may create a gigantic wave or cloud of dense and highly radioactive mist. This is called a 'base surge'. It apparently only occurs in deep water, and did not do so at *Hurricane*, which was a shallow water test.

The term 'fallout' refers to the radioactive material resulting from the explosion, and its magnitude depends on the process by which it is dispersed and deposited on the earth.

Firing conditions

Firing conditions were intended to ensure that early fallout beyond the prohibited area did not cause contamination that might deliver radiation doses above the level permitted for members of the public. This was the main purpose of theoretical prediction and meteorological forecasting.

If the wind direction varies at different altitudes—i.e., if there is windshear—fallout will be dispersed and will be thinly and widely spread over a comparatively short distance. But if there is little or no windshear (which is unusual) the fallout will extend much further, along the centre line of the wind, and will be more concentrated in a long narrow plume.

The meteorological conditions required for firing include suitable wind directions to carry fallout away from any inhabited areas, suitable wind speed, ample windshear and absence of rain. Since the trials director received the forecast several hours in advance of firing, he needed to be confident that favourable conditions would last throughout the firing phase and, ideally, for 24 hours after firing.

How fallout is dispersed

The distribution as fallout of the material in the cloud depends on four factors in conjunction:

(1) *The size of the particles*, since (other things being equal) large and heavy particles fall more quickly, and closer to ground zero, than do light particles. The more delayed the deposition, the more the short-lived radioactivity will have decayed and the more diffused the material will be.

(2) *The distribution of the material* in the cloud and its stem. Gases and very fine particles will usually rise to the top of the cloud, but some may be trapped in the lower layers. The various layers of the stem and cloud are affected by the winds at the corresponding altitudes, therefore the distribution of the particles is important.

(3) *The height and extent of the cloud*, which depends on the force of the explosion and also on meteorological conditions that may affect its

rise. For a 20-kiloton explosion, the cloud is likely to be 15 000 to 30 000 ft. Accurate estimates of the cloud height were important because they indicated the wind levels that were of concern; particles in the stem are transported by low level winds, and particles in the mushroom cloud by higher level winds at various altitudes. Clouds from kiloton explosions normally remain in the troposphere (the lower layer of the atmosphere extending to about 11 miles above the Equator and 4 miles at the Poles) in which 'weather' occurs. It is divided by the tropopause from the upper layer, the stratosphere; clouds from megaton explosions (or from very high altitude explosions) pass through the troposphere into the stratosphere.

(4) *Meteorological conditions*, especially wind structure and precipitation. In some meteorological conditions, a secondary cloud may be created as well as the primary cloud. Inversion conditions—in which a layer of air next to the Earth's surface is cooler than the overlying layer—may trap the cloud, or part of it. If the cloud encounters a rain area, material from the cloud may be washed out and deposited on the ground.

All these four factors work together; hence the importance of both theoretical predictions and meteorological forecasts in identifying safe conditions for firing.

Categories of fallout

Fallout has been categorized in various ways—as, e.g., on-site, local, early, close-in, intermediate, long-range or global. Four categories are noted below.

(1) *On-site fallout* This is fallout in the test-site area around and immediately downwind of ground zero, and it consists of the largest particles. In practice it is almost entirely an external radiation hazard, and then only for test participants carrying out re-entry sorties (with protective clothing, health escorts and other safety precautions).

(2) *Close-in or early fallout* This is fallout deposited within about 24 hours and within a few hundred miles of the explosion, but outside the protected area. It consists of the larger particles, mostly in insoluble form.

(3) *Long-range fallout* Finer particles of fallout may be distributed over a large part of the Earth's surface. The radioactive cloud from

an explosion in the kiloton range may travel many times round the Earth depositing tropospheric fallout in latitudes close to that of the original explosion. Deposition, which is very diffuse, is effectively complete within about 3 months, and occurs in the latitudes in which the explosion took place, in a relatively narrow band.

(4) *Global fallout* After a megaton explosion most of the fission products enters the stratosphere where they become widely distributed, and where they may remain for many months or even a few years. There is no precipitation (in rain or snow) from the stratosphere and the air mixes only very slowly with that of the troposphere. There is some transfer across the equator, but most global fallout reaches the Earth in the hemisphere in which it was created. The bigger the explosion the wider (and thinner) the diffusion of the fallout. Long retention in the upper atmosphere allows time for radioactive decay of all the shorter-lived radioisotopes. (None of the British tests in Australia was in the megaton range.)

The effects of fallout

There are several ways in which fallout can affect people and the 'pathways' have been intensively studied. People may be exposed to external beta or gamma radiation. They may inhale radioactive airborne particles. They may ingest fission products that have entered the food chain; e.g., by drinking milk from cows that have grazed on pasture contaminated by fallout. Two fission products that caused special concern were strontium-90 and iodine-131. Strontium-90 is a long-lived radioisotope (half-life 28 years) which is akin to calcium and therefore tends to concentrate in bone. There it can cause bone tumours or, by irradiating the bone marrow, leukaemia. Iodine-131 is a short-lived radioisotope (half-life 8 days); if ingested by grazing cows it passes into their milk and thence into the bodies of people drinking the milk. It then tends to concentrate in the thyroid and gives rise to a risk of thyroid cancer; it is a particular risk for young children.

Global fallout has resulted in very small radiation exposures to very large numbers of people. The total dose that people have received in the past and will receive in the future, from all the fallout from all the weapon tests carried out hitherto, has been calculated as about 4 millisieverts (0.4 rem) for each member of the world's present population. This is a total dose, not an annual dose, and is equivalent to about four years' exposure to external radiation from natural sources. (In the United Kingdom average background radiation is estimated at 1 millisievert (0.1 rem) from cosmic and terrestrial radiation and 1 millisievert (0.1 rem) from radon in buildings.) It is higher in the northern hemisphere (0.45 rem) then in the southern hemisphere (0.31 rem).

This total dose, over and above natural background and spread over a very long time, represents a very small increase in radiation exposure to very large numbers of people. For each individual person the risk is small, compared with the normal (non-exposed) incidence of those illnesses that may be attributable to radiation exposure. Recognition that contamination from atmospheric testing would increase the doses further was one of the factors that led to the adoption of underground containment for nuclear weapon testing.

Appendix J *Mosaic, Buffalo* and *Antler*

Atomic Weapons Tests Safety Committee reports to the Australian Prime Minister

Mosaic (G1)

The requirements of the Safety Committee for meteorological prediction of safe firing conditions and for examining the subsequent radioactive fallout by air and sea operations were fully met. The control of movements of shipping and aircraft worked smoothly. The air search of restricted areas showed with certainty that there was no shipping, other than that associated with the experiment, in the prescribed danger areas. The meteorological predictions were complete and accurate and the operation was carried out without there being any hazard whatsoever to life on the mainland, ships at sea, and to aircraft.

The whole operation proceeded with precision and was a complete success.

(Message sent by the AWTSC Chairman on 16th May 1956).

Mosaic (G2)

1   The Safety Committee unanimously concurred in the firing of the device after arriving at a considered opinion that no dangerous effects would arise in the Commonwealth. The meteorological requirements for the safe firing of the weapon were stringent. The conditions during the critical hours of firing and during the significant days following the event were more favourable for the safety of the Commonwealth than the limiting requirements laid down before the test.

2   The radioactive cloud from the explosion travelled at an altitude higher than commercial aircraft fly and in a direction away from the NW coast of the mainland. Aircraft interceptions and coastal studies both in the air and on the ground demonstrated beyond question that

the cloud at no point approached the coast. The last aeroplane fix located the cloud 150 miles off the NW coast where it showed evidence of rapid dispersion. The immediate high activity fallout was as predicted and fell entirely into the sea.

3   Some long range fallout can arise from small particles falling from the cloud. In falling such particles can be carried considerable distances from the track of the cloud because they are acted upon by winds at lower levels which may be blowing in different directions from those carrying the high altitude radioactive cloud. As was anticipated, therefore, there was some fallout of low level activity in a restricted coastal region, and to a lesser degree in a band reaching towards the centre of Australia. Incontrovertible evidence has been obtained which shows that all contamination of the mainland was near the low limit of detection. The highest activity measured in Continental Australia was such that a person living 24 hours a day in the open would have received a total dose less than one three thousandth of that which the British Medical Research Council in its recent report to the British Parliament considered would be safe to an individual. This level was confined to one small locality. Over the rest of the whole area through which exposures were received, they were very much smaller. That is all exposures were biologically and genetically insignificant. Actually the vast majority of the Australian population including the cities of Adelaide, Brisbane, Melbourne, Perth and Sydney received no radiation. From analysis of the detailed data available to us the Safety Committee has satisfaction in reporting that the safety measures were completely adequate. There was absolute *no hazard* to persons or damage to livestock and other property.

> [signed]:   L H Martin
> Chairman
> *Atomic Weapons Tests Safety Committee*

Buffalo (Summary)

Four atomic weapons were fired in the series, R1 and 4 (on towers) being of approximately nominal yield, R2 (ground level) and R3 (air drop) being of much smaller yield.

Stringent safety conditions were imposed for the firing of all weapons and detonation only occurred after those Safety Committee members on the spot had, together with their United Kingdom colleagues, arrived at a considered opinion that no dangerous effects would arise in the Commonwealth or in the seas around.

Measurements of ground fallout were made at 86 monitoring stations throughout the Commonwealth, while rainwater samples were monitored and mud samples from reservoirs were tested for radioactivity. In addition, certain tests were carried out on sheep to confirm that no untoward biological effects had occurred.

After a careful analysis of all these data, the Safety Committee has satisfaction in reporting to you that the safety measures taken were entirely successful and that there was absolutely no risk to any individual, livestock or property at any time during the series of test.

Note At R1, L H Martin, E W Titterton, W A S Butement and L J Dwyer were all present.

At R2, E W Titterton, L J Dwyer and D J Stevens were present.

At R3, E W Titterton, and L J Dwyer were present.

At R4, L H Martin, W A S Butement and L J Dwyer were present.

Antler (Summary)

1   Three atomic weapons were fired in this series, the first two being of small yield, fired on towers, and the third a weapon of approximately nominal yield, fired from balloons and suspended 1000 feet above ground level.

As on all previous occasions, stringent safety conditions were imposed for the firing of the weapons and, in fact, the Committee on two occasions vetoed possible firing conditions because they were not considered to be entirely satisfactory.

Eighty-six monitoring stations located through-out the Commonwealth measured ground fallout, while air contamination and rainwater samples were taken from selected stations. In addition, in the near vicinity of the test site, detailed tests were carried out on sheep to confirm that no untoward biological effects had occurred.

The Safety Committee has satisfaction in reporting to you that, after analysis of all these data, it can assert that the safety measures taken were completely successful. The fallout on the occasion of this trial was considerably less than in any previous trials and there was absolutely no risk to any individual, livestock or property, at any time.

2   The Committee feels this to be an appropriate occasion on which to inform you of two other continuing investigations it has instituted.

Firstly, seventeen fallout stations have been kept in operation since the Buffalo trials and twenty four will operate continuously from November 1957 unless there should be an international agreement to cease weapon testing. These fallout stations are used to determine background radioactivity; they allow a determination of the levels of activity in Australia resulting from overseas weapon tests. In particular fallout from British tests at Christmas Island may be detected, but that from the recent series was found to be trivial.

Secondly, a major investigation has been instituted to determine the levels of strontium-90 fallout in a wide variety of inert and living matter. These include samples of soil taken in appropriate places, samples of dried milk, samples of vegetable material, a systematic sampling of sheep bones and in the future some human bones. The early work reveals that the strontium-90 levels in Australia are considerably lower than those obtaining in the USA, the United Kingdom and Japan. Because of the political and scientific importance of the strontium-90 fallout problem, we regard the investigation as essential and it will be carried through in detail over a considerable number of years. However the work is necessarily slow and the full scientific report will not be available in less than a year.

E W Titterton   L J Dwyer   D J Stevens   J H Martin

Bibliography

Australian Commonwealth Department of Health: *Health of Atomic Test Personnel* (November 1983).

Australian Ionizing Radiation Advisory Council: *Radiological Safety and Future Land Use at the Maralinga Atomic Weapons Test Range* (AIRAC No 4: Australian Government Publishing Service Canberra, January 1979).

Australian Ionizing Radiation Advisory Council: *British Nuclear Tests in Australia—a Review of Operational Safety Measures and of Possible After-effects* (AIRAC No 9: Australian Government Publishing Service Canberra, January 1983).

Australian Ionizing Radiation Advisory Council: *AIRAC Report 1983–84* (AIRAC No 10: Australian Publishing Service, Canberra 1985).

Australian Radiation Laboratory: *Residual Radioactive Contamination at Maralinga and Emu 1985* (ed. Keith H Lokan. ARL/TR070, April 1985).

Barker, Elizabeth: *The British Between the Superpowers 1949–50* (Macmillan, 1983).

Bartlett, C J: *The Long Retreat: A Short History of British Defence Policy 1945–70* (Macmillan, 1972).

Beadell, Len: *Blast the Bush* (Rigby Ltd, Adelaide, 1967).

Bryant, F J *et al.*: *Strontium-90 in Fallout and in Man in Australia January 1959–June 1960* (*Nature*, May 27, 1961).

Butement, W A S *et al.*: *Radioactive Fallout in Australia from Operation Mosaic* (*Australian Journal of Science*, December 1957).

Butement, W A S *et al.*: *Radioactive Fallout in Australia from Operation Buffalo* (*Australian Journal of Science*, October 1958).

Carter, Melvin W and Moghissi, A Alan: *Three decades of nuclear testing* (*Health Physics*, **33**, p. 55–71, July 1977. Pergamon Press).

Cockburn, Stewart and Ellyard, David: *Oliphant* (Axion Books, Adelaide, Brisbane, Perth, Darwin, 1981).

Divine, Robert A: *Blowing on the Wind: The Nuclear Test Ban Debate 1954–1960* (New York, Oxford University Press, 1978).

Driver, Christopher: *The Disarmers: A Study in Protest* (Hodder and Stoughton, 1964).

Dwyer, L J *et al.*: *Radioactive Fallout in Australia from Operation Antler* (*Australian Journal of Science*, September 1959).

Glasstone, Samuel (ed): *The Effects of Atomic Weapons* (McGraw-Hill Book Company Inc., 1950).

Gowing, Margaret: *Britain and Atomic Energy 1939–1945* (Macmillan, 1964)

Gowing, Margaret: *Independence and Deterrence: Britain and Atomic Energy 1945–1952* (2 volumes, Macmillan, 1974).

Gowing, Margaret: *Britain, America and the Bomb* (*in* Dilkes, David (ed.) *The Retreat from Power* Macmillan, 1981).

Groom, A J R: *British Thinking about Nuclear Weapons* (Frances Pinter, 1974).

Keam, D W *et al.*: *Experiments on the 'Sticky Paper' Method of Radioactive Fallout Sampling* (*Australian Journal of Science*, November 1958).

McKay, Alwyn: *The Making of the Atomic Age* (Oxford University Press, 1954).

Macmillan, Harold: *Tides of Fortune 1945–1955* (Macmillan, 1969).

Macmillan, Harold: *Riding the Storm 1956–1959* (Macmillan, 1971).

Marston, H R: *The Accumulation of Radioactive Iodine in the Thyroids of Grazing Animals Subsequent to Atomic Weapon Tests* (*Australian Journal of Biological Science*, II(3), August 1958).

Medical Research Council: *Hazards to Man of Nuclear and Allied Radiations* (Cmnd 9780, June 1956, HMSO).

Medical Research Council: *Second Report on Hazards to Man of Nuclear and Allied Radiations* (Cmnd 1225, December 1960, HMSO).

Menaul, Stewart: *Countdown: Britain's Strategic Nuclear Forces* (Robert Hale, 1980).

Pierre, Andrew J: *Nuclear Politics* (Oxford University Press, 1972).

Pochin, Edward: *Nuclear Radiation: Risks and Benefits* (Oxford University Press, 1983).

Reissland, J A (ed.): *Protocol for a Study of the Health of UK Participants in the UK Atmospheric Nuclear Weapons Tests* (NRPB–R154, National Radiological Protection Board, September 1983).

Seaborg, Glen T: *Kennedy, Kruschev and the Test Ban* (University of California Press, 1981).
Simpson, John: *The Independent Nuclear State* (Macmillan, 1983).
Symonds, J L: *A History of British Atomic Tests in Australia* (Australian Government Publishing Service Canberra, 1985).
Symonds, J L: *British Atomic Tests in Australia—Chronology of Events 1950–1968* (1984).

Tame, Adrian and Robotham, F P J: *Maralinga—British A-bomb Australian Legacy* (Fontana Books, Melbourne, 1982).

United Nations: *Reports of the United Nations Scientific Committee on Effects of Atomic Radiation* (1959 and 1982 especially).

Ward, Russel: *The History of Australia—The Twentieth Century 1901–1975* (Heinemann Educational Books, London, 1978).
Wise, Keith N and Moroney, John R: *Public Health Impact of Fallout from British Nuclear Weapons Tests in Australia, 1952–1957* (Australian Radiation Laboratory (unpublished)).

York, Herbert: *Race to Oblivion* (Simon and Schuster, New York, 1971).
York, Herbert: *The Advisors* (W H Freeman and Company, San Francisco, 1976).

This list does not include any of the numerous scientific and official reports, mostly produced at AWRE Aldermaston, that have recently been declassified and will shortly be open.

Issues of the *Bulletin of Atomic Scientists* throughout the period provide invaluable background reading on nuclear weapons, testing and fallout. The articles are too numerous to be listed here.

Index

Printed in the UK for Her Majesty's Stationery Office
by Eyre & Spottiswoode Ltd at Grosvenor Press, Portsmouth
Dd 239192   GP3932/1   C35   2/87